Quality Management (Tools & Techniques)

Geoff Vorley MSc, MIQA
and
Fred Tickle BA, CEng, MIMechE, MIEE, MIQA

Founding Directors of Quality Management & Training Limited
Associate Lecturers at University of Surrey

Geoff Vorley

Fred Tickle

Q
M & T
Quality Management & Training (Publications)Limited

Quality Management & Training (Publications) Limited
PO Box 172 Guildford Surrey United K
Telephone: +44 (0) 1483 453511 **Fax:** +4
E-mail: help@qmt.co.uk **Website**: w

Quality Management & Training (Publications) Limited
PO Box 172 Guildford Surrey GU2 7FN

First Published by Quality Management & Training (Publications) Limited 2002

Reprinted 2005

British Library Cataloguing in publications data

A catalogue record for this book is available from the British Library

ISBN 1-904302-04-1

Printed and Bound in Great Britain at
the University Press, Cambridge

Quality Management (Tools & Techniques)

Table of Contents

Introduction to Quality Management (Tools & Techniques)

This book Quality Management (Tools and Techniques) is intended to provide quality professionals and students with a clear and comprehensive understanding of the tools and techniques of quality. It delivers an exploration of the applicability and effectiveness of different quality tools and techniques for all organisational types. The intention being to encourage and stimulate the reader to feel sufficiently confident to use the tools and techniques in a practical and rewarding way.

Quality Management (Tools and Techniques) is part of the Quality Management series which includes; Introduction to Quality, Quality Management (Principles and Practice) and Quality Management (Communications and Projects). For clarity and continuity purposes, there is correctly some overlap between these titles. However, this book is expected to be 'stand alone' and a comprehensive and practical reference to all the major quality management tools and techniques.

The overall aim of this book Quality Management (Tools and Techniques) is to:

- provide a clear awareness and understanding of the disciplines, tools and techniques of quality improvement.
- enable the user to be capable of practical evaluation of the tools and techniques for variety of situations.
- enable the confident application of the appropriate quality tools and techniques for the selected activities in the business or organisation.

Detailed below, is what could reasonably be expected to be appreciated and be competent in performing, as a consequence of studying this book.

- Demonstrate and present an argument for the use of the tools and techniques of quality improvement.
- Evaluate the applicability of tools and techniques of quality.
- Appropriately apply the quality tool or technique.
- Appraise the effectiveness of individual applications of the quality tool or technique.
- Analyse the contribution to quality improvement of the tools and techniques in a variety of organisational settings.
- Understand and develop the relationship between an organisation and its suppliers.

The book is broken down into six sections

Section 1 - *Process Improvement;* this section addresses the following tools and techniques:

Kaizen	Kaizen is Japanese for Improvement or Continuous Improvement. In a business setting, it means on-going never ending improvement, involving everyone.
5S Methodology	The 5S is a systematic approach to establishing and maintaining housekeeping standards. With this method, divisions or departments within organisations adopt and implement their own housekeeping programme, used as a means of improving quality, safety and productivity.
Value Analysis	Techniques used to investigate the function of a system, process or equipment with the objective of achieving the intended function at the lowest overall cost.
Failure Mode and Effects Analysis (FMEA)	Risk analysis technique used to identify and eliminate possible causes of failure.
Poka Yoke	Fool proofing - a technique for avoiding and eliminating mistakes.
Process Capability (Cp, Cpk)	An evaluation of process performance against specification.

Section 2 - *Improvement Techniques;* this section addresses the following tools and techniques:

Quality Circles	A small group of employees, doing similar work, voluntarily meeting regularly, learning to identify and analyse work related problems and recommending solutions.
Gemba Gembutsu	Gemba is Japanese for the place where the problem has happened, and gembutsu is the actual information at gemba.
Muda	OPTIMUM - Classification and avoidance of the seven wastes.

Balanced Scorecard	A communication, informing and learning system. Used to help concatenate and to communicate strategy by aligning individual, organisational, business unit and cross-functional objectives to achieve common goals and mission.
Six Sigma	Six Sigma is a business strategy and quality improvement technique. Six Sigma performance means reducing defects to less than 4 per million.

Section 3 - *Quality by Design*; this section addresses the following tools and techniques;

Taguchi Design of Experiments	A process using orthogonal arrays to analyse a problem, which could have a number of different contributory factors or variables.
Ishikawa's 7 Tools of Quality	Seven tools of quality control that need to be taught to all circle members.
Quality Function Deployment (QFD)	"The voice of the customer" - a technique, which seeks to understand the basic function or customer requirements and determine how best these functions can be achieved.

Section 4 - *Analysis and Mapping Techniques;* this section addresses the following tools and techniques:

IDEFO	Integration DEfinition for Function Modelling level 0. A method developed by the USA Air Force to graphically represent process activities, showing process activity inputs, outputs, controls and resources.
Fault Tree Analysis	A method for calculating the frequency of a undesired event, which if occurs could cause; danger, expense or downtime.
Nominal Group Technique	A process for idea generation or braining storming.
Flowchart	Means of diagrammatically representing a process
Benchmarking	A means of establishing, quantifying and comparing one activity's performance against another.

Section 5 - *Optimisation Techniques;* this section addresses the following tools and techniques:

MRP	A (usually computer based) system which calculates the total material requirements (quantities, time scale) to meet a predetermined set of customer requirements.
MRP II	A (usually computer based) system which integrates manufacturing data to calculate the total resources required to manufacture a product in specified time scales, in order to meet customer requirements.
JIT (Just in Time)	An approach to ensuring that the customer's requirements in terms of quality and service (deliveries and quantities) are exactly matched.
Total Productive Maintenance	An approach similar to Total Quality Management in its philosophy, supporting the initiative to keep equipment and facilities to a defined standard.

Section 6 - *Suppliers and Distribution*; this section addresses the issues associated with supply chain management including:

Supplier Partnerships	A means of developing relationships with suppliers to ensure that they understand the customer's specific requirements and needs. Further reducing the number of suppliers provides better control and fosters a mutually beneficial climate of continuous improvement.
Supplier Associations	Supplier associations or "Supplier Clubs" are similar or like minded suppliers who form a group to mutually help and learn from each other.
Integrated Supply	Management of the supply chain.

The book was intended to be written in a way that hopefully makes the various tools, techniques and approaches to quality assurance self explanatory. However, if the reader has any problems with the contents or has a quality problem or issue that they would like to discuss further, please do not hesitate to contact us. We can be contacted via the publishers, or email us on help@qmt.co.uk. We welcome the opportunity to discuss quality issues.

The book has been written by Geoff Vorley and Fred Tickle with contributions from Mary Brightman, Mary-Clare Bushell and Penny Simmons.

SECTION 1 - PROCESS IMPROVEMENT

Kaizen

"If you are content with the best you've done, then you'll never do the best you can do"

Introduction

Kaizen is Japanese for Improvement or Continuous Improvement. Although, in Japan the concept applies to all aspects of life, in a business setting it means on-going, never ending improvement, involving everyone. The approach has been credited with being the single most important concept in Japanese management. Meeting specification is often considered good enough - there is no value in making further efforts at improvement. In contrast, Kaizen requires on-going, never ending efforts at improvement, no matter how good the product, process or service may be considered. The progress and refinement of the Kaizen approach has resulted in the development of an outstanding collection of management tools which, incidently, still continue to be evolved and polished. The application and use of these tools is an important element in the Kaizen approach. The Kaizen approach is not looking for the big initiative or project but optimisation and small improvements to existing systems. There are two dimensions to processes; the control and the improvement. Control is usually described in the procedures or Standard Operating Procedures (SOPs). Improvements can be described as experiments or studies on the process, which if successful bring about a better quality or productivity, or both. Once understood these improvements can be incorporated into the SOP. Role and responsibilities for improving the process and maintaining the process against the SOPs can be structured and classified as seen in **figure 1**.

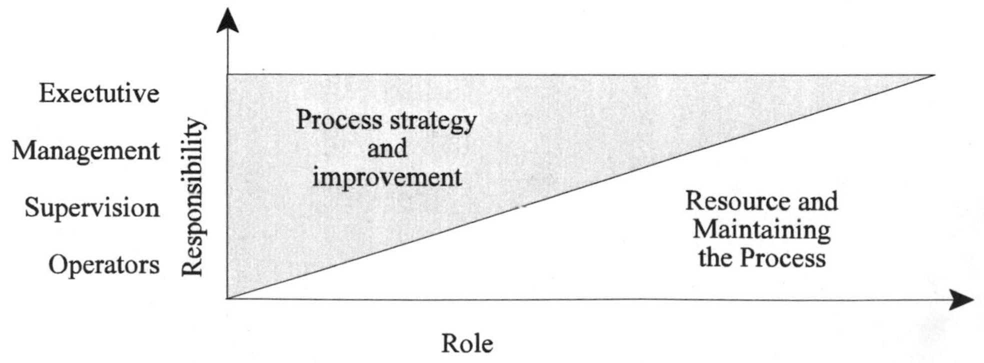

Figure 1 Changing Responsibilities

Whilst with Kaizen the executive role is more associated with setting strategy and large innovative projects, where as the management and operative role is achieving continuous improvement - See **figure 2**.

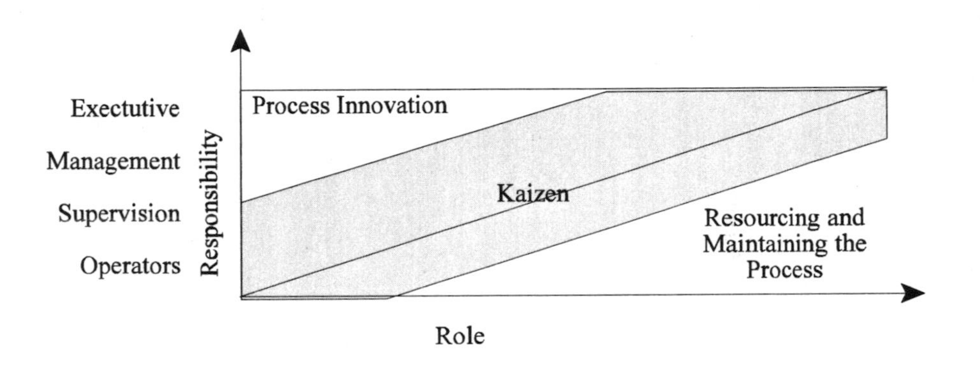

Figure 2 Kaizen Roles and Responsibilities

The Practice of Kaizen:

These Kaizen roles and responsibilities in practice consist of:

Area	**Executive & Management Kaizen**	**Kaizen Team**	**Kaizen Worker**
Respon-sibilities	To make Kaizen the corporate goal and mission To provide resource and training to implement To goal set To motive and encourage	To achieve the goals and targets set by management To improve process and workmanship standards To develop and use the tools of quality	Involvement and participation in the Kaizen objectives and team. Self improvement and development in the seven tools of quality and others quality techniques as appropriate.

Area	Executive & Management Kaizen	Kaizen Team	Kaizen Worker
Role	Identification of the overall improvement strategy (not only for Kaizen Team but for innovation). Establish the improvement strategy in action. Develop systems and structures to communicate and integrate this strategy across the organisation (Balances Scorecards).	Implementation of the Kaizen strategy in action. Development of local plans. Ensuring cross functional support and integration. Maintaining the Kaizen philosophy though the Kaizen workshops. Provide and implement Kaizen Suggestions.	Practice the seven tools of quality and other self taught skills in the Kaizen Team workshops.
Tools and techniques	Balanced Scorecards Management by objectives. Total Preventive Maintenance	Seven tools of quality plus other techniques as appropriate. Root cause analysis 5 Whys Gemba Gembutsu	Problem solving techniques Suggestion schemes. Overall equipment effectiveness
Cost	Can be large innovative projects and investment.	Low cost solutions.	Resourced by the organisation.

Note; all of the above mentioned tools and techniques can be found by reference to the contents list or index.

Kaizen and Quality Circles

The Kaizen approach, whilst similar to Quality Circles differs in a numbers of important ways.

Area	Quality Circles	Kaizen Teams
The group	Do similar work Tends to be the workers not management Voluntary	Multi-disciplinary and multi-function Chosen for the task
The Leader	Usually the Supervisor	As appropriate
The Problem	Chosen by the group	Imposed externally

Area	**Quality Circles**	**Kaizen Teams**
Meeting frequency	Regularly	For the duration of the project
Tools	Seven tools of quality	Seven tools plus Affinity Diagram Tree diagram (Systematic diagram) Matrix diagram Relationship diagram Process Decision Programme Diagram (PDPC) Matrix analysis diagram Arrow diagram Business Process Analysis

Exercises

1. Describe how Kaizen teams and Quality Circles differ.
2. Describe how the executive and workers role differ.
3. Describe five ways in which management could demonstrate active commitment to the Kaizen Philosophy.
4. Provide a check list to evaluate an individual's or your level of quality commitment to the organisation.
5. Provide a check list to evaluate an individual's competence.

Answers

1. See text.
2. See text.
3. Management commitment:
    a. Strategy determined
    b. Goals set
    c. Communicated and agreed
    d. Resourced
    e. Monitor and participation

4. Quality Commitment:

"If you are content with the best you've done, then you'll never do the best you can do"

Area \ Degree	Never satisfied	Content	Casual	Indifferent
Learning				
Participation				
Self-improvement				
Personal goals				
Quality of work				
Customers				
Deliverables				

5. Competence

Degree / Area	Can teach others	Good	Limited experience	Undergoing training
Process skill				
Task skill				
Process controls & resources				
Task controls & resources				
Process improvement				
Task improvement				
Knowledge product				
Knowledge competition				
Problem handling &solving				
Deliverables quality				
Process input quality				
People				
Communication				

5S Technique and Approach

Introduction: The 5S is a systematic approach to establishing and maintaining housekeeping standards. With this method, divisions or departments within organisations adopt and implement their own housekeeping programme, for means of improving quality, safety and productivity.

The Programme: This programme is based on the Japanese 5S Housekeeping programme[1] which has been successfully adopted in a number of organisations. Although originally the programme was mainly applied to manufacturing organisations, it has relevance to service organisations as well. Below is an interpretation of the 5S programme for a service organisation. The 5Ss referred to are based on the Japanese words:

i) Seiri or Sorting (clearing out or arranging).
ii) Seiton or Simplifying (configuring or tidying).
iii) Seiso or Sweeping (cleaning).
iv) Seiketsu or Standardising (clean condition or cleanliness).
v) Shitsuke or Self Discipline (culture, training or breeding).

The benefits in an office environment are that this approach has the potential to reduce the number of ledgers, forms and documents. It can improve file retrieval and archiving times. Possibly and most importantly, it provides a catalyst for team building and office process improvement. Offices often provide the customer with their first impression of the organisation and this may reflect (in the customer's view), our approach to work.

The overall aim is to encourage a "*one is best*" campaign of the office: one item of equipment, one file and one filing system, one-page memos, one-hour meetings, one -minute telephone calls, one-day processing.

Seiri or sorting (Clearing out or arrangements)

This refers to clearing out anything and everything that is not required in the workplace. Photographs (coloured with photograph dates) can be taken of the workplace before starting the clearing out process. This is to benchmark or identify the current status in order to show what improvements have been made. A tagging system can be used by the personnel responsible for the area to identify any items or documents not directly involved with their work place or surrounding area.

---

[1] Samuel K Ho - TQM An Integrated Approach

Seiton or simplifying (Configuring or tidying)

The tasks or activity area needs to be organised or configured in order to ensure that items are located correctly and can be easily found. Every desk and storage area could have its own address. In this way the whole area can then be organised into an address grid. The various work areas, desks, copying, stores, cabinets, etc. could be (colour) coded.

Seiso or sweeping (Cleaning)

The purpose of cleaning is to maintain the workplace in a suitable condition for the activities and tasks that need to be performed. This is achieved by ensuring that all excess material or documentation is suitably located or disposed of. All areas that have to be cleaned should be clearly identified with responsibilities allocated and frequency pre-determined.

Seiketsu or standardising (Clean condition or cleanliness)

The work area needs to be maintained in a clean and tidy condition at all times, with no accumulation of unnecessary items or documentation.

Shitsuke or self discipline (Culture, training or breeding)

A working environment needs to be created that welcomes constructive criticism and an improvement culture. This environment is essential if problem points are to be quickly and easily identified and rectified. All work areas need to be clean and tidy and should be free of unnecessary materials and product. Only machines, tools, instruments and equipment which are actually used should be in place. There should be techniques for removing unnecessary items. Work areas should be organised and all machines/equipment labelled and easily identified. All stored and necessary items should be immediately visible. Maximum and minimum stock levels of consumables needs to be clearly visible. All work areas and passage ways should be clearly separated. The storage location of tools/instruments should be clearly labelled for ease of operation and return. The work place should be free of dirt, spills, clothing, and other extraneous materials. All machines, tools, equipment and containers should be clean and in good condition. Responsibilities for cleaning and the state of items should be allocated and cleaning should be a regular part of work. The work place should be standardised and there should be a system for regular clearing up, organising and cleaning. There should be training and discipline in housekeeping. All staff should be aware of procedures and all procedures should be strictly followed. All housekeeping actions should be taken promptly and all actions and controls should be effective. Audits should be conducted against housekeeping procedures.

All Shitsuke should be practised until it has become second nature.

Following is a detailed check list which could be employed when conducting a 5S assessment.

5S Check List			Section:	Checker:				
Marks: . . . . %			Previous Marks: . . . . %	Date:				
5S	#	Checking Item	Evaluation Criteria	0	1	2	3	4
Clearing Up (20 Marks)	1	Task inputs & Deliverables	No unnecessary paper work or finished documentation left lying around.					
	2	Equipment (utilisation)	All equipment is in regular use.					
	3	Equipment (condition)	All equipment is regularly serviced & maintained.					
	4	Visual control	There are no unnecessary items left lying around on tops of desks, cabinets or chairs.					
	5	Standards for disposal	Items and documentation are properly disposed of, e.g. tag items.					

5S	#	Checking Item	Evaluation Criteria	0	1	2	3	4
Organising (20 Marks)	1	Equipment labelling	Equipment is clearly labelled.					
	2	Necessary items	All necessary items can be quickly identified and located.					
	3	Consumables	Minimum and maximum stock levels are established and visible.					
	4	Dividing lines	Work areas and passageways are clearly divided.					
	5	Equipment and tools	Storage locations of tools and equipment are clearly marked for ease of use and return.					
Cleaning (20 marks)	1	Floors	Clean and clear					
	2	Equipment	Tidy and serviceable					
	3	Desks and cabinets	Clear and tidy					
	4	Computers and ancillaries	Tidy and serviceable					
	5	Health and safety	Fire, protective equipment, lifting & handling, COSHH, disaster recovery.					
Standardising (20 Marks)	1	One method of working, e.g. one day processing	Process based procedures available Targets set and records kept of processing performance.					
	2	One set of files, e.g. one location, one copy, one minute file storage and retrieval	Examine file condition Test ability to store and retrieve records in one minute.					

5S	#	Checking Item	Evaluation Criteria	0	1	2	3	4
	3	One set of documentation e.g. forms and one-page memos	Examine forms Examine memos					
	4	One piece of equipment	Examine equipment availability and quantity					
	5	One-minute telephone calls, one-hour meetings,	Review telephone call practice and duration Review meeting times.					
Training & Discipline (20 Marks)	1	5S Programme and audit results	Results published, reviewed and improvements made.					
	2	Team building	Process improvement. Meetings held and real solutions identified.					
	3	Team briefing and communication	Team briefing held.					
	4	Absenteeism and employee turn over	Review records.					
	5	Recognition	Recognition for achievement is observed.					
Total								

Key

Scores	
0	Very Poor
1	Poor
2	Average
3	Good
4	Very Good

These audit check lists could be reviewed and analysed at a pre-determined frequency to show the improvements made.

Value Analysis

Introduction

The aim of Value Analysis (VA) is to investigate the function of a system, process or equipment with the objective of achieving the intended function at the lowest overall cost. The technique is a logical, disciplined approach that can be applied from individual components or stages up to complete systems or processes. It consists of five basic phases:

a. Information phase
b. Function phase
c. Speculation phase
d. Evaluation phase
e. Implementation phase

Sometimes, when systems or products are designed, certain key customer requirements can be overlooked, also not all the design options may have been considered. VA provides the opportunity for a team of people to critically review the system or product design to establish simpler, cheaper and more effective ways of achieving the design's intended function. This technique has provided some astounding successes in reducing design and manufacturing costs. Savings of tens of thousands of pounds per month is not unusual. It is particularly successful where the system or product has never been Value Analysed before.

Guidelines for Value Analysis

Value Analysis is a team approach, although the first stage (information) may be completed by one person, subsequent stages are a team effort.

Information Phase: This phase involves gaining as much information as possible about the item under evaluation to enable a complete understanding of the system being studied.

Table 1 Sheet 1 - Information Form

INFORMATION PHASE	
Basic Data	Information
Title Drawing Number and issue no.	
Design Data Design Material Quantity	
Process Data Process Costs Volumes/batch sizes	 Materials Labour Sub-Contract

This can include: obtaining drawings and parts lists, diagrams and photographs, descriptions of the process, flow diagrams, customer specifications, costs, budgets, time scales or quantities. It may be that some of this information is sketchy or unavailable. This phase can be a very lengthy stage involving a number of man hours (100 man hours is not unusual). (See **Table 1**)

Function phase: This phase involves defining the basic function of the item under evaluation.

The function being the purpose for which the item exists, the purpose for which it was designed and manufactured. The function can be broken down into two parts - the basic and secondary function.

Table 2 Sheet 2 - Function Form

Purpose	Information	
What does the item do? Operation & Performance Is this task necessary? Can another method or component perform this function?		
Function Basic Secondary	Verb	Noun
Are all these functions necessary		
Other major design requirements		

The basic function is the specific feature which must be attained. It may be that the item has two basic functions to perform.

The secondary function is the features other than those which must be attained. To help in clarifying the basic and secondary function, it may be helpful to express the function of the item in terms of a verb and a noun. This ensures an exact understanding and statement of the function of the item, which provides the opportunity for exploring many possible approaches to achieving the function. (See **Table 2**)

Table 3 opposite shows this function definition. Using a screw driver as an example the basic function is to convey torque (including the handle) and the secondary function is to aid friction. If the screw driver was an electrician's screw driver then another basic function would be to protect the user/electrician.

Table 3 Screw driver

Function	Verb	Noun
Basic Function	Conveys	Torque
Secondary Function	Aids	Friction

Speculation phase: This phase involves speculating as many problem solutions as possible. Often this phase is called Brainstorming. Brainstorming can be used to generate possible solutions and latterly to develop possible action plans.

Brainstorming

Firstly, a full understanding of the function of the item will have been gained by the completion of the information and function phases. Having clearly stated the function the next stage is for the team to propose as many different solutions as possible. To get accustomed to the concept of brainstorming it may be helpful for the team to brain storm a trivial problem like "Name as many different uses of a brick as possible" before moving on to the actual problem. It is important that this speculation is performed freely with no evaluation or criticism of the proposed solutions or approaches. During the Brain Storm all of the team's suggestions are written on a flip chart with the objective that the team may develop other ideas.

Evaluation phase: Having generated a list of possible solutions these solutions require evaluation to determine the most appropriate approach.

The list of solutions is initially reviewed to remove ones which can obviously be rejected. Next, the list is rewritten and the team awards marks for each suggestion in terms of cost, simplicity, ease of application and introduction. A scale of 1 to 10 can be used. For example:

Highest cost award 1, lowest cost award 10
Most Complex award 1, most simple award 10
Difficult to implement award 1, easy to implement award 10

These numbers can be multiplied together to give an overall score for each suggestion.

This should reduce the list down to the final few where upon the Evaluation Form can be employed. Each of the remaining solutions are listed on the left-hand side of the form. On the right-hand side each solution's good and bad features are listed, e.g. costs (material and manufacturing) etc. At this stage other information may be required (costings, feasibility studies etc) and action may need to be taken away from the VA team's meeting. (See **Table 4**)

Table 4 Sheet 3 - Evaluation Form

Evaluation Phase		
Possible Solution	Advantages	Disadvantages

At any time during the Evaluation phase it may be appropriate to return to the Speculation phase to refine some of the ideas but it is important to remember not to criticise or evaluate while speculating.

Implementation phase: This is probably the most difficult of all the phases discussed, but the most important as the Value Analysis Team has not completed its task until the proposed solution has been implemented. There will be numerous reasons (or negative attitudes) put

Table 5 Sheet 4 - Approvals Form

Implementation Phase		
Features	Proposed	Current
Cost Analysis Material Cost Labour Cost Sub-contract Cost		
Implementation Cost Detailed Design Product Development Equipment Design & Manufacture Other Costs		
Approvals Quality Purchasing Design Marketing Customer Service Production		

forward as to why the proposed solution will not work or not be acceptable. "We've done it before, the customer won't accept it, too difficult, too expensive" etc. All of these problems need to be addressed before implementation can be achieved. Many key people will need to be convinced of the viability of the proposed solution. The Approvals Form **Table 5** shown opposite is one method of clearly listing the benefits gained by the implementation of the solution. The Approval Form can also be used to record acceptance of the approach by the relevant personnel.

A clear implementation programme is required and again the Brainstorming techniques can be employed. (**Table 6** - Implementation Form may be used to provide guidance in establishing the Implementation Programme.)

Table 6 Sheet 5 - Implementation Form

Implementation Phase		
Stage	Date	Duration
Submit VA proposals		
Approve VA proposals		
Produce Specification		
Review & Approve specification		
Design FMEA		
Produce prototype		
Test prototype (Lab & field)		
Produce process plan		
Process FMEA		
Produce Inspection & test plan		
Process Approval		
Purchase items		
Process capability studies		
Produce		

Overall Equipment Effectiveness

"If you do not measure it, you can not improve it"

In order to establish the effectiveness of the Total Productive Maintenance (TPM) programme it is necessary to measure performance. Usually organisations have some kind of performance measurement system on their equipment that measures criteria such as; quantities, operating time, cycle time, etc. These criteria are fine but they are measures of equipment output and not necessarily capability which is what TPM requires. I.e how much more could we achieve from this equipment? How effective is this equipment? - overall equipment effectiveness.

Overall Equipment Effectiveness (OEE) provides a metric to continually monitor how effectively the equipment is performing and where the losses are with the potential for improvement.

For more information see Total Productive Maintenance on page 250 and for a more fuller description of Overall Equipment Effectiveness see page 255.

Failure Mode and Effects Analysis (FMEA)

Introduction

Failure Mode and Effects Analysis (FMEA) is a logical technique used to identify and eliminate possible causes of failure. The technique requires a sequential, disciplined approach by engineers to assess systems, products or processes in order to establish the modes of failure and the effects of failure on the system, product or process. This is to ensure that all possible failure modes have been fully identified and ranked in order of their importance. The FMEA discipline requires the engineers to document their evaluation with regard to the failure mode, effect and criticality. The analysis work can be applied at any stage; design, manufacture, test, installation or use; but is best performed at the design stage. In a simple system the study may be performed on the total system or product, but with more complex systems it may be necessary to break the product down into various sub-systems or sub-assemblies.

The addition of the "C" in FMECA refers to the criticality analysis and risk priority number generated when carrying out this analysis. The calculation of the risk priority number is included in the Guidelines for FMEA. For further information on FMEA and other Risk Analysis techniques see page 199.

Poka-Yoke

"Those who are not dissatisfied will never make any progress"

Dr Shigeo Shingo

Introduction

Poka-Yoke is fool proofing, which is the basis of the Zero Quality Control (ZQC) approach, which is a technique for avoiding and eliminating mistakes. Generally this technique is used in manufacturing process but has much wider uses, such as; offices - order and invoice processing, hospitals - drug dispensing, aircraft maintenance - particularly with processes having the potential of inducing catastrophic in-service failures. The term Poka-Yoke is Japanese and can roughly be translated as mistake or fool proofing. It is derived from 'poka' - inadvertent mistake and 'yoke' - avoid. Of course, the concept of fool proofing processes and mechanical devises has been around for many years (e.g. see photographs of floppy disk drive and electrical plugs) but is was the Japanese Matsushita Industrial Engineer Dr. Shigeo Shingo who was probably most prominent and influential in developing it into a technique. He turned the idea into a powerful approach for eliminating mistakes and achieving zero defects. Dr. Shingo used the phrase "error avoidance", as he recognised that people, or more specifically Japanese workers, may take offence at the term fool, particularly when associated with mistakes. This is especially important when considering the technique and approach requires the workers active participation in the error cause removal programme[2].

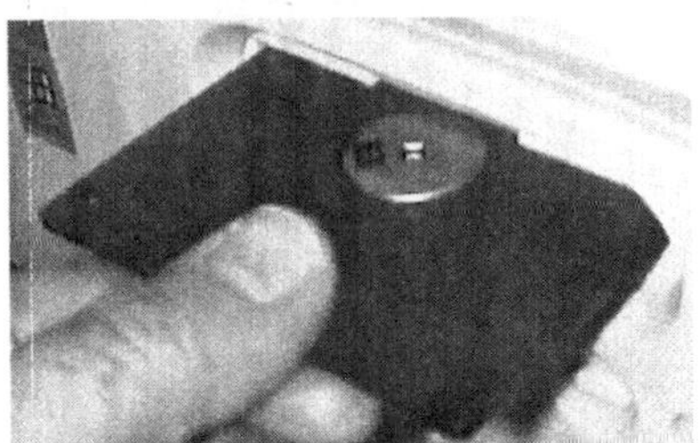

Figure 3 Floppy disk

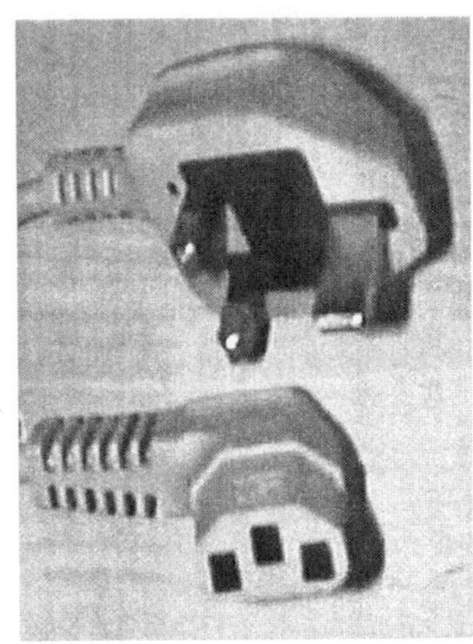

Figure 4 Electrical Plug

Dr. Shingo wrote the book "Zero Quality Control: Source Inspection and the Poke-yoke system" in 1986. This original source material defined the basic approach. However, the technique has been extensively developed since. Dr. Shingo also suggests that statistical process

[2] Note: error cause removal and zero defects are phases first used by Philip Crosby but the approach is very different and should not be confused..

control (SPC) cannot achieve zero defect because by its very nature it is a sampling technique which must inevitably allow defects. SPC also implies a feedback control loop which may be too slow in preventing defects from being made. See figure 5, Statistical Process Control. With the process shown in figure 5 it is conceivable that the process could have gone out of control before the "gather information" and "action" stages had been completed. Consequently defects could have been produced. Contrast this with ZQC which eliminates the causes of mistakes and consequently defects.

A study by Grout and Downs (1995) indicated that:

- ZQC is not as effective as SPC where the defects are as a result of process variation.
- ZQC is effective as a means of eliminating special causes[3] of variation as identified by SPC attribute data.
- ZQC can effectively be combined with SPC to eliminate special causes of variation.

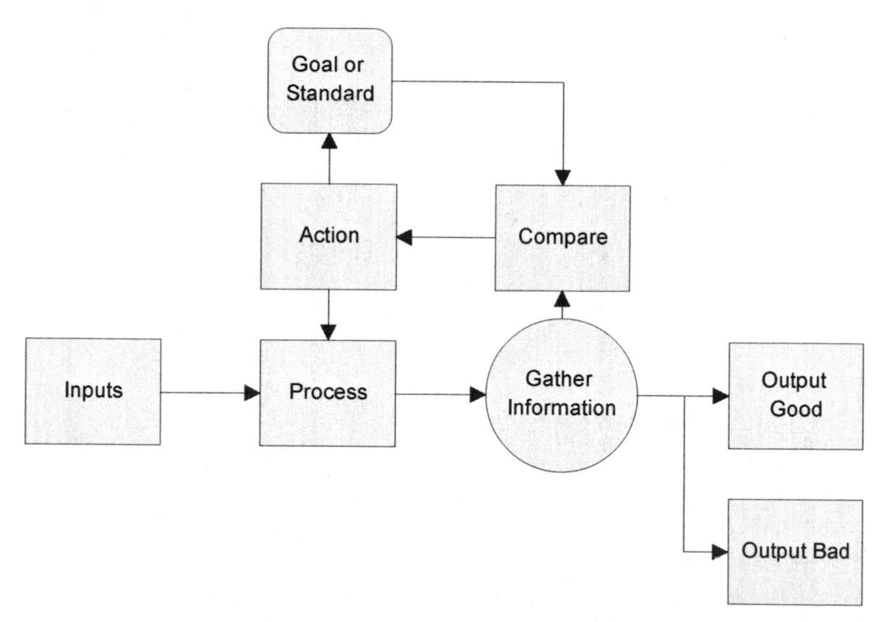

Figure 5 Statistical Process Control

3 Special causes of variation are non random events identified by data which has failed one of the four tests of variation. See Statistical Process Control

Errors & mistakes

The ZQC approach recognises that work can be repetitive and because it is difficult to maintain concentration, particularly over long periods of time, mistakes can be made. Certain processes may also be very complex and require considerable dexterity which can increase the pressure on a busy operator and provide further opportunity for errors. In these situation it may be considered that mistakes are inevitable and consequently defects will be produced. So Acceptable Quality Levels (AQL) targets need to be established. For example a batch is accepted on 2 defects rejected on 3, but this flies in the face of concepts like zero defects and provides the potential for at least 2 customers being dissatisfied with their product or service. Possibly Poka-Yoke is even more important when considering safety critical processes like drug dispensing, aircraft servicing or atomic weapon assembly, where this level of defects would simply be unacceptable. Some people even seem to take a perverse pleasure in rushing around resolving the consequences of errors, mistakenly believing that the error source can never be identified or the causes prevented - there are simply too many and the issues too complex. ZQC shows mistakes are not inevitable and steps can be taken to; eliminate the causes of mistakes, introduce devices that automatically stop error inducing conditions or stop the process immediately when a mistake is made.

There are a number of potential errors and Juran spoke of three: technical, inadvertent and wilful errors. Nikkan Kogyo Shimbun speaks of ten: forgetfulness, misunderstanding, identification, amateurs, willful, inadvertent, slowness, lack of standard, surprise and intentional errors. Philip Crosby talks of two: lack of knowledge and lack of attention, all other errors are as a result of these two types. Confused? Well it may not matter too much as long as error causes are understood and an approach is adopted to prevent errors occurring.

Types of errors:

- *Forgetful errors* - Absent-mindedness can happen for a number of reasons: lack of concentration, a moment's inattention could cause an error to occur. Possible prevention methods are; check lists, automatic safe guards, work reorganisation, Poka-Yoke, etc.
- *Misunderstanding* - It is easy to misconstrue instructions or commands if they are not clear (*"Into the valley of death rode the five hundred"*) and as a consequence, take the wrong action. Possible prevention methods are; written instructions, training, first off checks, etc.
- *Wrong Identification* - Wrong categorisation or designation of an item, file or quantity can result in expensive errors. Clear methods of identification need to be established;. tagging or labelling, colour coding (although one in ten are colour blind to some degree), photographs, examples, etc.

- *Lack of Experience* - Lack of preparation for tasks and activities not only extends the start up time but also makes errors more likely. Possible prevention methods include: induction training, improved selection procedures, skill building, certification of inspectors, competent employees.
- *Willful Errors* - Intentional errors can occur either due to deliberate mistakes or just because the rules were ignored. Possible prevention methods include: education, discipline.

The ZQC approach is based around understanding these basic errors and mistakes and the establishment of an improvement method that will eliminate the causes and prevent defects. In order to establish this improvement method it is necessary to understand the basic inspection techniques which can be used to avoid errors and mistakes.

Inspection techniques

There are three basic inspection techniques which can be employed in quality controlling processes. These are described in the following table.

Inspection Technique	Description
Sorting or judgmental inspection	Sorting Inspection - is a sorting process which segregates the defects from the acceptable items. This action prevents defects from being received by the customer but does not prevent further defects from being made. This is the traditional approach.
Detection inspection - informative inspection	Detection Inspection - is an investigation of the causes of defective items with the objective of eventually taking corrective action to prevent recurrence.
Preventive inspection - source inspection	Preventive Inspection - is inspection of the potential causes of defects preventing sources of defect occurring, avoiding the production of defects in the first place. Poka-yoke may be considered one method which could be employed to achieve this objective, i.e. automatically 100% inspecting or eliminating the potential causes of defects. There are three stages or elements to the Preventive Inspection approach factors that lead to the elimination of mistakes and the achievement of zero defects: ○ Error elimination - An understanding of the factors that can cause the defects. ○ Error proofing - Fail safe techniques which prevent the factor which cause defects. ○ Error avoidance - Immediate action which stops the process in the event of a mistake being made, until the causes of the mistake are understood and fail safe mechanisms are established.

Defect causes

In order to evaluate errors, mistakes and help determine the most appropriate course of action it is necessary to understand the likely causes of defects. Listed below are just some possible defect causes.

Possible defect causes

Omitted operation	Faulty processing	Wrong location
Missing parts	Wrong part	Equipment adjustment fault
Incorrect set up	Faulty equipment	

Shown in table 7 is an analysis between the above defect causes and the types of error (discussed previously). Table 7 shows the strength of the relationship between defect causes and types of error. This analysis can be used to help determine the most suitable course of action for a particular defect cause. For example, according to table 7, a missing part is likely to be caused by forgetfulness. Now what steps can be taken to avoid forgetfulness? Well that is the next step in our ZQC approach.

Table 7 Comparison of error types with causes

	Forgetful	Misunderstanding	Wrong Identification	Lack of Experience	Willful Error
Omitted Operation	◙	⊡	⊡	⊡	◙
Faulty Processing	◙	◙	⊡	◙	◙
Wrong Location	◙	⊡	◙	◙	◙
Missing Part	◙	□	◙	□	□
Wrong Part	⊡	□	□	□	□
Equipment Adjustment Fault	□	◙	□	◙	□
Incorrect Setup	□	◙	◙	⊡	◙
Faulty Equipment	◙	□	□	□	□

Key

Strong Link	◙
Medium Link	⊡
Weak Link	□

ZQC approach

ZQC principles; There are three basic principles behind the ZQC approach:

Firstly do not manufacture any more products than are actually required (See Just in Time). The principle being that finished products have a greater opportunity to be damaged than in the component or sub-assembly form. In other words - ‘Do not produce’.

Secondly use the product as soon as possible, as the user is an expert in finding defects. This is particularly important if the product cannot be manufactured to withstand abuse. In other words 'Once made - use it'.

Thirdly ensure the product can withstand use and abuse. This may involve building in poka-yoke devices into the manufacturing process that will safe guard the production process. In other words 'User-friendly manufacture'.

Poka-Yoke function and devices

The Poka-Yoke function needs to address two possible states; errors which are about to occur and errors which have occurred.

In the case of errors which are about to occur prevention is necessary to;

- stop the process from producing a defect,
- control the situation so that a defect is not produced and
- provide a warning that a defect is about to occur.

In the case of errors that have occurred then detection is necessary to;

- stop further defect items being produced,
- ensuring that the defect item does not get further processed and
- provide a warning alert indicating that a defect has occurred.

Poka-Yoke devices fall into two main classes; prevention and detection. Prevention devices are usually the best as they prevent an error from happening and usually the operation cannot be completed until corrected, e.g. our electrical plug and floppy disk drive, see figures 3 and 4. Other examples include limit switches, stops and counters. The filing cabinet in the photograph has a safety stop device on the draws. This safety stop will only allow one draw to be opened at a time, avoiding the dangerous situation of the cabinet over balancing.

Figure 6 Filing Cabinet

Detection devices are classified as devices which by some means advise that an error may occur but do not necessarily prevent it. For example, on some cars, if the car door is opened with the lights left on, a buzzer will sound alerting the occupants. However, the car occupants can still leave the car with the lights on. Other examples could include warning lights and checklists.

Table 8 shows an example of a checklist a lecturer may use in preparation for a lecture.

Table 8 Lecturers Checklist

Reserve the room	✔
Order participant course notes	✔
Confirm course objectives with Business Unit Manager	✔
Obtain list of attendees	✔
Communication with attendees & supervisors (time, place, pre-course work (if any))	✔
Check teaching materials (pens, pencils, notes, blank and completed overheads, white board markers, highlighter, writing paper, hole punch)	✔
Order refreshments	✔
Check condition of overheads and assemble exercise material	✔
Prepare course certificates	✔
Check meeting room (white board, flip charts *2, overhead projector (including spare bulb), screen, room layout (horse shoe?)	✔
Prepare for presentation	✔
Arrive 45 minutes early	✔

ZQC implementation

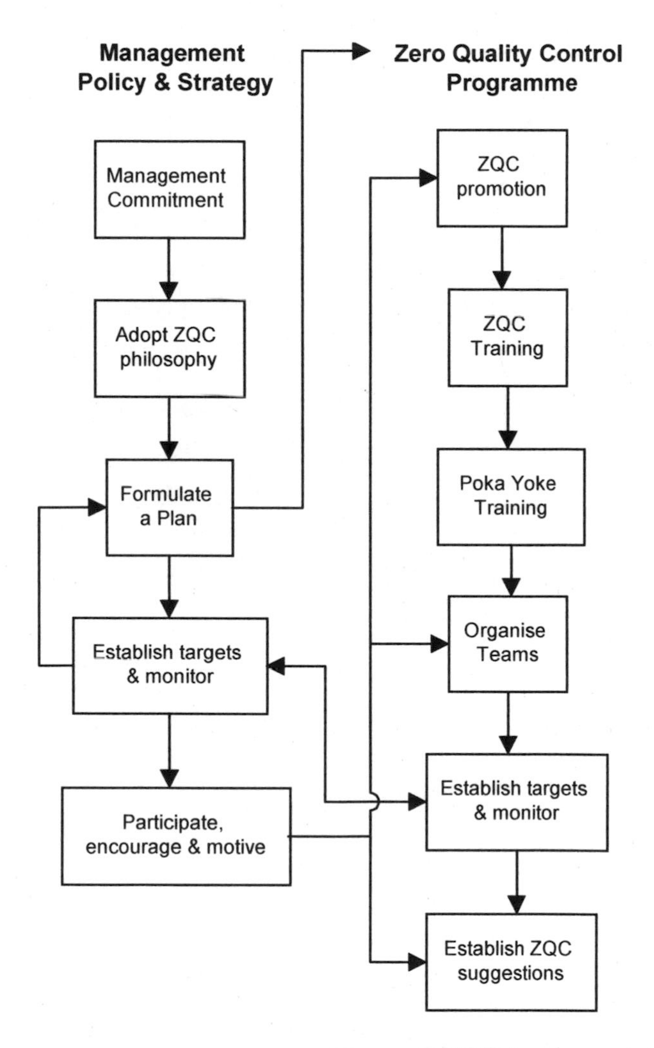

Figure 7 ZQC Implementation

See figure 7. As with all quality improvement initiates the first stage is Management Commitment, committing management to adopting the new philosophy and cementing this philosophy in a set of policies and strategy. This new philosophy will need to embrace concepts such as 'zero defects', which shows mistakes are not inevitable and errors can be eliminated. Investment needs to be made (both financial and human) specifically in ZQC, Poka-Yoke, 5S and problem solving training. An action plan needs to be formulated which will drive the ZQC programme, involving all levels of the organisation, motivating them to participate in the ZQC programme. Targets for this programme need to be established not only in terms of projected error reductions but also in terms of ZQC programme milestones, take up, levels of participation and involvement. More over the management needs to be proactively enthusing and rewarding those participating in the ZQC programme and encouraging those that are not.

Table 9 Typical Poka-Yoke improvement form

Process: Packaging	**Prevent Error**:	**Shut Down**:
Problem: Missing or too many items in packaging	**Detect error**: ✖	**Control**: ✖
Solution: Weight completed and assembled package	**Key Improvement**: No more shortages in presentation package	
Description of Process: Camera presentation box packaging including; User Manual, Batteries * 2, Film *2, Camera and Strap		
Before Improvement: It was possible to miss certain items out of the box e.g. batteries or film	**After Improvement**: A weighting stage was added to the process. Once the package was completely assembled the package would be checked for over or under weight.	

Exercises:

1 Identify and describe the differences between Shigeo Shingo and Philip Crosby views on Zero defect.

2 Four Poka-Yoke devices have already been identified (an electrical plug, a floppy disk drive, filing cabinet and a lecturer's checklist). Identify an example of a prevention and detection Poka-Yoke device for each of the headings below.

Heading - Device type	**Prevent Error**	**Detect Error**
Location		
Alarms		
Limit switches		
Counters		
Checklists		

3 Identify a process or activity that has been the cause of errors in the past and design a Poka-yoke device that is cheap, simple[4], part of the process[5] and placed close to where the error is likely to occur[6].

4 Define:
- 4.1 Zero Quality Control
- 4.2 Poka-Yoke
- 4.3 Sorting inspection
- 4.4 Detection inspection
- 4.5 Preventive inspection

---

[4] Cheap and simple or the implementation will not be a cost effective exercise.

[5] This means that Shigeo Shingo version of 100% inspection will automatically take place. The Poka-yoke device provides a 100% check that prevents or detects the error.

[6] Providing immediate feedback to the operator that an error has or is about to take place.

Process Capability

No matter what precautions are taken, no two items are absolutely identical. Differences may be barely measurable but they exist and that is why tolerances are allowed on drawings and specifications.

A manufacturing process, no matter how precise, is subject to a very large number of random disturbances, each so small as to be individually insignificant, but which in combination cause the results of the process to deviate slightly from the objective.

The inherent variability thus caused is a characteristic of the process. It is the basic variability which is always present when that particular process is in operation and is called the RESIDUAL variability.

The causes of variation can be divided into machine and process variations.

Machine variations

Machine variations are purely and simply those variations attributable to the machine only. It is the best that a machine can be expected to produce given ideal the conditions. Machines vary in their capabilities owing to their age and condition or the tolerances to which the machine was constructed. For a given machine some functions may be more capable than others. For example, a drilling machine will generally be more precise (have a better capability) on hole diameter than on position. Some examples of the relative capabilities of common manufacturing processes are shown below.

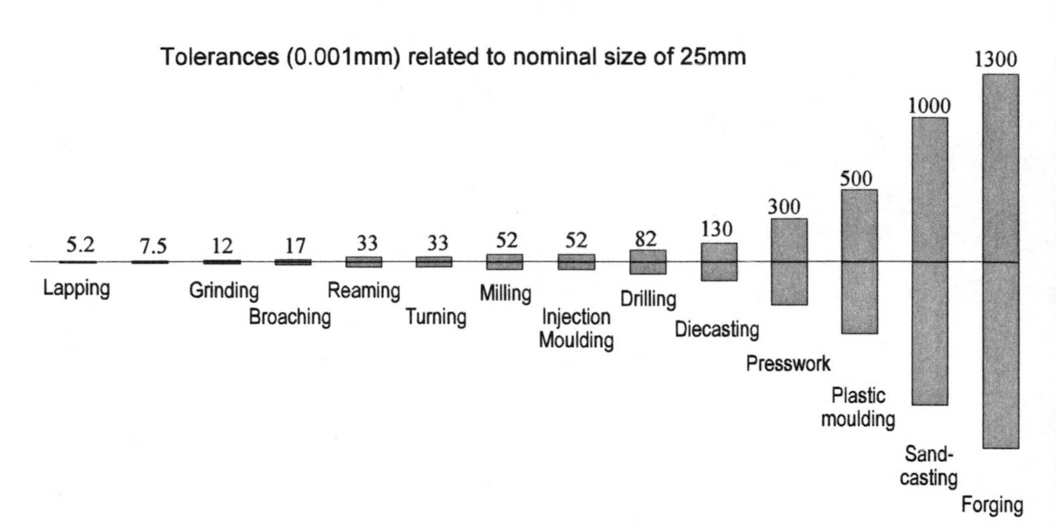

Figure 8 Process Capabilities

Process variations

Process variations are those over and above the machine variations which are attributable to circumstances around the machine. They include the effect of environmental fluctuations such as temperature and humidity, variations in raw materials, variations in operator attention, variations from shift to shift and so on.

The first important check, therefore, is to consider whether the machine and subsequently the process, are both capable of doing the job to the specification. This will require machine and process capability studies to be carried out.

The sources of variation can be further categorised into two types:

i) Common causes, otherwise known as random causes.
ii) Special causes, otherwise known as non-random or assignable causes.

i) Common causes

Common causes appear to follow a random pattern and are due to inherent variations in the machine or process. For a particular machine or process, the pattern of variation will be characterised by its location, spread, and shape. The combination of these characteristics is called the machine capability in the case of the machine and the process capability in the case of the process. It is the natural tolerance of a stable machine or process.

In general, improvements in machine and process capabilities having only common cause variations, can only be achieved through detailed analysis to identify and isolate particular causes. This usually requires managerial action such as overhauling or replacing a machine, changing to more reliable supplies of materials, providing better tooling, providing further training for operators and so on.

ii) Special causes

Variations due to special causes do not form a random pattern but quite definitely indicate a shift, trend, cycle or otherwise systematic variation such as peaks or troughs. For a stable process, two thirds of the measurements should lie within the middle third of the capability band, with the other third being equally divided into the outer two thirds. In addition, no more than seven points in a row should be consistently above the mean, below the mean or progressively up or down.

In general, variations due to special causes can be controlled by local actions such as resetting the machine controls, taking a lighter cut, providing more immediate feedback of performance to the operator etc.

Process capability studies

Before allocating a job to a given machine or process, it is necessary to establish whether the process is capable of meeting the specification. A simple approach is described below:

a) Set the process to meet its target figure. This would normally be its mid point of specification.
b) Ensure the process is stable and under control.
c) Take 50 consecutive units from the process and measure them accurately to one more decimal place than the specified tolerance, e.g. if the specified tolerance is ±0.01mm, then measure to the nearest .001mm.
d) Assuming that the distribution of results forms a smooth bell shaped curve (approximating a normal distribution - see section normal distribution), calculate the arithmetical mean $\overline{X}$ and the standard deviation σ of the 50 units.
e) The process capability (C_p) is considered to be six standard deviations (6σ). Now compare the six standard deviations with the specified tolerance thus:

$$Cp = \frac{\textit{specified tolerance}}{6\sigma}$$

The potential process capability

The potential process capability is the best that the process can achieve having eliminated special cause variations. The process is said to be stable when the variations are due to random causes only. Six standard deviations are considered to contain 99.7% of all items made. To determine if a process is capable the statistic Cp needs to be calculated. If Cp = 1 then approximately 3 in every 1,000 will be outside the specification. This means that values of Cp greater than 1, say 1.5 or even 2.0, are desirable. Diagrammatically this may look like this:

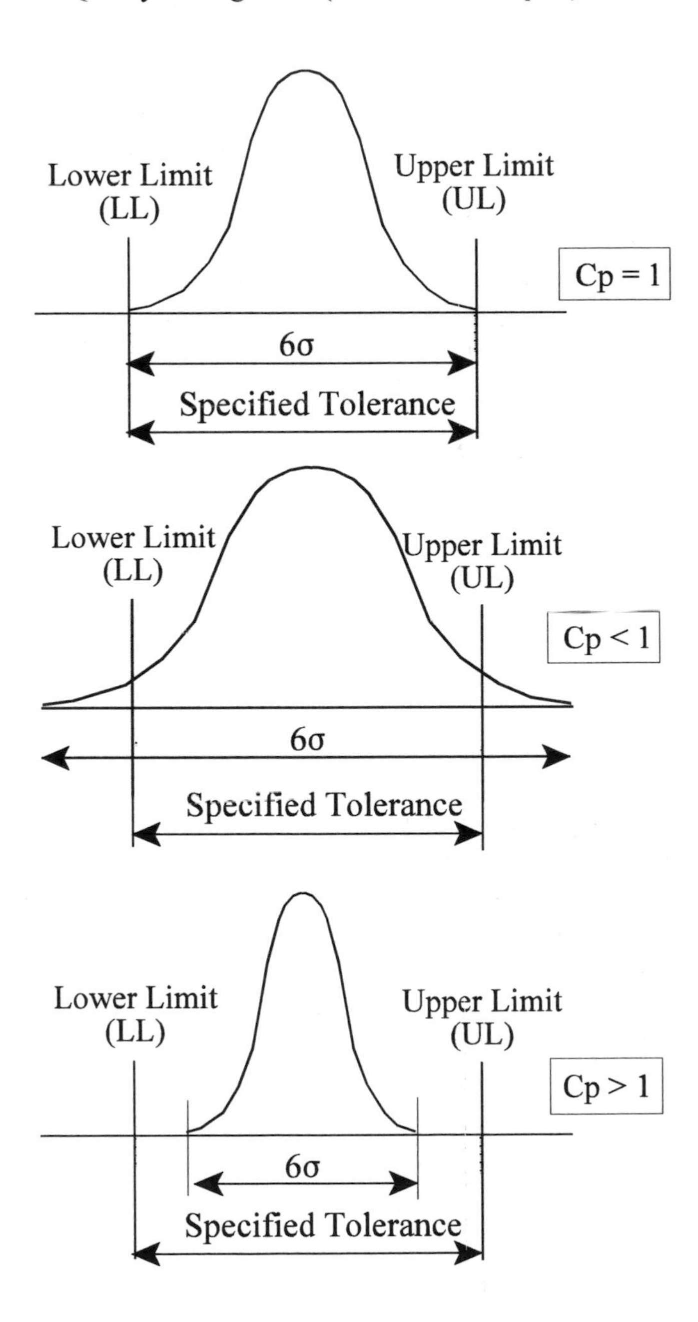

Figure 9 Process capability

Example

We are now going to work through an example based on the inspection results of a sample of 40 bolts. The following shows how raw data is turned into meaningful information. The diameter of a sample of 40 bolts was measured with the following results:

7.31	7.47	7.55	7.20	7.45	7.49	7.62	7.86	7.44	7.39
7.38	7.57	7.63	7.24	7.76	7.55	7.56	7.18	7.00	7.83
7.57	7.24	7.32	7.39	7.42	7.35	7.63	7.41	7.40	7.30
7.48	7.49	7.27	7.51	7.51	7.73	7.12	7.37	7.48	7.14

A chronological plot is produced to establish that there are no trends or patterns:

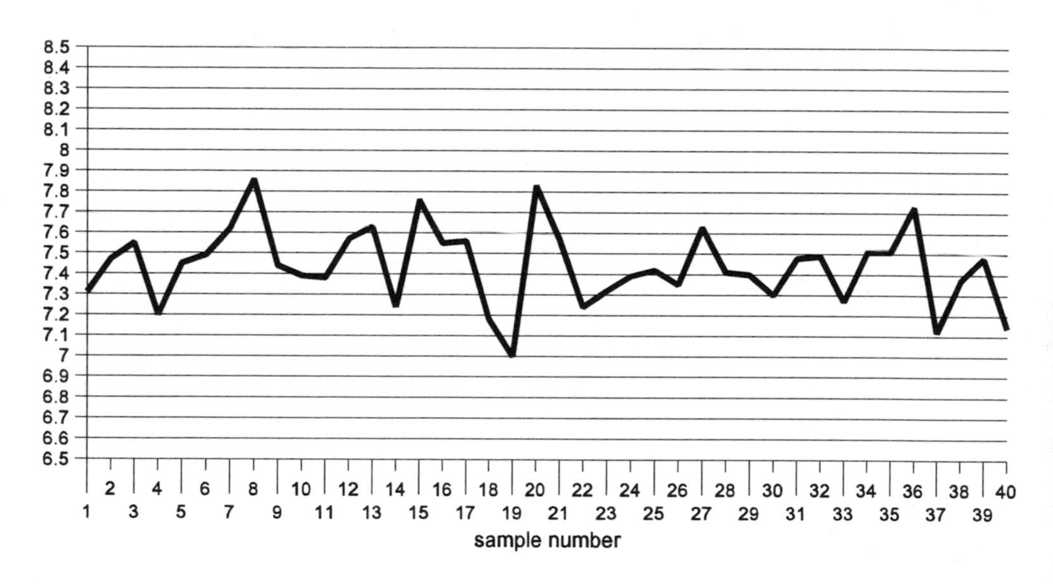

Figure 10 Chronological plot of data

By drawing a frequency distribution we can confirm that it approximates to a normal distribution. The data must be grouped into approximately 10 intervals to create a frequency diagram. The boundaries of these intervals are called the *class limits.* The nominal value for each class interval is used to represent its respective class. A tally chart is used to record the number of items within each class.

Class limits	Nominal value N_i	Tally	Freq. X_i
7.80-7.89	7.845	11	2
7.70-7.79	7.745	11	2
7.60-7.69	7.645	111	3
7.50-7.59	7.545	~~1111~~ 11	7
7.40-7.49	7.445	~~1111~~ ~~1111~~	10
7.30-7.39	7.345	~~1111~~ 111	8
7.20-7.29	7.245	1111	4
7.10-7.19	7.145	111	3
7.00-7.09	7.045	1	1

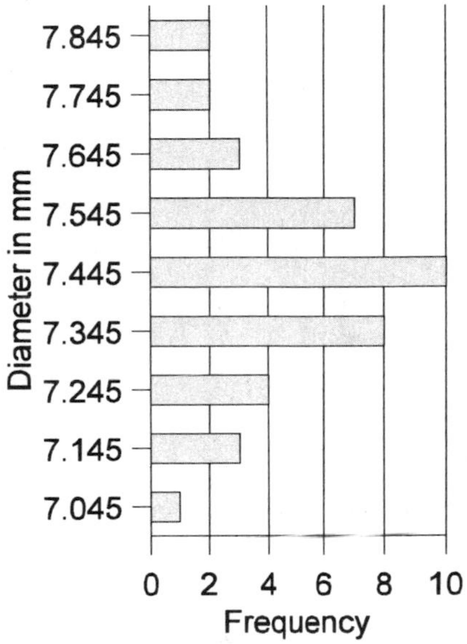

Figure 11

To determine the process capability we need to calculate the mean and hence the standard deviation of the raw data.

$$Mean\ \bar{x} = \frac{\sum_{i=1}^{i=40} x_i}{n}$$

$$\bar{x} = 7.440$$

$$Standard\ deviation\ \sigma = \sqrt{\frac{\sum_{i=1}^{i=40} \left(\bar{x} - x_i\right)^2}{n}}$$

$$\sigma = 0.1899$$

Process Capability = 6σ = 1.139

In other words, the process is currently producing components in the range:

$$\bar{x} \pm 3\sigma$$
$$= 6.8703 \text{ to } 8.0097$$

Now suppose that the specified tolerance was, say, 7.5 ± .5 then clearly the process is not capable of producing 100% non-defectives. For one thing, the mean is offset from the nominal and secondly, the spread is wider than the specified tolerance.

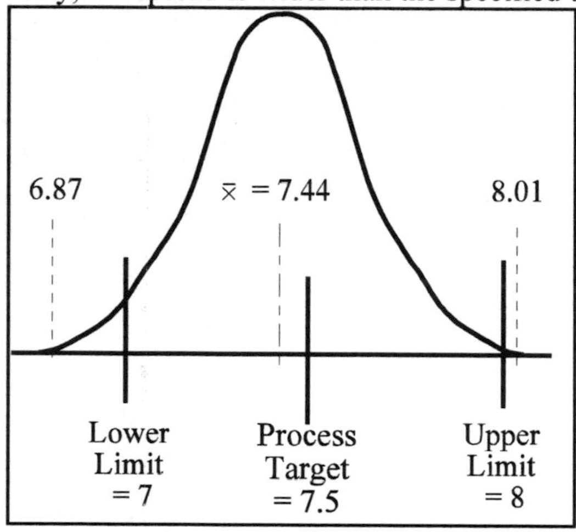

Figure 12 Process in relation to specification

Process Capability Index

A Cpk value, called the process capability index, may also be helpful, as this takes into account the *accuracy*, i.e. the location of the mean, of the process.

$$Cpk = \frac{UL - \bar{x}}{3\sigma} \quad or \quad \frac{\bar{x} - LL}{3\sigma} \qquad \textbf{(1)}$$

whichever is the smaller

As with the Cp, the Cpk must be greater than 1 to avoid defectives being produced.

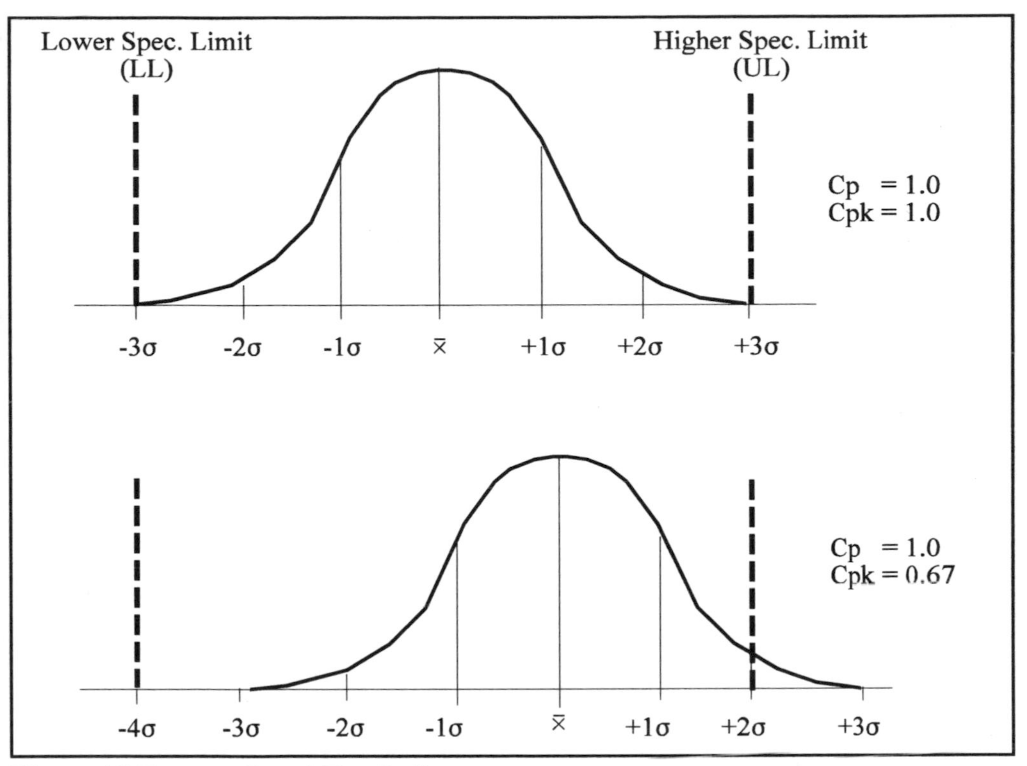

Figure 13 Process Capability Indices

At this stage, a basic knowledge of capability will suffice - see the following examples. Long term movement and variation of the process is possible and further control of processes will be discussed later.

Examples

Example 1

Specification = 1000±50
σ = 20 units

Assuming a stable process, which has been adjusted to be central between the specified limits, calculate the Cp and Cpk.

Tolerance = 100 units

$$Cp = \frac{100}{6 \times 20} = 0.83$$

process is not capable of meeting the specification, rejects will be inevitable.

Process Capability (Cpk)

$$Cpk = \frac{\text{upper limit - mean}}{3\sigma} \quad \text{or} \quad \frac{\text{mean - lower limit}}{3\sigma}$$

whichever is the smaller

$$Cpk = \frac{50}{3 \times 20} = 0.83$$

Note, since the process is assumed to be central, Cpk is equal to Cp, i.e.0 .83

Example 2.

$$\begin{aligned} \text{Specification} &= 115\pm5 \\ \overline{X} &= 112 \text{ units} \\ \sigma &= 1 \text{ unit} \end{aligned}$$

Calculate Cp and Cpk.

$$Cp = \frac{10}{6 \times 1} = 1.67$$

$$Cpk = \frac{112 - 110}{3 \times 1} = 0.67$$

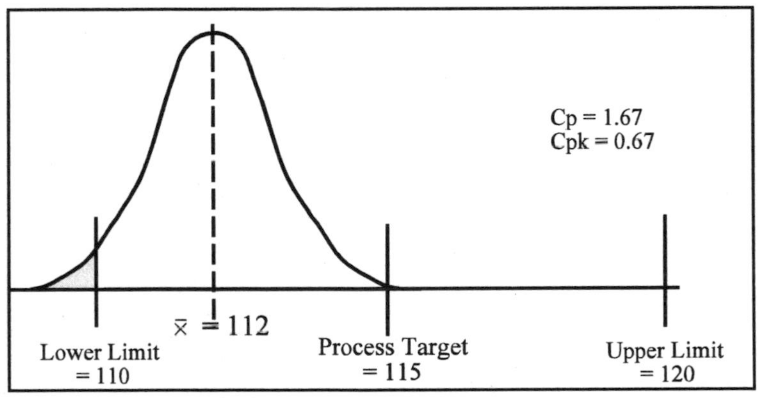

Figure 14 Example 2

Process is capable but requires adjustment

Example 3

UL = 50 units, LL = 45 units
$\sigma = 0.2$ units, $\bar{x}= 48.5$ units
Calculate Cp and Cpk.

$$Cp = \frac{5}{6 \times 0.2} = 4.17$$

$$Cpk = \frac{50 - 48.5}{3 \times 0.2} = 2.5$$

therefore process is capable

Example 4

Target value		=	6 units
Tolerance		=	±6 units
Process mean	$\bar{X}$	=	6 units
Process sigma	σ	=	2 units

Calculate Cp and Cpk.

$$Cp = \frac{\text{Tolerance}}{6\sigma} = \frac{12}{6 \times 2} = 1$$ therefore process is capable.

$$Cpk = \frac{\text{upper limit - mean}}{3\sigma} \quad \text{or} \quad \frac{\text{mean - lower limit}}{3\sigma}$$

whichever is the smaller.

$$Cpk = \frac{12 - 6}{3 \times 2} = 1 \quad \text{or} \quad \frac{6 - 0}{3 \times 2} = 1$$ therefore process is set correctly

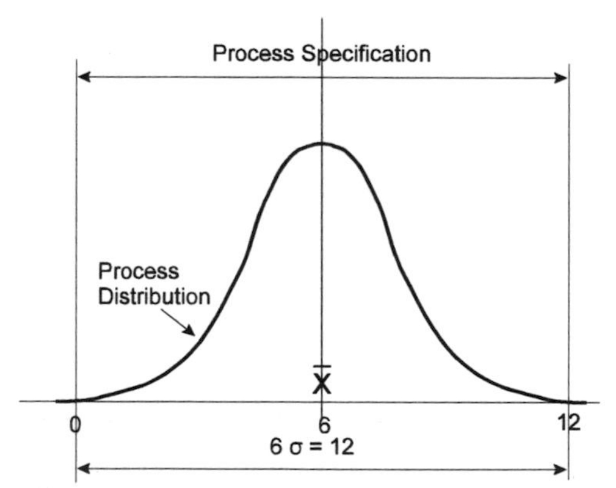

Figure 15 Example 4

Example 5

Target value	=	5 units
Tolerance	=	±5 units
Process mean $\overline{X}$	=	7 units
Process sigma σ	=	1.67 units

Calculate Cp and Cpk.

$$Cp = \frac{\text{Tolerance}}{6\sigma} = \frac{10}{6 \times 1.67} = 1$$ therefore process is capable

$$Cpk = \frac{\text{upper limit - mean}}{3\sigma} \quad \text{or} \quad \frac{\text{mean - lower limit}}{3\sigma}$$

whichever is the smaller.

$$Cpk = \frac{10 - 7}{3 \times 1.67} = 0.6 \quad \text{or} \quad \frac{7 - 0}{3 \times 1.67} = 1.397$$

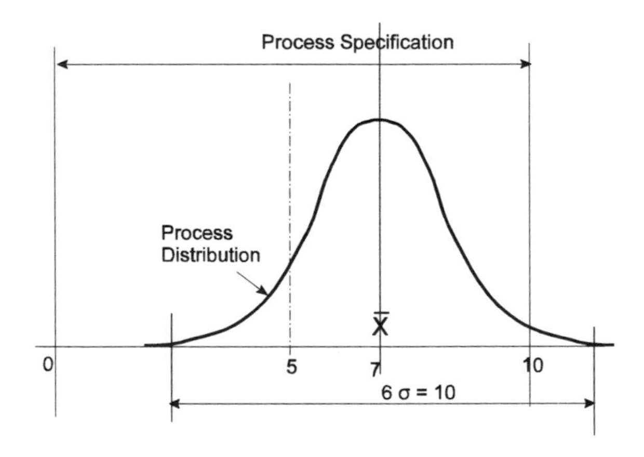

Figure 16 Example 5

therefore process is not set correctly.

Example 6

Target value		=	3 units
Tolerance		=	±3 units
Process mean	$\bar{X}$	=	3 units
Process sigma	σ	=	3 units

Calculate Cp and Cpk.

$$Cp = \frac{\text{Tolerance}}{6\sigma} = \frac{6}{6 \times 3} = 0.33$$

therefore process is not capable.

$$Cpk = \frac{\text{upper limit - mean}}{3\sigma} \quad \text{or} \quad \frac{\text{mean - lower limit}}{3\sigma}$$

whichever is the smaller.

$$Cpk = \frac{6 - 3}{3 \times 3} = 0.33 \quad \text{or} \quad \frac{3 - 0}{3 \times 3} = 0.33$$

therefore process is set correctly since Cpk = Cp

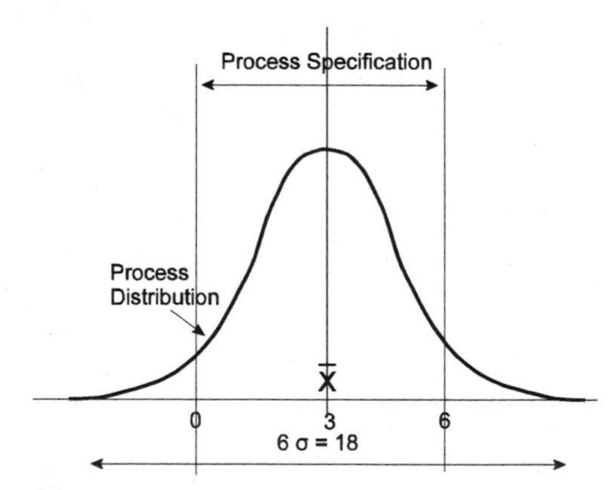

Figure 17 Example 6

The Specification, Measurement and Process Capability relationship

Since measurement is itself a process, it will have its own process capability. This is referred to as the uncertainty of measurement. The relationship between the process capability and the uncertainty of measurement may be appreciated in the following graphical representation.

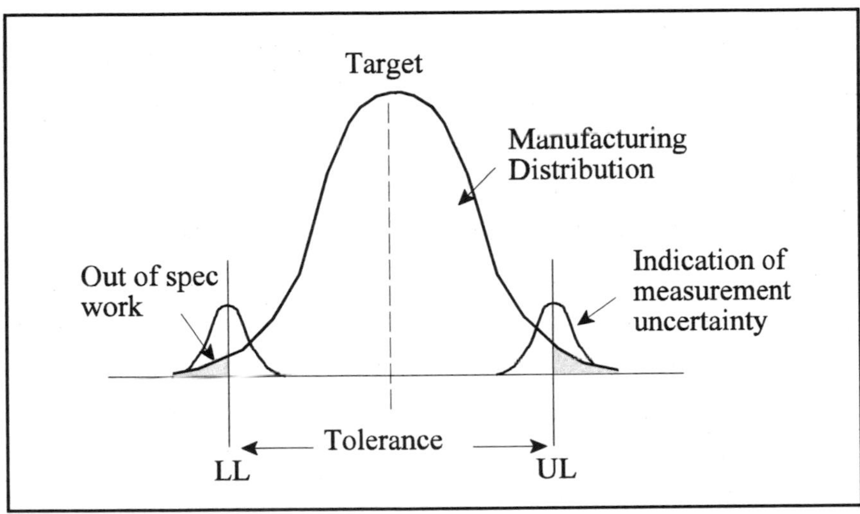

Figure 18 Uncertainty of measurement

A number of important features may be observed:

- The specification is the working tolerance with associated upper and lower limits.
- Capability is the relationship between the tolerance and manufacturing distribution given as Cp or Cpk from which the areas in the tails of distribution may be calculated giving out of spec work.
- Measurement uncertainty results in inspection error - passing defective work and failing adequate work. To ensure this error is minimal, a ratio of 10:1 between the working tolerance and measurement uncertainty is desirable.

Business Process Analysis

Introduction

Organisations are full of processes, not only manufacturing processes but processes for purchasing, warehousing, handling orders etc. These processes can involve moving and manipulating data and information as much as material. They can also involve various departments and specialists in completing tasks and activities, making decisions, filling out forms, filing and retrieving information. The processes can also involve complex parallel and serial activities interconnected and dependant on tasks being completed satisfactorily. Very often these processes have evolved as the organisation has grown, sometimes keeping pace, sometimes overwhelmed by the sheer size of the organisational growth. To solve growth problems - such as maintaining the throughput a quick fix solutions may be used, e.g. increasing the labour resource rather than improving or overhauling the process. Sometimes this can just make the situation worse. (If it takes one man one day to dig a hole, then one hundred men can dig the hole in one hundredth of the time - Oh I wish). Another and possibly a more powerful way of describing a similar situation is 'if it takes one woman nine months to produce a baby how quickly can you do it if I give you nine women - one month?'
In other words, increasing the labour resource will not necessarily result in quicker throughput. Some jobs just cannot be done by more than one person. Not only can processes be very complex and involved but they can also be very inefficient; responsibility ownership can be unclear. This is because it can be very difficult to understand, control and manage all the tasks involved in a process from start to finish.

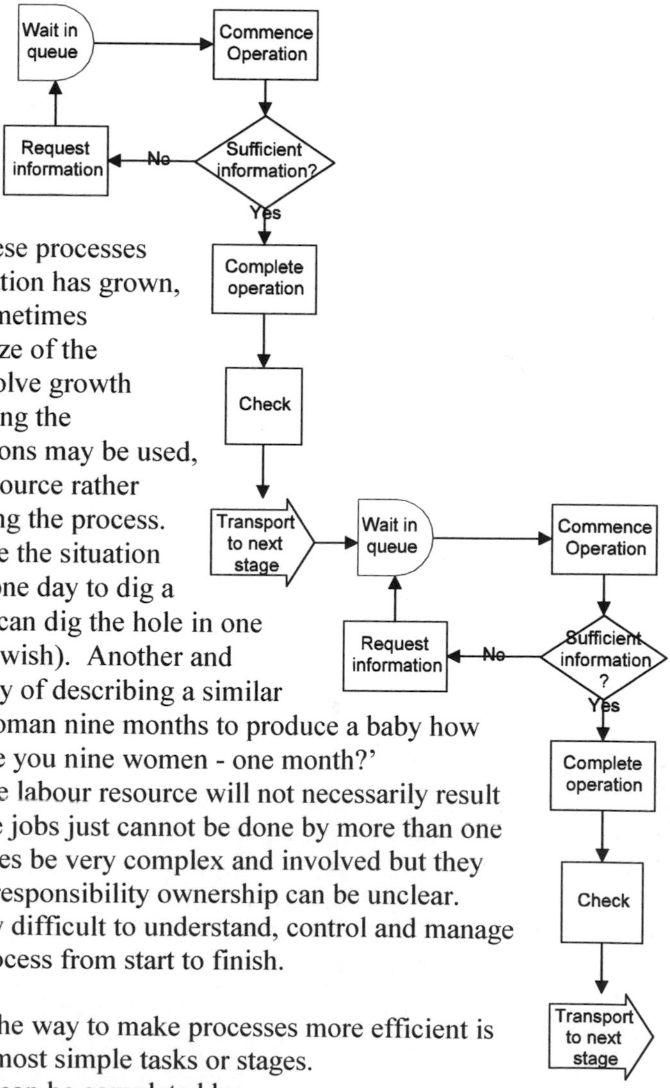

Analysis has suggested that the way to make processes more efficient is to break them down to their most simple tasks or stages.
In this way the process tasks can be completed by

Figure 19 Typical process

unskilled labour. Having sufficiently de-skilled the tasks, then the work can be distributed to a team of semi-skilled people so that the work is equally shared between each team member. (Adam Smith - Wealth of Nations)

The de-skilling and fine balancing of the tasks between the workers involves many specialists and technicians who analyse the process and determine the most efficient way to complete the process. To purchase the equipment, install and commission to make the process run successfully. This divides responsibility between several specialists:

- Engineers to develop the process
- Engineers to plan the process
- Engineers to develop the equipment or identify the supplier of the required equipment
- Buyers or purchasers
- Trainers to train the process operators
- Managers or supervisors to coordinate the labour, material, equipment, process output, transportation etc.
- Inspectors, checkers or approvers to check the process and allow it to run and confirm the output is to requirements

This may seem efficient, as it breaks the process down to its smallest element, allowing the specialists (knowledgeable in their particular field) to decide the best way to do things. One problem however is, that the responsibilities for the process can become unclear. An example of this could be, who is responsible for the quality of the output? Is it the engineer who designed the process and provided the equipment? The purchaser who supplied the material? The operator who produced the item? The supervisor responsible for the process? The inspector who checked the output?

Ownership is just one problem with this specialisation approach. Another problem can be the total process itself which can be very slow and unwieldy, as it can involve several sequential operations, each operation with its own inherent delays and transportation between each stage (see **Table 10**). The actual action (value added) time for each of the process tasks can be very small compared with the waiting and transportation time. Waiting, queuing and transportation can take up a significant proportion of the time to complete the whole process. The process tasks can consist of three basic elements; wait (queue), action and transport - performed by four departments. See **Figure 20**.

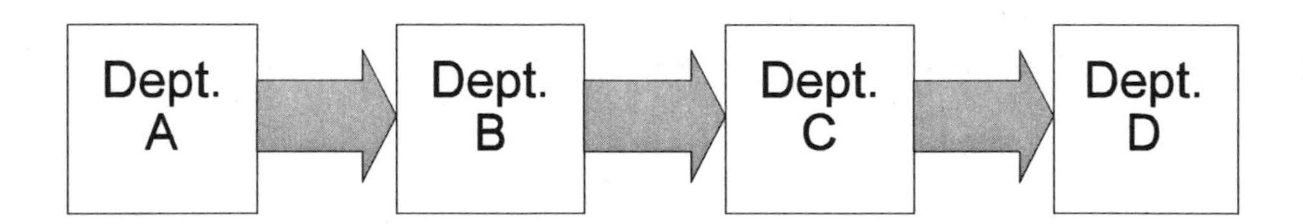

Figure 20 Typical Process

Table 10 Process Time Table

Activity	Department A	Department B	Department C	Department D	Total Time
Queue	500 mins	500 mins	500 mins	500 mins	2000 mins
Action	5 mins	5 mins	5 mins	5 mins	20 mins
Transport	20 mins	20 mins	20 mins	20 mins	80 mins
Total	525 mins	525 mins	525 mins	525 mins	2100 mins

Table 11 Total Process Time taken

Activity	Total (Min)
Total waiting/reconciliation time	2000 (≈4 days)
Total transport time	80 (≈0.17 day)
Actual work time	20 (0.04 day)
Total Process Time	2100 (≈4 days)
Possible World Class Time	20 (0.04 days)

So for this process the work or value added time is 20 minutes but completion of the process will take some 360 hours to complete. If the process was completed efficiently, it could be completed in 20 minutes.

Note, the waiting/reconciliation time could consist of:

- Reconciliation of various pieces of information. For example Goods Inwards Data, Invoice and Delivery Note
- Resolving any problems concerning inaccurate data etc.

Why is Business Process Analysis Important?

The previous section described some of the reasons why Business Process Analysis is important (ownership and responsibility, improvement in lead time, reduction in the amount of reconciliation work etc.) but there are other factors that may be the motivation for embarking on a Business Process Analysis exercise.

i. *Customer focus - Customer focus in all that we do*

The aim of customer focus is to continually understand the customers' needs and expectations, using our customers' perceptions to guide our improvement activities. *The customer* is not necessarily an external customer but could equally be an internal customer, i.e. one who within the organisation is the recipient of your product or service. Business Process Analysis helps in ensuring that the customers receive timely, defect free products and services that meet or exceed their expectations - improving the processes to reduce variation and waste. Flexible and responsive processes that respond quickly to customer demands and consistently meet the customers' expected delivery target.

Some spin offs from these process improvements are better teamwork, communication, and training.

Quality is judged by the customer and the judgements the customer makes are; Value, Satisfaction and Preference. It is therefore essential that the customer has:

- Trust and confidence in products and services
- Unique product-service combinations
- Sensitivity to customer and market information
- Rapid response to requirements

Business Process Analysis is the process improvement catalyst that can be used to focus attention on these issues.

ii. *Non-Value Added Activities*

The objective with Non-Value Added Activities is to identify and eliminate those activities that do not contribute towards the customer requirements. With many processes there can be activities which may be considered worthwhile but may not add any value to the finished product or service. Consequently these activities will not be something the customer wishes to pay for. Unfortunately these activities do have to be paid for and will become an overhead to the running of the process. A non-value added activity is an activity that is costing money but does not add value to the item or service. It is an activity that is not a direct requirement of the customer and usually the consequence of poor planning or systems. Value-added activities, however, are activities that the customer is prepared to pay for. This is because the customer accepts their effect as value obtained for the money.

Business Process Analysis, with its detailed analysis of the key process, gives the opportunity to identify any activities that may be considered Non-Value Adding.

iii. *An organisation provides its external customers through a small number of key processes*

Although there are many processes running in and through organisations there are only a few (possibly five[7]) which are key in delivering the organisation's product or service. These processes often provide 80% of a business turnover but only constitute 20% of their costs.

The processes running through an organisation can be complex, cross functional and sometimes wasteful. This waste can manifest itself in terms of:

- Cost to run the process (number of transactions per employee).
- The length of time to get from one end of the process to the other (lead time).
- The quality of the service provided e.g. errors, response or delivery times.

Organisations structured along functional lines do not always reflect the need for efficient process flow.

---

7 Bidding to Winning - Enquiry/Quotation to Customer Order
Product or Service delivery - Providing the product or service
Product or Service Development - Product or Service Improvement
Supplier Development - Improving the Performance of Suppliers
Customer Support - Technical or service support

Other Business Processes

Order Processing

Figure 21 shows the sequence of events associated with processing an order. The initial enquiry will go into the Sales Department. Sales will need to review the enquiry, identify to see if there are any special requirements that they cannot deal with and compile a quotation. If there are special requirements then the Technical Department may need to be involved to advise on the solution. Once the order arrives, then again the order will need to be reviewed but this time by the Order Processing Department, the Technical (technically correct), Financial (credit worthiness and payment terms) and Legal (penalties, consequential damages and insurance) Departments will re-review the order. Having completed these stages the order can be acknowledged and fulfilled. Note, throughout this process the people completing the individual tasks are probably

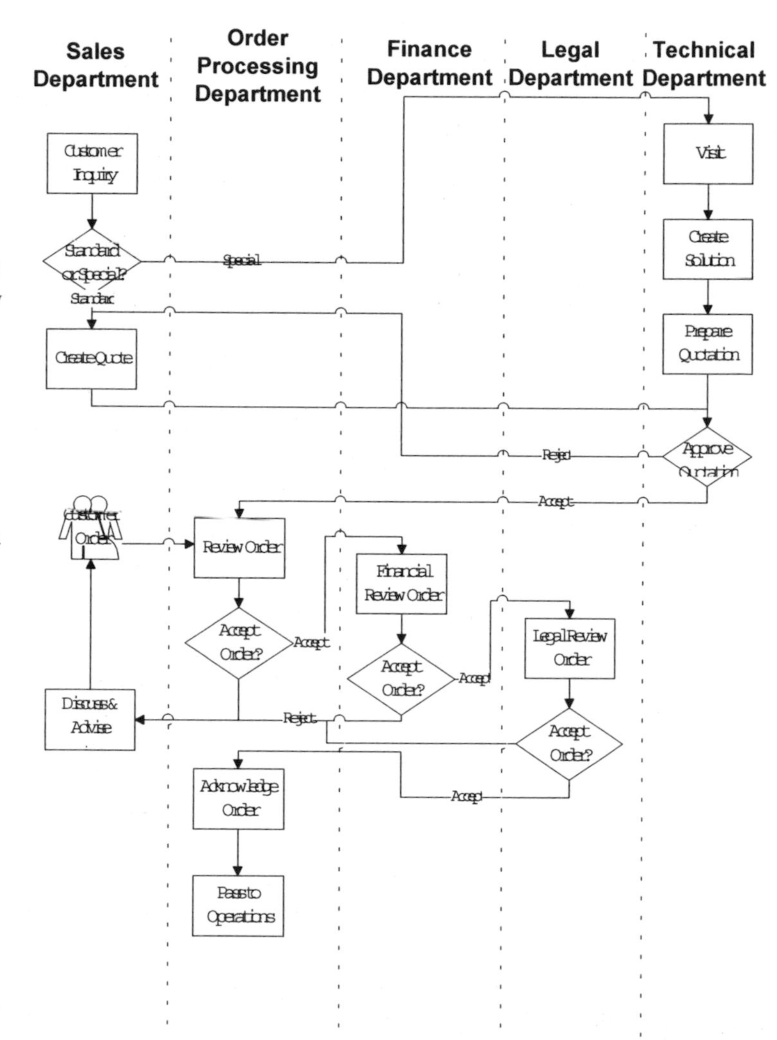

Figure 21 Current Order Processing Process

working hard and efficiently as they can in isolation. The process works vertically - functionally based rather than horizontally - process based.

What now needs to happen is a complete review of the process. What are the process objectives? Who is best placed to achieve these objectives? Who in this process adds value? Who is responsible for the complete process? Is the process being completed correctly? What errors are made when completing the process? Full use needs to be made of techniques and methods such as information technology, process cost modelling, ownership, skills levelling etc. to re-engineer the process.

Figure 22 shows what the new process diagram might look like after Business Process Analysis. Order Processing now handles all the stages and tasks associated with processing a customer enquiry and order. The process has been re-engineered to make it the central focus, rather than the departments or functions which were previously the central focus. The process is now not about single tasks but single process and multi-tasking.

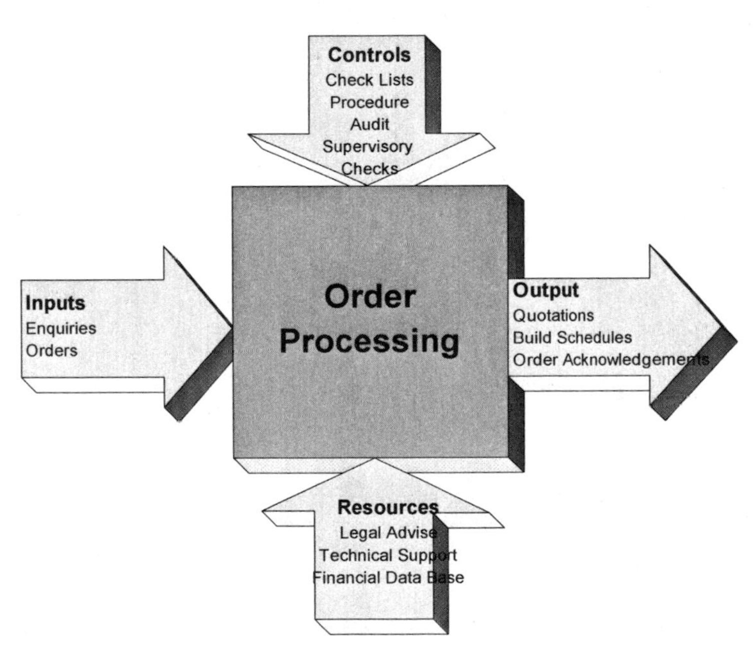

Figure 22 Order Processing Re-engineered

One of the key objectives is to change the process into its natural order rather than its functional order. This gives the opportunity to combine jobs, getting the workers to make the key decisions - real empowerment. Managers often emphasise empowerment but this approach gives the chance to change talk into action. Managers are understandably nervous regarding empowerment, as it can be seen to give the power to make change without the responsibilities for the consequences of change. The functional manager will still be responsible and held accountable for the resulting mess. The process can be organised on its natural process lines with the emphasis on results rather than transactions. (Results - Average time to place orders. Transactions -

Number of orders handled per Individual). Results are the processes performance rather than the performance of individuals within the process. The performance of individual activities may be seen as unimportant, as it is the performance of the complete process that counts. The workers will be responsible for both the decisions and the consequences of that decision - Ownership.

However, there are certain implications with this new approach. The order processors will need all the skills, training and facilities to fulfil this new approach. Procedures and check lists will need to be created which describe the tasks to be completed. Checks and monitoring will need to be carried out to ensure the tasks are being completed in a satisfactory manner.

Product Development

When developing a new product, the associated sequence can be lengthy and complex. Usually the development of a new product can involve the development of various product sub-systems. For example, when developing a new Overhead Projector, the lens system, the electrical system and the mechanical arrangement of all the parts will need to be considered.

The development sequence can look like development of the lens system first, then the electrical system and finally the mechanical box to hold all the elements in place. These sub-systems will then require integrating to form the completed overhead projector. Suppliers of the various parts then need to be identified and the production or build and testing method established. The figure Product Development, shows such a sequence.

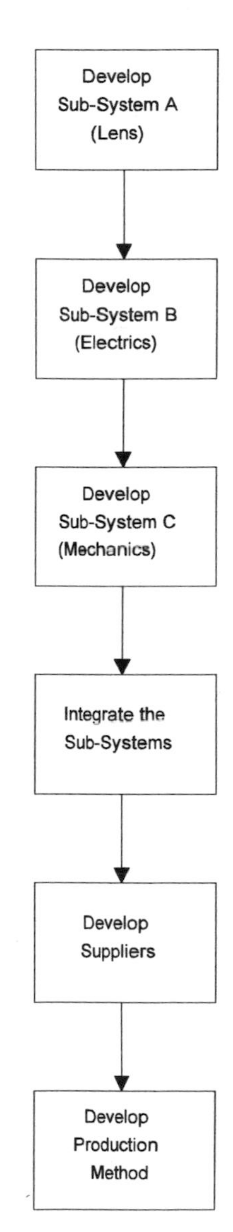

Figure 23
Product
Development

The problem with this process is that it can be difficult to coordinate - one team not knowing what the other team is doing. Management is difficult because if one team falls behind the whole project will be placed in jeopardy. There is a technique that is gaining favour called concurrent engineering which means instead of doing the stages in series some elements can be completed in parallel.

The examples are two totally different approaches to re-engineering the process. The approach necessary to arrive at these solutions would also have been unique for each situation. There is no one approach to review and re-engineer processes. Each situation must be evaluated according to the process needs. However, there is a general shape to Business Process Analysis that can be adopted. Business Process Analysis could be a zero based approach - tear it up and start again, or an attempt to optimise the process using techniques such as Information Technology, Automation, Special Skills (up skilling) etc.

Procedure for Business Process Analysis

The figure opposite shows a typical overview of the implementation of Business Process Analysis. Additional detail on the sequence is shown in **Table 12**.

Step A: The most suitable process for evaluation needs to be selected. The process selection can be one of the organisation's key processes. Another method of selection may be a frequently run process where any inefficiencies can be dramatically multiplied by the frequency with which the process is run. The process needs to be detailed using flow diagrams. The criteria by which the process is to be measured needs to be determined and evaluated. This requires presentation and agreement with the key personnel associated with the process.

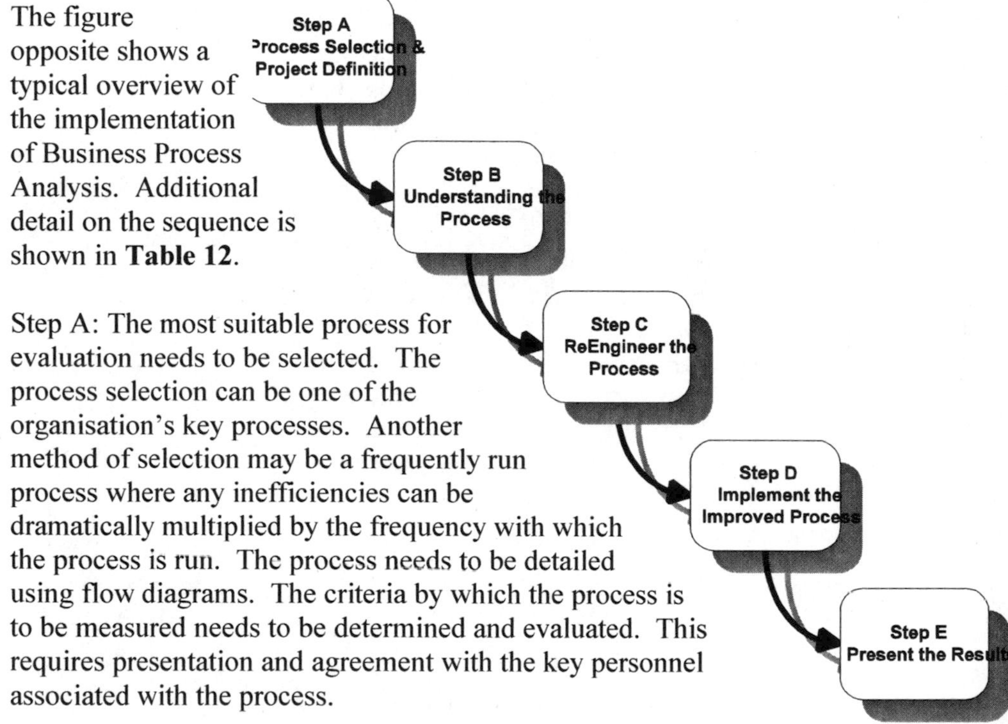

Figure 24 Business Process Analysis Overview

Step B: Further information regarding the process needs to be established: The process objectives. The standards expected from the process need to be agreed, e.g. the quality standards of the quotations - levels of detail, quantity of information etc. What are the inputs, outputs, controls and resources required to run the process? What are the projected new targets that should be achieved following the re-engineering of the process? E.g. What is the ideal number of people to run the process?

Step C: All this information now needs to be evaluated, discussed and agreed, with a view to establishing a better solution - brainstorming, tree diagrams and other problem solving techniques.

Step D: The new agreed solution now requires implementation, with the necessary project plan, procedure writing and training to ensure the successful start of the re-engineered solution.

Step E: Finally, and most importantly, recognition via presentation to management to show changes, successes and failures with the new process.

The above sequence has been described in greater detail in **Table 12**. The table shows the stage number and objectives, what the inputs to completing the stage are and the output expected from satisfactory completion of that stage.

Table 12 Procedure for Business Process Analysis

#	Stage	Inputs	Outputs
1	Identification of the Organisations Key Processes and determination of the process current status A Key Process[8]. i.e. A process that is regularly repeated (e.g. Order Processing) or a project that follows a series of similar activities (e.g. Research Projects).	Process Scope[9] Process Boundaries[10] Process Benchmarking[11] Process Requirements Process Customer Process Problems[12] Process Support Process Procedures Process Custom & Practice[13] Process Versions or Variety[14]	A Business Process Analysis Team (BPAT)

8 Often the key processes are; Enquiry to Order Acceptance, Product or Service Development, Supplier Development, Product or Service Delivery

9 Process Scope can include the geographical or physical location, products or services delivered and the aim of the process etc.

10 Process Boundaries: Identification of the start and end point of the process, e.g. receipt of an enquiry to Contract Acceptance. It may assist in determining this point by identifying the finished product at the successful completion of the process.

11 Identification and measurement of the key factors to measure the performance of the process and then to quantify these factors, e.g. cycle times, lead times, response time etc.

12 Process problems need to embrace not only the obstacles and difficulties with existing process (common mistakes, inadequate information, rejects, rework etc.) but also problems with suppliers and customers. These problems will need to be categorised in order to identify the important few from the trivial many (Pareto Analysis)

13 Custom & Practice could be the various methods of offering customer discounts

14 Process Versions: These can be categorised in a number of ways. Repeaters or jobs which are effectively the same, e.g. repeat orders. Runners or projects which involve a number of other functions or disciplines. Stranglers or jobs which clog up the process to the detriment of the other jobs. Alternatively, the process version may be categorised into; Small - a job which can be completed in the normal way, Medium - a job which requires a project manager to progress the job and Large - a job which requires the formation of a project team.

#	Stage	Inputs	Outputs
2	Commitment to the future objectives and vision for the process	Understanding of the Process Current Status	Establish and confirm process objectives and vision Process Owner Establishment of targets Development of possible approaches Establish the process control and resource requirements Service Level Agreements - Measures & Targets
3	Short term solutions	Process objectives and vision Process targets Possible approaches	Identify areas for short term improvements in the process performance
4	Re-engineering the Process	Process objectives and vision Process targets Possible approaches Value and Non-value added activities	Business Process Analysis Solution Process inputs, outputs, control and resource requirements[15] Cost Benefits System Model Information Model Documented Procedures Validated Process Logic[16]
5	Agreement to Change	Process Re-engineered Solution	Agreed solution management Communicated

15 In the style of the input/output diagram, identifying any non-value added activities

16 Taking due account of commercial, political and cultural changes that may be necessary

#	Stage	Inputs	Outputs
6	Implement Solution	Agreed solution management Communicated	Training Migration Plan System: Specification Testing New Technology: Specification Prototype & Test Install & Commission Organisational Responsibilities: Effects Interfaces Skills Structure Management Reporting System: Service Level Agreements Source of data and method or recording and reporting Method of review
7	Project Review	Changes and Benefits	Presentation to Key Personnel

SECTION 2 - IMPROVEMENT TECHNIQUES

Quality Circles

K. Ishikawa is generally credited with being one of the key developers of the quality circles approach although his work (as is often the case) relied heavily on the work of other quality philosophers, mainly W. E. Deming. Ishikawa was involved with the Japan Union of Scientists and Engineers (JUSE) and helped write JUSE's book on Quality Circles.

Motivation for quality: In the 50's and 60's the Japanese were going through a reconstruction of their industry in an attempt to remove the image the Western World had of them as being producers of poor quality products. They set up teams, groups, sections and departments with defined objectives to be achieved. These teams then met voluntarily, in their own time initially, to discuss how to overcome and solve problems affecting them as a group. These meetings became known as Quality Circles.

Quality circle definition:

1. A small group of employees
2. who do similar work
3. voluntarily meeting regularly
4. on company time
5. with their supervisor as their leader
6. learning to identify and analyse work related problems
7. recommending solutions to their management and, where possible, implementing their own solutions.

Introducing and implementing quality circles - **The FACILITATOR**

The facilitator must be carefully selected, for he becomes the focal point and will largely determine the future success of the programme. The facilitator requires a personality that will allow him to get on well with people at all levels within an organisation. Once a facilitator has been appointed, they should be capable of training the Circle leaders, coordinating the activities of all the Circle groups and assist in inter Circle investigations acting as say the 'go-between' to ensure lines of communication are maintained. The facilitator is generally responsible for obtaining any specialist advice from other departments or sections required by the Circle. Although the term facilitator is used in the UK, the role is usually performed by a Supervisor in Japan.

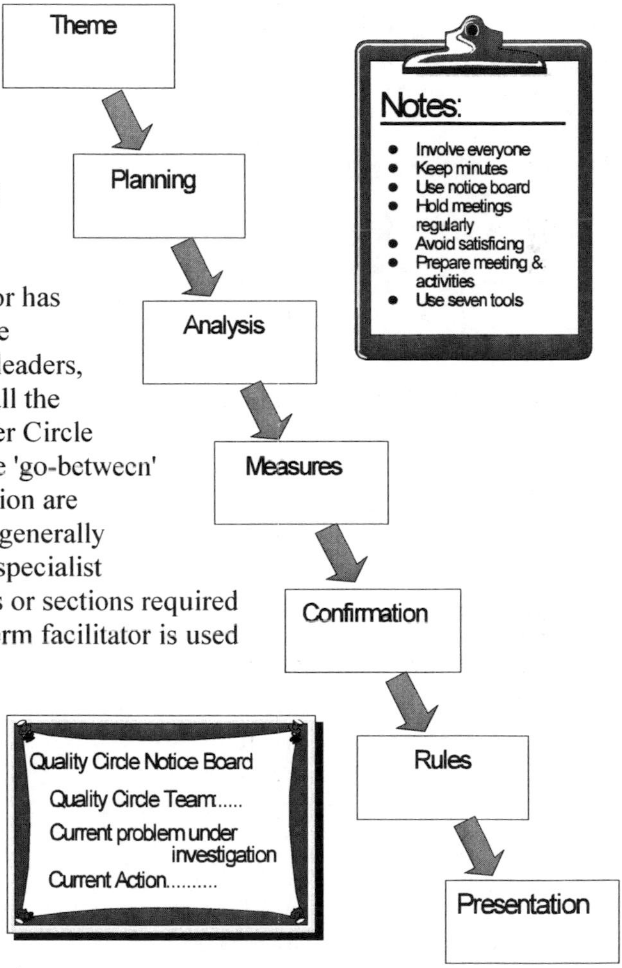

Figure 25 Typical Quality Circle Sequence

Training for the Quality Circle members: Training of the group leaders is essential to the success of the Circle. The 'quality' of their leadership will determine the level of subsequent achievement. The training should expose the group leader to the basic Quality Circle problem solving techniques to the extent that he is able to pass this training onto the other members of his Circle. To start a Circle the level of knowledge need only be a good understanding of the basic techniques. During the course of running the Circle it may be found that further training is required to update members on the latest problem solving techniques, for example statistics, process capability, etc. In Japan now foremen are often capable of using degree level statistical techniques for problem solving activities.

Training of the group leaders in other skills is also important as they need to retain their position as leaders. Training should cover such topics as control of meetings, encouraging development of the other members of the Circle and most importantly to develop the members as a team and not as a group of individuals.

There are seven tools of quality control that need to be taught to all circle members:

1. Pareto analysis - see section Pareto Analysis
2. Cause and effect diagrams
3. Stratification (see Sampling)
4. Check sheets
5. Histograms
6. Scatter diagrams
7. Shewhart's control charts and graphs (see Statistical Quality Control)

For more information on the seven tools or techniques, see the corresponding sections.

Starting a Quality Circle: There are 7 stages of activity involving members of the Quality Circle, although these stages sometimes merge and are repeated. **Figure 25** shows a typical sequence:

a. Selection of the theme or problem.
b. Plan the approach to the problem.
c. Analysis of the problem.
d. Determination of the measures to take to avoid the problem occurring.
e. Confirmation that the measures were successful.
f. Determination of the rules that need to be applied to avoid recurrence and finally.
g. Presentation of the Quality Circle activities.

a. ***Theme*** *or Select the problem:* Once the Circle members are chosen the first stage is to select the problem. Problems may be identified by anyone within the company and may be the result of customer complaint data, management information, quality control feedback, production engineering or design. Circles often identify problems themselves of which Management are sometimes unaware, problems such as handling, damage and short comings on route cards or specification sheets etc. The problem may be identified by the use of Pareto Analysis.

   It is vitally important that the Circles should be free to choose their own problems for solution.

Table 13 Typical Quality Circle Minutes Form

Minutes of Quality Circle			Circle Leader:	Facilitator:
Department:	Group:	Date:	Time:	
Attendance %	Absent:	Quality Circle Steps		
1 Theme ☐	2 Planning ☐	3 Analysis ☐	4 Measures ☐	5 Confirmat'n ☐
6 Standard'n ☐	7 Presentat'n ☐	8 Study QCC ☐	9 Others ☐	
Proceedings				
Overall decision or conclusion for next stage (who, what, when, how, why, where)				
Comments by Facilitator or Supervisor				
Next meeting date/time				

b. ***Planning**:* The Quality Circle's meeting is an important part of the Quality Circle activities. A well organised and prepared Quality Circle's meeting will help in the smooth operation of the Quality Circle. To help in the coordination of the Quality Circle activities it is useful to plan the meeting and to take notes regarding the agreed actions and responsibilities. **Table 13** shows one way of recording the actions agreed by the Quality Circle's Team. The 15 to 45 minute meeting can be held in working hours. As well as the minutes it may also be appropriate to use a notice board to communicate and detail the Quality Circle; members, theme, activities, action, responsibilities, progress etc.

State and re-state the problem It is often easy to jump to conclusions about what the cause or solution to a problem may be, i.e. Satisficing - using the first solution that comes to mind. It is important to make sure that the chosen problem is a problem and not a symptom of a problem. Curing or solving a symptom will not solve the problem and a lot of time and effort could be wasted resulting in loss of enthusiasm or disillusionment for the Quality Circle. Cause and effect diagrams may help in understanding the problem.

c. ***Analysis*** **-** *Collection of facts*: The collection of all the facts is a key part of the problem solving process. An inaccuracy in information or data could cause the group to 'head in the wrong direction'. Information and facts to be collected, which includes all data relating to the identified problem and possible related problems elsewhere. Information should also be gained, via the use of histograms, scatter diagrams, check sheets, stratification and Statistical Quality Control Charts, so that any limitations are known, for example, the cost to be incurred, timescales, space available, etc.

Organised Brainstorming - writing down all ideas: Almost all Quality Circles around the world make use of the cause and effect diagram. This is also known as the Ishikawa diagram or fish bone diagram. After the problem has been selected then the Circle may produce one of these diagrams.

Build on each other's ideas: Having identified the main causes and sub-causes the members can start to build upon each other's ideas. One idea may lead to a new line of thought or it may spark off another and so on. It is important never to ridicule any member's ideas.

d. ***Measures*** **-** *Choose a course of action:* Once the main causes and sub-causes have been found it is generally possible to identify which of the causes, if removed, would solve the problem. A course of action to be taken can then be planned and prepared. The course of action determined could include details regarding the steps or measures to be taken to eliminate the causes of the problem.

e. ***Confirmation:*** After the measures have been determined and implemented the success of the adopted approach needs to be established. Again, check sheets and Statistical Quality Control Charts can be employed to confirm the resolution of the problem.

f. ***Rules:*** Having confirmed the success of the suggested solution then rules or control methods need to be established that will avoid the problem ever happening again. These rules may be a new set of procedures or regulations but these procedures need to include the monitoring activities that ensure the new procedures are consistently and reliably observed.

g. ***Presentation:*** This is possibly the most important stage where the Quality Circle Team has the opportunity to demonstrate their achievements to management and colleagues. It is also an opportunity for management and colleagues to show approval and recognition of a job well done and to praise the achievements of the Quality Circle Team. This recognition does not have to be in the form of monetary reward - in fact this may be counter productive.

It may be worth noting that, for various reasons, it is not always possible for the Circle to actually implement the chosen solution. Various reasons could be; significant costs may be incurred or additional staff will be required, the solution lies within another area of the company, etc. Quality Circles can often realise the solution by gaining support from Management. This could be achieved through well planned presentations of the problem and recommended solutions to Managers.

Gauges of success: The success of the Quality Circle can be gauged in a number of ways, for example:

Quality - Which can be measured by defects/man hour, scrap/unit manufacture, customer return data etc.

Cost - Which can be measured by failure cost, cost of manufacture, cost of quality etc.

Attitude - Which can be measured by improvements in labour turnover, absenteeism, reduction in accidents, stoppages etc.

Companies have found the following benefits:

- Savings of time lost due to conflicting job instructions
- Savings of time in locating precision tools
- Elimination of oil leaks contaminating materials
- Savings of money on tin-plate finish problems
- Savings of money by changing processes
- Savings of money by changing handling and packaging methods
- Productivity is boosted
- Lower product defects
- Enhanced job involvement and work running more effectively
- Workforce more conscious of problem spotting and solving
- Improvements in communications and manager-worker relationships company-wide etc.

Failure of Quality Circles: While a lot of companies have experimented and subsequently failed with Quality Circles it is invariably found that they did not follow the recognised 'rules', e.g.

The group was mixed, i.e. different disciplines
The group was not allowed to choose their own problem
The group had to meet in their own time
Not all the information had been collected or was inaccurate etc.

Also see Deming's points on "Drive Out Fear".

Gemba Gembutsu

Gemba is Japanese for the place where the problem has happened.
Gembutsu is Japanese for the actual information.

Consequently, gemba gembutsu is actual information obtained at the scene of the problem. Therefore gemba gembutsu kaizen would be improvement established as a consequence of information from the problem scene.

The five Gemba Maxims

1. When a problem or abnormality occurs, go to the Gemba (scene) first.
2. Check the Gembetsu (information).
3. Take temporary countermeasures at the Gemba (scene).
4. Determine the root cause.
5. Define the rules to prevent reoccurrence.

Below is an explanation of these maxims with examples to help application.

1. When a problem or abnormality occurs, go to the Gemba (scene) first. Going to the scene of the problem immediately after it has happened means that real data can be obtained at a point closest to the abnormality. Rather than the manager requesting a report of events (which may include second or third party accounts) the manager should personally go to the Gemba. This has a number of advantages; it shows concern, provides clear accurate information to determining a suitable (rather than remote) plan of action, clearer understanding of what is going on and indicates an immediate response avoiding the issues becoming clouded. It also has a number of disadvantages as well; time, undermines the supervisor's authority, the supervisor does not learn about the problem or how to handle such an issue in the future, doing the supervisor's job.

2. Check the Gembetsu (information). This is the real information regarding the abnormality. The manager should initially just stand and observe what is happening at the Gemba. This in itself is not necessarily something that comes naturally, it is a skill which often has to be taught. Observing is not just about standing and watching, there is a logic and a process to the observing. Possibly say, in the case of an incorrect invoice. Initially the manager could observe the invoice creation task or process. Then when the task is fully understood, a none punitive discussion with the process or task owner can be facilitated by the manager's presence, to comprehend the details of the abnormality.

Possibly employing the five whys approach (also see section Root Cause Analysis).

i. Why did the customer complain?
 Because they had been invoiced incorrectly again.
ii. Why was the invoice incorrect?
 Because the prices were wrong.
iii. Why were the prices wrong?
 Because the price lists are incorrect and difficult to follow.
iv. Why are the price lists incorrect and difficult to follow?
 Because they have not been up dated.
v. Why have they not been up dated?
 Because the person responsible for them left and has not been replaced and nobody else understands how to up date the database.

3. Take temporary countermeasures at the Gemba (scene). Having now observed and obtained clear valuable information associated with the abnormality, an immediate remedy can be developed in conjunction with the task and process owner. Management problem solutions are often criticised as having no relevance to or effect on the initial problem. *'The further away from the problem source the solution is determined, the less likely that the solution will be effective'*. With the Gemba Gembutsu approach hopefully this effect is far less likely. In the case of the invoice and price lists the countermeasure could be to immediately bring the price list up to date, which will temporarily be effective.

4. Determine the root cause. The countermeasure may not resolve the root cause but only temporarily avoid the problem reoccurring. So an evaluation of the root cause needs to be undertaken . (See root cause analysis) The objective being to determine the most probable underlying causes of the problem or abnormality, with the aim of formulating and agreeing corrective actions to at least mitigate if not eliminate those causes and so produce significant long term solutions. Again, in the case of the price list this could involve the establishment of a price maintenance process.

5. Define the rules to prevent reoccurrence. Having confirmed the success of the suggested solution then rules or control methods need to be established that will avoid the problem ever happening again. These rules may be clear process owners and process metrics and a new set of procedures or regulations. It should be remembered that this newly defined process and associated procedures need to include the monitoring activities to ensure the new procedures are consistently and reliably observed, e.g. audit.

OPTIMUM - The Seven Wastes (Muda)

OPTIMUM can be defined as;

The waste of **O**verproduction

The waste of **P**rocessing

The waste of **T**ime

The waste of **I**nventory

The waste of **M**otion

The waste of **U**nacceptable items (defects)

The waste of **M**ovement (transportation)

The origins of OPTIMUM or seven wastes were from the Toyota engineer Taiichi Ohno who, in Toyoto Production System - Productivity Press 1988, described what he felt were the key wastes, that occurred in manufacturing. The original titles used by Ohno were the waste of; overproduction, inventory, waiting, motion, transportation, defects and processing but hopefully using OPTIMUM may make the seven titles a little more memorable. These seven wastes were initially intended to be applied to the manufacturing environment but then more recent additions (see below) has made the approach suitable to any organisation, including service.

i) The waste of under utilised human resource
ii) The waste of the environment (energy)
iii) The waste of lost opportunities
iv) The waste of duplication
v) The waste of misdirection

Introduction of methodologies such as Just in Time and reducing lead time and inventory has the effect of making quality problems much more visible. This is because quality problem are more likely to be immediately apparent with leaner and fitter organisations and systems. This can be demonstrated by, say, in the case of an assembler finding a faulty item, they may think it was just a one off or just throw away the faulty item and try another one. With precise batch quantities this cannot be afforded. Whole assemblies will have shortages and will not be able to be built or fail tests. With large inventories and long lead time rectifying such problems can be expensive (huge quantities of work in progress to be sorted for a start). Whereas with small batches and short lead time, problem identification and resolution can be much easier. In fact just solving the quality problem will in itself further reduce lead time. This is the concept 'quality is free' - it takes time and money to make things wrong and still more time to rectify. Do it right or correctly and you get quality for free.

So identifying and tackling waste becomes an essential element in the integrated approach to introducing leaner and fitter organisations, system and processes. This integrated approach would usually include attempting to identify "muda[17]" or activities that have no added value. Tom Peters may refer to it as MBWA (Management By Wandering About).

i) Customer OPTIMUM: For example this could include looking at processes from a customer's perspective. What activities are not OPTIMUM? How long are they waiting for the telephone to be answered when they wish to place an order? What is the average and maximum time for order delivery? How many customer queries are open and for how long? Or for hip replacement operations how long is the queue? What is world class performance in terms of cost of operation, success and time? Can our organisation emulate these world class performers?

ii) Internal OPTIMUM: Now try looking at the processes from an internal customer's perspective. What activities are not OPTIMUM? How many times does activities have to be rescheduled because key people are not available? In one process £250,000 was spent (wasted) just because data collection visits were aborted, due to doctors being unavailable at the prearranged time. How often is it necessary to chase information or data? How often, when is does arrive, is this data or information wrong? How many mistakes are there in the quotation and tender submission?

iii) Personal OPTIMUM: What about looking at tasks and processes from our own perspective? How much time is spent finding mis-located or misfiled data? How much time is wasted redoing misdirected work? One software project spent (wasted) £10M just because the specification was incorrect. Why had the responsible people not approved and checked the specification correctly ? - "We have not got time for that, we need to get on with the project". Well after spending (wasting) £10M they may not have had time to do it right but they certainly had time to put it right!

OPTIMUM should not be seen as individual specific activities, reviewed in isolation, but as a whole approach, supporting the just-in-time and zero defect philosophy. Consequently, OPTIMUM (together with the other additional five "waste" topics)

---

[17] Japanese word for uselessness and futility

often forms the basis of awareness training for all staff and have been developed as the foundation of many checklists for specific processes; administration, manufacturing, distribution, etc.

Wastes; **Description**	**Causes**	**Consequences**	**Solutions**
Overproduction; Making too many of an item	Poor scheduling and production planning, caution	Longer lead times and storage times, larger stores, higher transportation costs, more staff, excessive work in progress	Reduce set up times and change over times, improved requirements production planning, kanban, just in time,
Processing; Unnecessary or over processing	Inability to achieve the required quality standard, mistakes in processing	Non value adding activities, excessive plant utilisation.	Combining activities, ensuring process activities have the correct methods, equipment, materials and trained operators, value analysis[18]
Time; Unnecessary waiting. Waiting means everyone and item in the queue is waiting.	Poor planning, process bottle necks, poor process planning	Customer dissatisfaction (effecting all customers in the queue), poor operator and plant utilisation, items not moving	Identification of bottle necks, work flow analysis
Inventory; Inventory - Not making money work - having pound notes tied up in the stores or sorted under the bed rather than in the bank gaining interest.	Poor planning, caution, poor quality, inventory safety net, volatile demand	(Quality) problem identification more difficult, increased space and storage capacity, large buff stocks	Kanban[19], Deliberately, continually reduce stocks until stoppage occurs - thereby exposing system weaknesses, synchronisation of work flow, reduce set up and change over times, smooth demand

18 Value analysis - Technique for reducing costs and mechanism complexity.

19 Kanban - System of only allowing work to be processed when required by the next operation.

***Wastes;* Description**	**Causes**	**Consequences**	**Solutions**
Movement; Excessive transportation and handling of goods and materials. A non value adding activity[20]	Poor communication, poor siting, poor layout.	Damage and product deterioration, poor communication (of quality information) poor product and process awareness.	Review work layout, trace spaghetti diagram of material and customer flow to determine best office layout
Unacceptable items; Defects, errors, faults, mistakes and failures	Incapable non fool proofed processes	Scrap, rework, concession, regrading, cost of quality	Zero defects, zero quality control, statistical process control, process cost modelling
Motion; Ergonomically unsound activities and tasks	Poor work place layout.	Poor productivity, operator fatigue, poor quality, moral, ethical and safety issues	Time, method or motion study, mechanisation or automation, training, work place planning, video, snitch line.
Human; Resource; Under utilisation of the skill and latent potential of the work force	Unclear roles, responsibilities, objectives and targets	Lethergy, lack of motivation, poor performance, missed targets	Quality circles, team building, appraisal, suggestion schemes
Energy; Environmentally unsound activities	Poor environmental management systems. Lack of awareness.	Too high energy costs. Environmental damage.	Energy assay, environmental audit, environmental management system
Lost opportunities; Missed openings to improve processes and customer satisfaction	Poor planning, poorly motivated or educated staff.	Loss of business growth	Quality improvement schemes, empowerment
Duplication; Unnecessarily repeated activities and tasks	Poor process control and project management	Too high process costs.	Business process analysis, process charting, project quality control.
Misdirection; Unnecessary activities and tasks	Poor process control and project management	Too high process costs.	Business process analysis, process charting, project quality control.

20 Non value added activity - something the customer does not want to pay for.

Balanced Scorecards

Introduction

It was about ten years ago when the Harvard Business Review first published David Norton and Robert Kaplan's study and introduced the concept of the Balanced Scorecard (BSC). Since then it has continued to be a popular performance measurement tool. A measure of the BSC success can be seen from some 50% of US listed companies who use the technique.

The Balance Scorecard is a communication, informing and learning system. It is intended to help concatenate and communicate strategy by aligning individual, organisational, business unit and cross-functional objectives to achieve common goals and missions. It enables organisations to clarify and quantify their vision and strategy and translate it into action. It provides a common feedback route, not only regarding external outcomes, but also about internal business processes in order to continuously improve strategic performance and results.

Norton and Kaplan still run a Balanced Scorecard Collaborative - see http://www.bscol.com/ - which is a consulting, education, training, research and development organisation.

Approach and description

The Balanced Scorecard provides an organisation with fa ramework of four perspectives; financial, customer, learning & growth and internal business processes. Four questions associated with these perspectives needs to be addressed:

- *Financial*: to achieve financial success - how should we satisfy our stakeholders? This financial data should be readily available in the company database and financial reports. It may also include other financial-related data, such as risk assessment and cost-benefit data, in this perspective.
- *Customer*: to realise the customer's vision - how should we satisfy our customer? Customer focus and customer satisfaction are important indicators. If customers are not satisfied, they will eventually find other suppliers that will meet their needs. Poor performance from this perspective is an indicator of future decline, even though the current financial picture may be good. There is a need to understand and develop measures from the customer's perspective, regarding types of customers and the processes by which we provide products and services to the customer groups. See section customer satisfaction.
- *Learning and growth*: to realise the organisation's vision - how will we manage change and continually improve? Understanding this perspective includes

analysing employee training and corporate cultural attitudes related to both individual and corporate self-improvement. Measures should be established which guide managers in focusing on training funds, thus providing the foundation for a knowledge-worker organisation. This could include the concept of mentors and tutors within the organisation, as well as systems which readily allow workers to get help on a problem.

- *Internal business processes*: to satisfy our stakeholders - which process should we excel at? This perspective refers to the key internal business (mission oriented and support) processes. The mission-oriented process (usually six) include; Bidding to winning, Product or service development, Product or service delivery, Supplier development, Customer support and Invoice to cash. The Support processes support the mission oriented processes and are often more repetitive in nature and easier to measure. Measures based on this perspective allow the managers to know how well their process and consequently their business is running. These measures can also be related to the organisation's mission and confirm the organisation's ability to meet customer requirements.

These perspectives need to be described in terms of objectives, measures, targets and initiatives, the cause and effect and interrelationships between the various perspectives understood. **Figure 26** shows a balanced scorecard framework with the interrelationship between the perspectives; Customer, Financial, Processes and Learning & Growth.

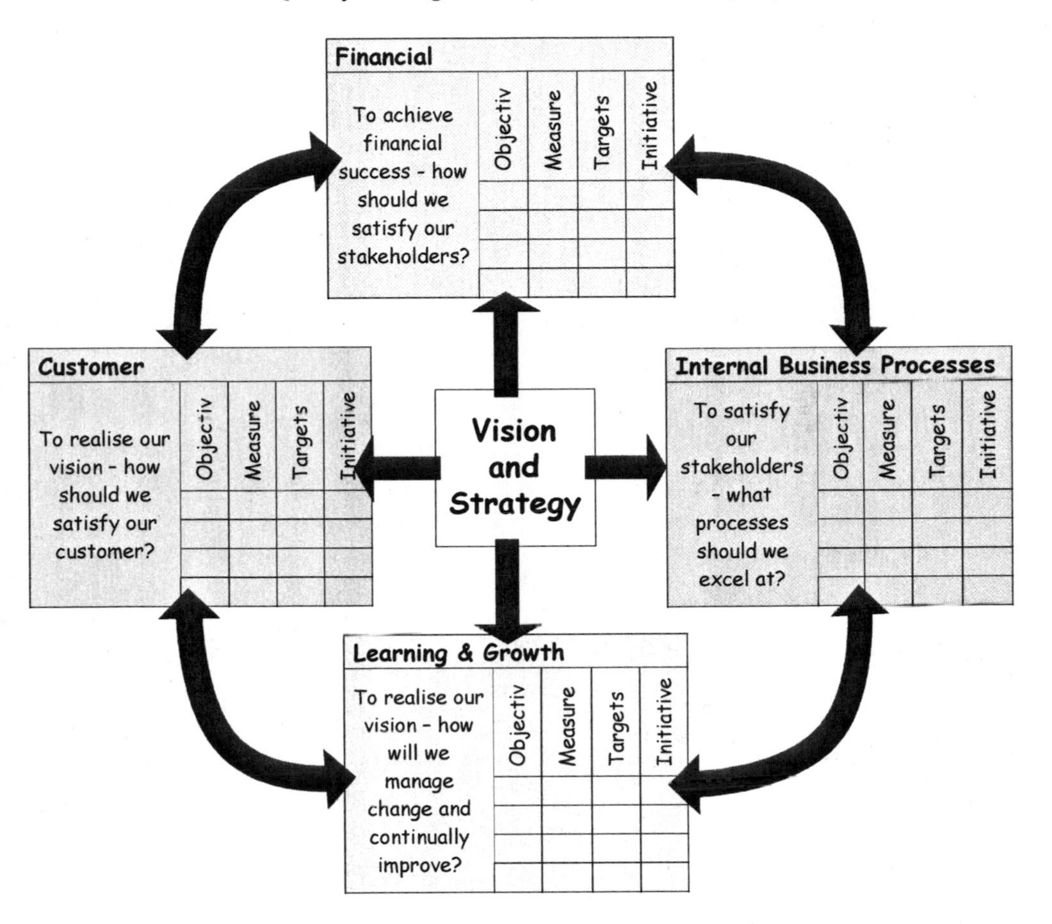

Figure 26 Balanced Scorecard Framework

The balanced scorecard does more than indicate the measures of success. The Balanced Scorecard provides the vehicle to help understand the relationship between the outcomes that we will achieve in the future and the measures we choose to apply today.

Figure 27 indicates the balance between outcome and performance. Outcome being previous results and performance being desired results.

Balanced Score Cards

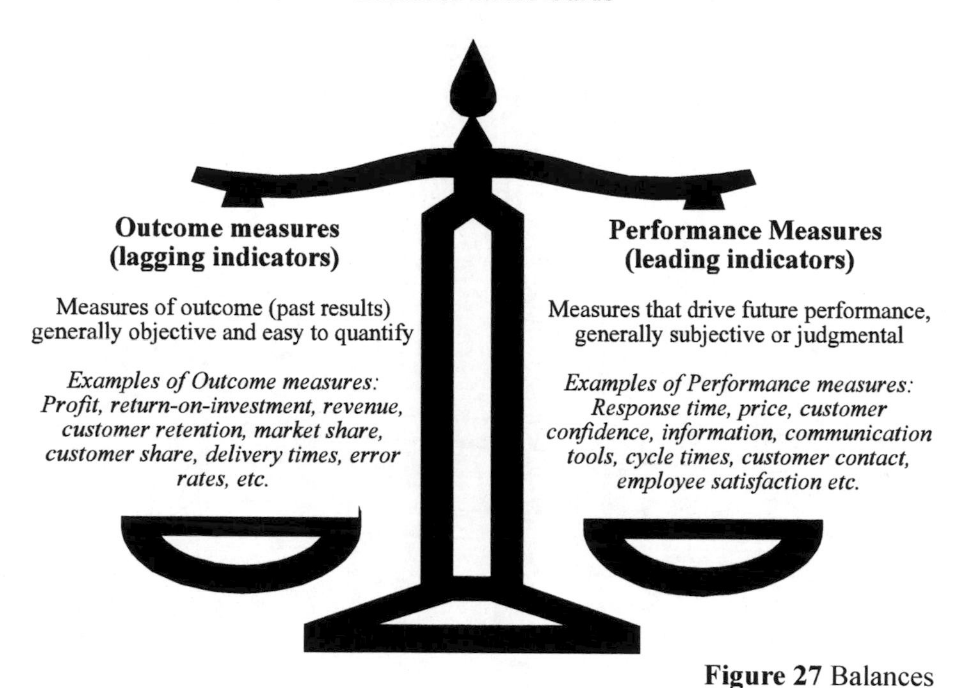

Figure 27 Balances

The Balanced Scorecard process

The scorecard process starts with the senior executive management team agreeing to the balanced scorecard methodology and then cascading the principles and their enthusiasm for the approach to the workforce to gain the worker's commitment.

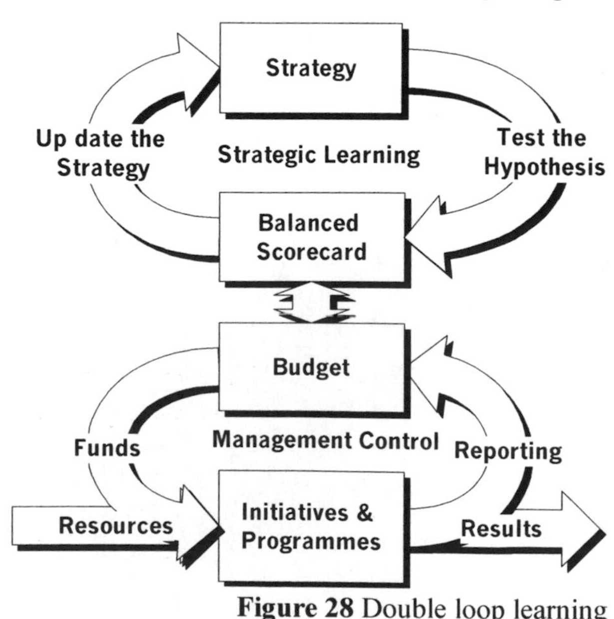

Figure 28 Double loop learning

The senior executive management then work together to translate its business unit's strategy into specific strategic objectives. This team work leads to an agreed model of the business for which the senior team is jointly responsible. The balanced scorecard approach encourages "double loop learning[21]". The idea is that time is better spent on developing and implementing strategy than on debating the results. The double loop is an approach for achieving the results. Examined here is both where the results differ from plan and also the degree to which the strategy remains viable. Consequently, the management emphasis shifts from reviewing the past to learning about the future. "What you measure is what you get"[22]. The suggestion is that using traditional financial accounting measures like return on investment and earnings per share can give misleading signals for continuous improvement. These traditional financial performance measures were fine for the industrial era, but they are out of step with the new skills and competencies companies need.

The Balanced Scorecard is a communication tool, informing and learning system, not a means of control. It is intended to help describe and communicate strategy by aligning individual, business units and cross-functional objectives with the organisation's goals and missions. This enables organisations to clarify their vision, strategy and translate them into action. It provides a common feedback about external outcomes (past results) and internal business processes in order to continuously improve strategic performance and results. In this way long-term strategies can be linked to short term actions.

Balanced Scorecard forms

Critical process

Perspectives	Objectives	Measures	Targets	Initiatives
Financial				
Customer				
Internal Business Process				
Innovation & Learning				

---

21 Developed by Chris Argyris, who found that organisations spend 80% of their time looking at results and 20% at strategy and implementation. With balanced scorecard methodology this is reversed with 80% on strategy and implementation and 20% on results. Double loop learning; Reviewing the past and learning about the future by reviewing figures and determining future strategy.

22 Robert Kaplan

Measurements Form

Administration and Finance Division				
Balanced Scorecard Metrics				
(Critical Function)				
Updated (Date)				
	Financial	Customer	Internal Business Process	Innovation and Learning
	(Description of Measure)	(Description of Measure)	(Description of Measure)	(Description of Measure)
	Target:	Target:	Target:	Target:

Although most reports discuss BSC successes, this has not always been the case. For example, a recent APQC (American Productivity & Quality Centre) benchmarking project said *"When properly implemented, the Balanced Scorecard can help steer an organisation and its employees toward profitability and growth. However, discussions with those using the scorecard process suggest that realising its full potential, often proves elusive."*

Exercises:

Describe the four perspectives associated with Balanced scorecard:

1. Financial: to achieve financial success - how should we satisfy our stakeholders? This financial data should be readily available in the company database and financial reports. It may also include other financial-related data, such as risk assessment and cost-benefit data, in this perspective.
2. Customer: to realise our vision - how should we satisfy our customer? Customer focus and customer satisfaction are important indicators. If customers are not satisfied, they will eventually find other suppliers that will meet their needs. Poor performance from this perspective is an indicator of future decline, even though the current financial picture may be good. To develop measures from the customer's perspective, the types of customer and the processes by which we provide products and services, to these customer groups needs to be understood. See section customer satisfaction.
3. Learning and growth: to realise our vision - how will we manage change and continually improve? Understanding this perspective includes analysing employee training and corporate cultural attitudes related to both individual and corporate self-improvement. Measures should be established which guide managers in focussing on training funds thus providing the foundation for a knowledge-worker organisation. This could include the concept of mentors and tutors within the organisation, as well as systems which readily allow workers to get help on a problem.
4. Internal business processes: to satisfy our stakeholders - which process should we excel at? This perspective refers to the key internal business (mission oriented and support) processes. The mission-oriented process (usually six) includes; Bidding to winning, Product or service development, Product or service delivery, Supplier development, Customer support and Invoice to cash. The Support processes support the mission-oriented processes and are often more repetitive in nature and easier to measure. Measures based on this perspective allow the managers to know how well their process and consequently their business is running. These measures can also be related to the organisation's mission and confirm the organisation's ability to meet customer requirements.

Six Sigma

Introduction

Six Sigma is a business strategy as well as a quality improvement technique. It began in the 1980's at Motorola in the United States. Six Sigma performance means that there are almost 'zero defects' in the process producing a product, service or transaction. It shows the achievement and the maintenance of world-class performance. It could be considered as the standard required to win and keep customers in today's markets.

Six Sigma performance means reducing defects to less than four per million with the resultant reduction in costs giving big gains on the bottom line. Products and services fail to satisfy customer requirements if they are produced with large variations , that is the product is inconsistent. To compensate for these variations, which are caused by inefficient work processes, companies spend a great deal of time and money on 'fire-fighting'. This includes activities such as redesign, inspection and rework. Six Sigma uses these 'wasted resources' spent on putting things right and uses them to improve on 'getting it right first time' by limiting the variation in the process. The Six Sigma process encourages leanness, simplicity and means that waste and cost are driven out of the organisation. The process turns 'wasted effort' into increased productivity and improved products; it also acts as a culture change vehicle.

Six Sigma means overall excellence, not only in the finished product, but in the administration, service and the manufacturing process throughout the whole organisation.

Background

The term sigma is a letter in the Greek alphabet, and is used in statistics as a measure of variation. The original industrial terminology is based on the established statistical approach which uses a sigma measurement scale (ranging from two to six) to define how much of a product's or process's normal distribution is contained within the specification. Essentially, the higher the sigma value the less likely it is for a defect to occur, because more of the process distribution is contained within the specification. In fact under the assumption of normality, a product or process operating at six sigma would have 99.999998 per cent defects at two parts per billion. At a more typical 3 sigma level, the yield will be 99.73 per cent. See **Figure 29**. Taking into account that the product or process mean might vary from the nominal target by up to 1.5 sigma, this translates into a yield at six sigma of 3.4 defects per million - the target declared by Motorola and now regarded as 'Six Sigma' quality by the industry in general.

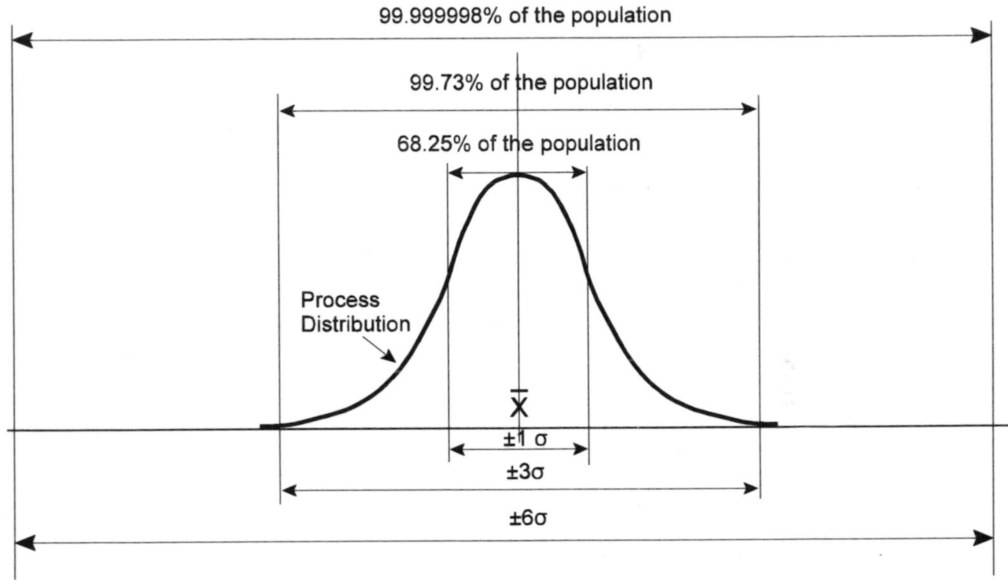

Figure 29 Areas in the population of a normal distribution

Benefits

Major US corporations have achieved significant financial benefits through their Six Sigma programmes. This has been seen in billion dollar savings and has strengthened their share values. For example, by 1998 GE announced programme savings of $1.2 billion, and between 1987 and 1994 Motorola increased employee production on a dollar basis by 126%. These 'Six Sigma companies' have made these savings by focussing on key issues that are crucial to their customers and driving for greater and greater efficiency in key areas.

Six Sigma projects can be identified in a wide range of areas in the company, for example:

- Can the understanding of customer requirements be improved? (See Section Quality Function Deployment)
- Can waste be reduced by reducing total defects, scrap & rework? (See Section OPTIMUM)
- Can delivery be improved by reducing delivery time cycle time? (See Section Business Process Analysis and Just in Time)
- Can Work In Progress (WIP) be reduced? (See Section Material Requirements Planning, Just in Time and Total Productive Maintenance)

- Can processes be simplified and thus operations simplified? (See Section Just in Time)
- What could be done to improve productivity? (See Section Process Improvement)
- Could product reliability be improved? (See companion book Introduction to Quality)
- Can the flow of a process be altered to improve cycle time? (See Section flowcharting and Business Process Analysis)
- How can changes in market requirements be monitored so that response to them can be faster? (See Section Quality Function Deployment)

Implementation

For an organisation to start a Six Sigma programme means aiming to deliver a top quality service and product, virtually eliminating all internal inefficiencies. In other words, it means having a common focus on excellence throughout the whole organisation.
Although most of the statistical and problem solving methods are found in other quality improvement strategies, Six Sigma uses these tools in a methodological and systematic fashion to create a culture that does not accept defects and provides major bottom line gains. What underlies this change in culture and makes Six Sigma work is the infrastructure that is built within the organisation. It is the infrastructure that motivates and produces a Six Sigma culture through the entire organisation.

As for all Quality Initiatives, Senior Executives must have a total commitment to the implementation of Six Sigma and establish a Six Sigma leadership team. A training programme must be instigated throughout the company. The investment in training is essential for staff to learn the appropriate methods and enable them to manage the programme and guide improvement projects. The staff trained in this way are now usually referred to as 'master black belts', 'black belts 'and 'green belts' and these staff are at the heart of the Six Sigma programme. The belt indicates the level of training that they have accomplished. Usually companies have about ten black belts per 1000 employees and one master black belt (the site expert and trainer) per 1000 employees.

For success in the Six Sigma programme, the Senior Executives must:

- Highlight key issues and set goals
- Help the masters and the leadership team to identify crucial projects that are tied to the important business issues
- Allocate time for culture change - try to find some fast successes to build on

- Provide the required finance and use financial measures to see the impact of the changes - try and find some early successes to encourage the teams
- Constantly review the Six Sigma programme and make changes where required.

There are several ways of implementing a Six Sigma programme and there are various versions of the stages which a process being 'improved' goes through. Whatever implementation programme is used the same type of questions must be answered.

- What are the end product requirements?
- What are the characteristics of these products which are key to satisfying these requirements?
- What are the processes that affect these characteristics?
- What are the target values for each characteristic that minimize the variation in the end product?
- What are the actual or expected variations in each characteristics?
- What are the controls in the process steps which will allow the target values, with minimum variation, to be met?

These questions must be answered and the resulting answers implemented with the help and guidance of the trained staff; every employee has a role to play.

These questions can be used in the basic approach (derived from Shewhart's - Plan ➡ Do ➡ Check ➡ Act cycle)

1. *Define*: The scope and project objects. E.g. Why is there such a large variation of Salesman performance?
2. *Measure*: Determine what and how frequently to measure. E.g. The top ten percent of our salesmen provide eighty percent of the sales volume. The bottom ten percent are failing to meet sale targets - A Sales Non-conformance - a defective unit.
3. *Analyse*: The collected data, evidence and information requires analysis to determine the root cause of the problem. E.g. Product and sales skills, experience, training, sales areas, salesmen profiles (age, time in the job, etc.).
4. *Improve*: Implement and agree action plan to improve or resolve the identified issues. E.g. Salesmen profiles indicate the skill set required for the job. Training existing sales people against the required skill set.
5. *Control*: Monitor the success and continued performance possibly by the use of control charts. E.g. Monitoring Salesmen's performance and use the Salesmens profile when selecting people for this function.

As everybody takes part, everybody can enjoy the successes that Six Sigma brings. This is good for motivation and it can be further emphasised by linking it to remuneration. The reward structure is a critical piece in a successful Six Sigma implementation. In one major US company promotion was linked to Six Sigma training and 40% of top management bonuses were tied to Six Sigma goals - this company had few problems in engaging the entire organisation in the initiative.

Six Sigma is for all functions within an organisation

Six Sigma is not just for manufacturing processes but it can be applied to every process and transaction within a company. Using the common measurement index of 'defects per unit', where a unit can be virtually anything such as; a line of code, a purchase order, an invoice, companies have started to use Six Sigma to reduce errors in non-manufacturing operations. Motorola has indicated that not implementing Six Sigma in their non-manufacturing areas early enough was a mistake that cost Motorola at least $5 billion over a four year period.

The point is that any process can be seen as a set of inputs and a set of outputs, thus a process is a process, regardless of the type of organisation or function. All processes have customers and suppliers and all processes exhibit variation. Since the purpose of Six Sigma is to gain the knowledge on how to improve these processes and do things better, faster and at lower cost, it applies to everyone.

Establishing Six Sigma throughout an organisation is a long term programme - essentially it is an ongoing process of continuous improvement, where even the most dedicated company sets goals of achieving Six Sigma within six to ten years. However, if properly introduced the companies should expect financial benefits shortly after they begin. In fact, management should engineer some early successes so that the motivation for the programme can be given a boost.

It should not be seen as just a measurement of quality but viewed as the basis of a best-in-class philosophy, and a long term business strategy, serving to further enhance the results of existing programmes. It is not just the US giants who recognise the benefits, increasingly UK businesses are following suit as they strive to become 'world class'.

Suggestion Schemes

Why Suggestion Schemes? - The Sell

Probably one of the most underutilised Quality Improvement schemes and yet possibly promises the greatest return with the least effort, with many spin off benefits. The set up and implementation cost are insignificant. It reinforces the idea of a listening management, as the management has now provided an additional communication route, where employees can not only exhibit their frustration but also provide a solution. It adds to employee esteem by providing an outlet for their talents and creativity, in an environment which provides rewards (not necessarily financial) and recognition.

The name itself 'Suggestion Schemes' is a barrier - it sounds stuffy and 50s in style. The tired suggestion box, full of complaint notes, that are ignored. Possibly, a new name is required to move the approach away from these connotations. Possibly 20 million Ideas, Team One Ideas or Team 1deas (sic). With the readers indulgence the name Team 1deas will be used in place of the name Suggestion Schemes. Although, providing a new name will not significantly change the approach described, which is largely based on Yuzo Yasuda, author of *"40 years 20 million Ideas*". In-turn the book *40 years 20 million Ideas* is based on the work of Taiichi Ohno, VP and 'father' of Toyota Production System. The fact that the suggestion scheme approach is based on Taiichi Ohno and actively and successfully employed at Toyota, should in itself be sufficient advertisement.

An explanation of Suggestion Scheme Idea

"Something is wrong if workers do not look around each day, find things that are tedious or boring, and then rewrite the procedures. Even last month's manual should be out of date". Taiichi Ohno, VP and 'father' of Toyota Production System.

The objectives of the scheme

Aims and Objectives

- Releases the inherent talents within the organisation
- Promotes business excellence
- Continuous improvement
- Promote staff recognition

Like all Quality Improvement schemes the basic aim is to promote excellence - "stand on the shoulders of giants". If we already have good processes and procedures what do we need to do to make them even better? Reinforcing the concept of continuous improvement. Some of the spin off benefits are that it provides a vehicle to release the inherent talents within the organisation and provide a method of recognising employees who have provided the ideas. The various means of recognition are described later.

Management commitment

> *"With no exaggeration, whether employees are independently involved in suggestion activities depends on whether managers are doing what they should do to stimulate these activities"* Yuzo Yasuda, author '40 years 20 million Ideas'

The six most important words associated with any Quality Initiative are Management Commitment, Management Commitment, Management Commitment. Without total and unequivocal Director and management commitment to the scheme do not attempt to start. At best it will be a waste of time and money, at worst it will cause serious damage to management reputation.

Having obtained this commitment, possibly by letting managers come up with the idea themselves in the first place[23], then it is possible to move into the operational planning phase.

Launching the scheme

There are two considerations to be made; launching the scheme and running or operation of the Team 1deas scheme. Detailed below is a successfully employed method launching and operating a Team 1deas scheme, although this is not the only approach that can be used.

Brief and agree with Directors - the launch approach and operation of the scheme, including their role and responsibility, the method of recognition, programme budget, programme steps and responsibilities.

Management Responsibilities

- Support & promote Team 1deas
- Adjudicate Team 1dea entries
- Review Team 1deas entries
- Guide, monitor, resource and support the 1dea implementation
- Ensure implementation is successful

---

[23] Suggesting the scheme to management has a 10% chance of success, management suggesting and resourcing the scheme has a 90% chance of being implemented but not yet necessarily working.

Distribute to the Managers briefing packs describing the launch, scheme operation and their role and responsibilities.

Produce for distribution to all employees the Team 1deas pack. This pack could include:

- A letter extolling the advantages and benefits to be gained from the Team 1deas scheme for both the organisation and the employees.
- A leaflet showing how the team 1deas scheme is operated, how to make a suggestion and what the recognition will be for accepted ideas.
- An entry form or Team 1deas sheet.

Launch Day

Managers brief employees on the Team 1deas using the briefing packs and distribute the Team 1deas pack.

Team 1deas scheme operation

The Team 1deas Operational method

Operational Method

- Receive and log Team 1deas
- Adjudicate and score
- Review, select and authorise
- Appoint 1deas Team Leader
- Implement Team 1dea
- Fast Track or Project Team
- Recognition
- Implemented Team 1dea

The employees submit their ideas using the Team 1deas form. Each form is then recorded, reviewed and scored by the Team 1deas Administrator. The selected ideas are then submitted to the review panel of managers for final adjudication and determination whether the idea can be fast tracked (possibly implemented immediately with little supervision) or whether the idea requires a team or project approach for implementation. The most appropriate level of recognition would also be determined and the award organised, for presentation, by the administrator.

Recognition methods

There are numerous recognition methods and just as many views on their value and suitability. It is not intended to discuss the merits of any particular method.

- A pat on the back from the management

- A medal, award, cup, etc.
- A prize (consumer goods, holiday, etc.)
- Entry into the next stage of the competition for a prize
- Money

These methods are not mutually exclusive, they can be used together, for example a pat on the back from management (it may be considered) should always be employed.

Problems with Suggestion Schemes

It may be seen as just another transient improvement campaign which, with lack of employee and management focus, will fail. The level of Director and Management active participation (ownership) may be inadequate to sustain the scheme. Implementation of the Team 1deas may be ineffective and poorly communicated. The volume of Team 1deas suggestion may be too high or too low, making the scheme operation difficult. There may be inadequate recognition or reward mechanisms. The scheme may only have a limited life, regular reviews and invigoration will be necessary.

SECTION 3 - QUALITY BY DESIGN

Design of Experiments

Genichi Taguchi - (Experimental Design and Analysis of Variance)

Dr. Genichi Taguchi was born in 1924 and in the 1970's developed the concept of the Quality Loss Function and had books published on Design of Experiments.

The Taguchi methodology is based on:

- Ensuring that quality is built into the product right from the design stage - with a bad or faulty design the best that manufacturing can do is make the design perfectly wrong
- Product optimisation prior to commencing manufacturing
- Avoiding 'inspecting the quality into the product'. I.e. Make the product right first time rather than using inspection to sort the good from the bad.

The methodology can also be used to identify and resolve manufacturing quality problems which cannot be solved by the normal routine problem solving methods.

Experimental Design

One of Taguchi's well-known writings is in the field of experimental design using orthogonal arrays. The problem solving techniques such as Pareto, Cause & Effect Diagrams, etc. as used in quality circles only go so far. These techniques provide a means of logically analysing a problem with a view to tackling the root cause. However, for sophisticated problems where there may be one or more causes and a number of variables, these techniques start to show their limitations. So it may be appropriate to use a more sophisticated problem solving technique like analysis of variance.

Analysis of variance can be used when there is a problem which could have a number of different contributory factors or variables. To study this situation, all of the factors except the factor currently under investigation will be held constant. The one factor is then varied and the effect on the problem monitored. No effect - then the next factor is selected - all of the other factors are held constant and the one factor varied and the effect on the problem monitored. This process is repeated until the factor causing the problem is finally identified.

There are certain difficulties with this approach:

- Two or more factors may be combining to cause the problem - so the problem may not be observed.
- Five variables tested at three points would require 50 tests.

- This is a very time consuming approach.
- It can be difficult or even impossible to hold the other variables constant while varying only one. Think about golf and trying to keep the swing constant while varying the grip. (I only wish I could keep my golf swing just slightly constant!).

Using Taguchi's matrices the number of tests can be greatly reduced. These matrices can be used to determine the main factors. It is this experimental design that provides considerable information concerning the best combination of levels of factors which will minimise process variation.

Taguchi Methods and Design of Experiments

As explained above one of the difficulties is that the more factors there are, the more combinations we have to test. For example, seven factors tested at two levels requires $2^7 = 128$ trials in a full factorial design. Genichi Taguchi developed a techniques called 'orthogonal arrays' to reduce the number of trials but still provide a balanced plan of experiments which would provide sufficient information to identify any interactions and further to identify the relative impact of the respective factors.

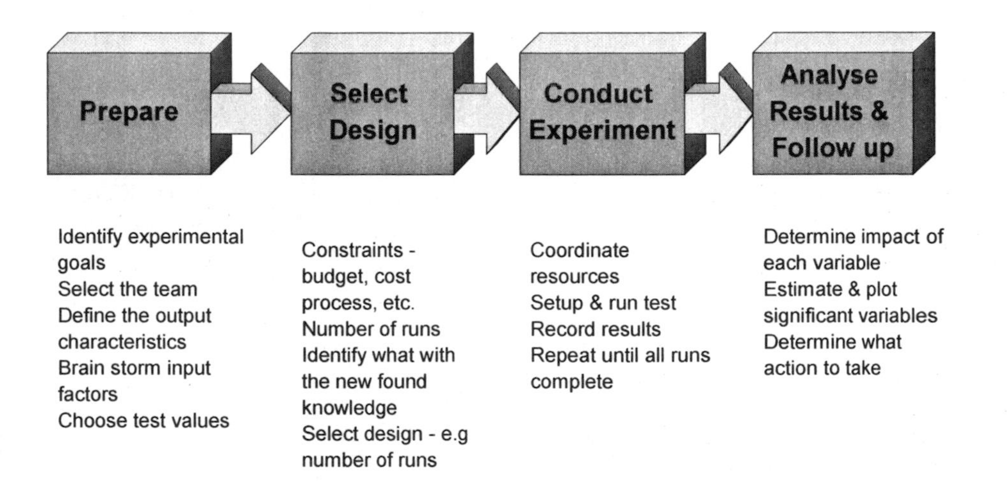

Figure 30 Taguchi Methods

Prepare - Choosing experimental parameters

Quality Characteristic

Prior to setting up and performing the experiment it is necessary to be clear what is to be studied. What quality characteristic is to be measured.

Trial Response

Next we need to identify what response (outcome) is to be used to measure our chosen quality characteristic. If, for example we were investigating the effect of various factors on customer satisfaction, we may look at complaints, goods returned, repeat orders etc. Each of these is a response which would require separate analysis. The responses may or may not be independent. For simplicity it is best to choose and stick to a single response if possible. The choice of response is most important. There is a story of the supermarket that monitored the speed of checking out goods (time taken from the first item entered to the 'total' key being pressed). Ostensibly this was intended to optimise customer satisfaction. In reality it annoyed customers, who found it difficult to keep pace in packing the goods into carriers.

Factors

Implicit in the above is the choice of factors to be investigated. Factors can be classified in to control factors and noise (uncontrollable) factors. Control factors are those which can be readily controlled for optimum results. Noise factors are those which are difficult, expensive or impossible to control. Noise factors may be internal such as the condition of plant or personnel, or external such as the condition of the weather.

- Factors are causes.
- Responses are effects.

Levels

The aim of the Taguchi analysis is to determine optimum levels for the control factors being least sensitive to the noise factors which are uncontrollable. Such a design is to be a robust design since it minimizes the effect of the noise factors and increases quality without any additional cost. Optimum levels may be to maximize a response, to minimize a response or to minimize variation about a preferred target value.

In theory there can be an infinite number of levels investigated. In practice it is found that the two extreme levels or alternative conditions are usually sufficient.

Select Design - Orthogonal Arrays

An orthogonal array is a table showing the various combinations for each treatment. For an experiment having 3 factors with two levels for each it looks like this:

	Factor 1	Factor 2	Factor 3
Treatment 1	level 1	level 1	level 1
Treatment 2	level 1	level 2	level 2
Treatment 3	level 2	level 1	level 2
Treatment 4	level 2	level 2	level 1

The thing to notice about this array is that

a) it does not include all possible combinations. That would require $2^3 = 8$ trials instead of four using this method.

b) the experiment is balanced so that each level of each factor will occur in the same number of trials and the effect of each factor can be analysed.

Conduct Experiment - Trials and Observations

Sampling Error

Earlier we suggested that single trials do not provide us with any information about sampling error. In other words how do we know the response is typical? For now we shall carry out each trial twice. That way we shall have information about variations 'within' the treatment as well as 'between' treatments. Repeating the experiment is called ***replication***.
We now carry out the trials for all the treatments in the table and record the responses.

Consider the following example:

It is required to investigate the relative effects of three factors on the stopping distance of a vehicle. The quality characteristic is brake efficiency and the response is the stopping distance. The factors under consideration are tyre pattern (P), tyre material (M) and road surface (S).

The orthogonal array for this experiment is:

	Tyre pattern (P)	Tyre material (M)	Road surface (S)
Treatment 1	pattern 1	material 1	surface 1
Treatment 2	pattern 1	material 2	surface 2
Treatment 3	pattern 2	material 1	surface 2
Treatment 4	pattern 2	material 2	surface 1

The observations are:

Treatments	P	M	S	Trial 1	Trial 2
1	1	1	1	190	210
2	1	2	2	210	215
3	2	1	2	210	220
4	2	2	1	225	240

Analysis of Results

Graphical Interpretation of Responses

For tyre pattern mean responses for level 1 (see shaded panel above)
(190 + 210 +210+215)/4 = 206.25
For tyre pattern mean responses for level 2 (see box with double border)
(210+225+220+240)/4 = 223.75

For material mean responses for level 1 = (190 + 210 +210+220)/4 = 207.5
For material mean responses for level 2 = (210+215+225+240)/4 = 222.5

For surface mean responses for level 1 = (190 + 210 +225+240)/4 = 216.25
For surface mean responses for level 2 = (210+215+210+220)/4 = 213.75

These values have been plotted in a response graph or Main Effects graph which can be seen in **Figure 31**.

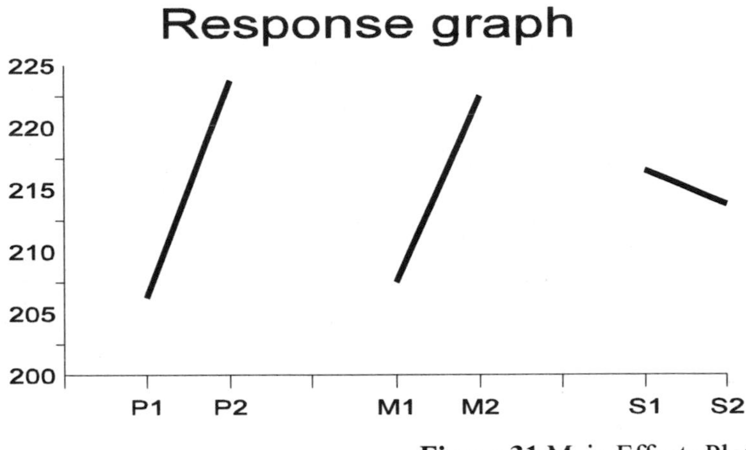

Figure 31 Main Effects Plot

Negative slopes indicate an improvement since the stopping distance is shortened. From this graph we can see that the tyre pattern appears to have the greatest effect with the road surface having negligible effect. However, we shall carry out an analysis of variance to distinguish signal from noise.

Analysis of Variances

Comparison of variation uses the sums of squares of deviations. The analysis consists of studying the sums of squares and using statistical methods to identify which sums of squares are large enough to be critical to our quality characteristic.

Coding

The mathematics of this can be considerably simplified by stating the response as deviations from an arbitrary datum without affecting the results. It makes sense to choose a datum as close to the mean as possible to minimise calculations. In this case 210 has been adopted as the datum.

Re-writing, the table becomes:

Treatments	P	M	S	Trial 1	Trial 2
1	1	1	1	-20	0
2	1	2	2	0	5
3	2	1	2	0	10
4	2	2	1	15	30

Calculate the Total Variation

This represents the total variation existing in the experiment. It comprises three types of variation:

a) Grand Mean Effect - mean of the sum of all observations squared. $S_{Grand\ Mean} = (\sum X_i)^2/N$
This is variation due to the specific and unique characteristics of the things being tested. It is inherent in the characteristic, in this case, this particular braking system.

b) Effect of the Factors - This is the variation that occurs as a result of changing each factor and are the 'Main Effects'.

c) Error Effect - This is the variation of unknown or uncontrolled causes. This is the random 'noise' due to uncontrolled and unknown factors. Already we can observe 'within' variations by studying the differences between replications.

Treatments	P	M	S	Trial 1	Trial 2
1	1	1	1	-20	0
2	1	2	2	0	5
3	2	1	2	0	10
4	2	2	1	15	30

The Total variation is $S_{total} = \sum X_i^2 = -20^2 + 0^2 + 0^2 + 15^2 + 0^2 + 5^2 + 10^2 + 30^2 = 1650$

Grand Mean Effect $S_{Grand\ Mean} = (\sum X_i)^2/N = (-20 + 0 + 0 + 5 + 0 + 10 + 15 + 30)^2/8 = 200$

Effect of Factors

First, tyre pattern:

$$S_P = (S_1 - S_2)_2/N$$

Treatments	P	M	S	Trial 1	Trial 2
1	1	1	1	-20	0
2	1	2	2	0	5
3	2	1	2	0	10
4	2	2	1	15	30

Now total the results observed for level 1 of P

$$-20+0+0+5 = 15$$

Treatments	P	M	S	Trial 1	Trial 2
1	1	1	1	-20	0
2	1	2	2	0	5
3	2	1	2	0	10
4	2	2	1	15	30

Now total the results observed for level 2 of P:

$$0+15+10+30 = 55$$

Now subtract the level 2 answer from the level 1 answer and square the result:

$$(-15-55)^2 = 4900$$

Finally divide this number by the total number of trials:

$$S_P = 4900/8 = 612.5$$

We now do the same for factor M (tyre material) using the level 1 rows:

Treatments	P	M	S	Trial 1	Trial 2
1	1	1	1	-20	0
2	1	2	2	0	5
3	2	1	2	0	10
4	2	2	1	15	30

$$-20+0+0+10 = -10$$

then using the level 2 rows we get:

$$0+15+5+30 = 50$$

Now subtract the level 2 answer from the level 1 answer and square the result:

$$(-10-50)^2 = 3600$$

Finally divide this number by the total number of trials:

$$S_m = 3600/8 = 450$$

Now doing the same for factor 3, the road surface:

Level 1	$-20+15+0+30$	$= 25$
Level 2	$0+0+5+10$	$= 15$
Subtract	$(25 - 15)^2$	$= 100$
Divide by N	$S_s = 100/8$	$= 12.5$

Notice the main effect is for tyre pattern, the effect of the road surface appears to have minimum effect.

We now need to calculate the error effect since this may be greater than the main effects and therefore render the main effects insignificant.

Since the error effect is the difference between the total effect and the sum of other effects and is given by the formula:

Error Effect = Total Variation - Grand Mean Effect - Sum of Main Effects

$$S_{error} = S_{total} - S_{Grand\ Mean} - (S_p + S_m + S_s)$$

$$1650 - 200 - (612.5 + 450 + 12.5) = 375$$

Summarising:

$S_{Grand\ Mean}$ = 200
$S_{pattern}$ = 612.5
$S_{material}$ = 450
$S_{surface}$ = 12.5
S_{error} = 375
S_{total} = 1650

At this stage it appears that since the effect of the road surface is lower than the effect of error we cannot conclude that road surface is significant. However we need to do this statistically.

So far the calculated values of S are total variations and not average variations. To get the average variations we need to divide by the degrees of freedom to obtain the Variances.

$$V_{effect} = S_{effect}/df$$

Degrees of Freedom

Each experiment possesses a total degrees of freedom (df) equal to the number of trials which in this case is 8. Since each of the degrees of freedom belongs to one of the three components grand mean, the factors and the error effect, we can deduce the individual degrees of freedom by subtracting one degree of freedom for each of the other effects:

$$df_{Error} = df_{Total} - df_{grand\ mean} - df_{factors}$$

$$df_{Error} = 8 - 1 - 3 = 4$$

Testing for significance

$$\text{Error Variance} = S_{error}/df_{Error} = 375/4 = 93.75$$

Now a rule of thumb states that to be significant the variance of an effect must be greater than 3.84 times the error variance, i.e. $V_{effect} / V_{error} > 3.84$. Therefore the minimum variance required for significance is 93.75 x 3.84 = 360.

Now Tyre Pattern variance = V_P = $S_{pattern}/df_{Pattern}$ = 612.5/1 = 612.5 which is > 360 therefore significant.

Tyre Material variance = V_M = $S_{Material}/df_{Material}$ = 450/1 = 450 which is > 360 therefore significant.

Road Surface variance = V_S = $S_{Surface}/df_{Surface}$ = 12.5/1 = 12.5 which is < 360 therefore not significant.

Having eliminated one of the effects we must add its values to the error values since it cannot be distinguished from error. Thus:

$$\text{New } S_{error} = S_{error} + S_{surface} = 375 + 12.5 = 387.5$$

$$\text{New } df_{Error} = df_{Error} + df_{Surface} = 4 + 1 = 5$$

We must now calculate the Error variance which will be 387.5/5 = 77.5

Now looking up the F ratio for 5 df gives 6.61 for 5% significance. These figure can be found from suitable statistical table such as Table "Percentage points of the F distribution" in "*Statistical Tables*" by Murdoch and Barnes.

Therefore to be significant the variance of an effect must be greater than 6.61 times the error variance, i.e. $V_{effect}/V_{error} > 6.61$ Therefore the minimum variance required for significance is 77.5 x 6.61 = 512.28

Finally, we can state that on this basis the only variable that appears to be significant is the pattern of the tyre.[24]

---

[24] The data used in the examples is fictitious and for the purpose of illustration only. No conclusions other than for this purpose should be inferred.

Follow up

The graphical presentation of the responses provides us with a good idea of the relative effects which are borne out by the statistical analysis.

Although the latter treatment of the Taguchi method of analysis of variance looks somewhat different to factorial design, it is essentially the same but presented differently. Either approach may be used, the only difference is full factorial design includes every possible combination, whereas the Taguchi approach limits the number of experiments to the orthogonal array.

Exercises

A food supplier produces Soup in a carton. The soup sometimes leaks from the carton which causes customers to complaint. A study was established to determine the likely cause. Using the data below draw the response plot

Soup Carton Experiment

	Levels	
Factors	Low	High
Filling Machine Speed	Slow = 1	Fast = 2
Glue Supplier	A = 1	B = 2
Pressure Applied	Low = 1	High = 2

Run to trial and measure seal strength:

Run	Filling Machine Speed	Glue Supplier	Pressure Applied	Seal Strength
1	1	1	1	56.2
2	2	1	1	55.6
3	1	2	1	54.0
4	2	2	1	50.0
5	1	1	2	61.6
6	2	1	2	52.2
7	1	2	2	60.3
8	2	2	2	51.1

Answer

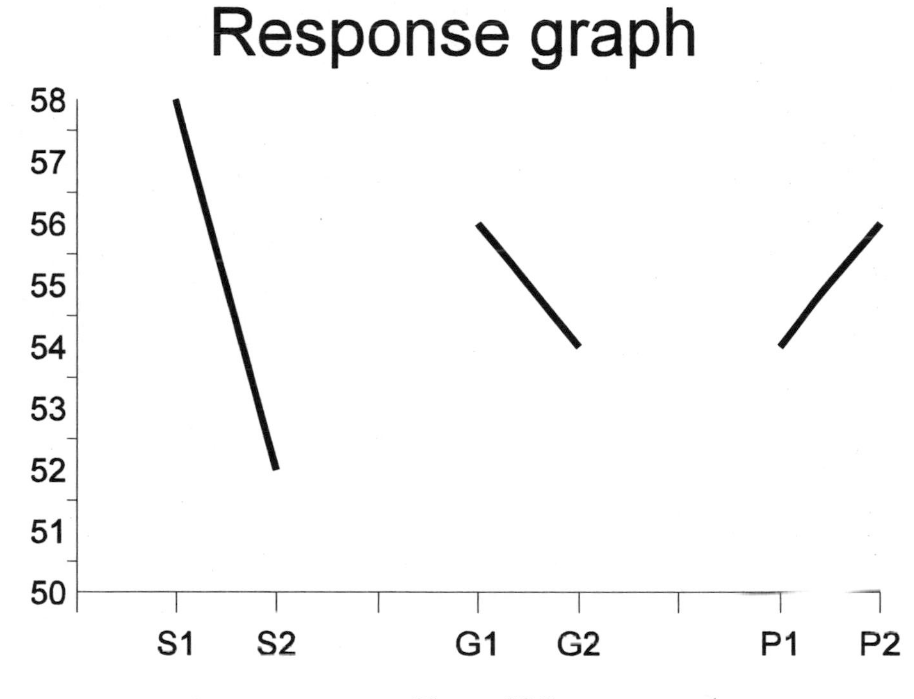

Figure 32 Response graph - soup cartons

Ishikawa's Seven Tools of Quality

1. Pareto analysis - See page 114
2. Cause and effect diagrams - See page 117
3. Stratification or Sampling - See page 119
4. Check sheets - See page 122
5. Histograms - See page 123
6. Scatter diagrams - See page 125
7. Shewhart's control charts and graphs (see Statistical Quality Control) - See page 135

Pareto Analysis

Introduction

Establishing the factors that together make up all the various causes of rejects invariably means that a considerable number of problems are discovered. To tackle all of these problems at one go would require enormous resources and in many cases, some of the problems may be trivial and not worth pursuing for the time being.

A technique invaluable in singling out those problems which have the greatest influence on the total reject quantity or costs is Pareto Analysis.

Very often when this type of analysis is conducted, the results show that when placed in order of importance out of a given number of causes, only a small percentage, usually around 20%, account for 80% of the total problem. For this reason the concept is often known as the 80 - 20 rule.

Table 14 Scrap records

Operation	Dept Resp	Scrap Qty	Cause	Value	Total Cost
Saw	105	50	Wrong Size	0.30	15.00
Turn	105	61	Wrong O.D.	0.40	24.40
Mill	103	87	Flat Position	0.50	43.50
Drill & Tap	120	230	Hole Position	0.60	138.00
Heat Treat	110	239	Wrong Case Depth	0.80	191.20
Cyl. Grind	110	320	Wrong O.D.	0.90	288.00
Bore Grind	103	616	Wrong I.D.	1.00	616.00
Hone	103	701	Over Size	1.50	1,051.50
Lap	103	1991	Surface Finish	2.00	3,982.00
Total		4,295			6,349.60

As an example of this technique the reasons for rejects or scrap from a process were recorded over a convenient period of time. This information has been tabulated. **Table 14** opposite shows the number of scrapped components found by inspection at each operation.

This information can be arranged in order and a graph plotted of the results, see **Figure 33** Graph Pareto Analysis. Examination of this graph reveals that approximately 20% of the causes of reject items are responsible for 80% of the total cost of rejects.

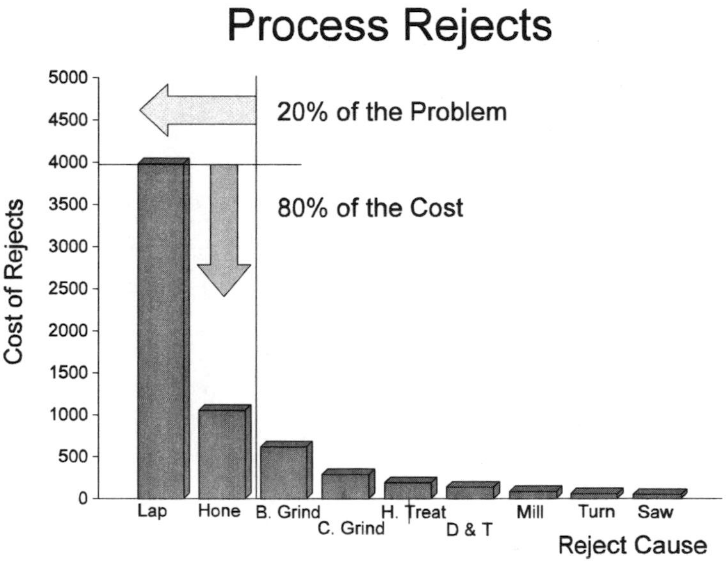

Figure 33 Pareto Analysis Graph

Guidelines for Pareto Analysis:

Select the factor to be analysed. Determine how the data is to be collected (possibly by the use of check sheets) and what the duration of data collection will be.

Rank the data in ascending order.

Establish the appropriate horizontal scale and vertical scale.

Table 15 shows other criteria which can be analysed using the Pareto technique depending on the nature of the problem.

Table 15 Pareto Graph Axis

Horizontal Axis	**Vertical Axis**
Part No./Machine No./ Operator or Dept. No.	Cost of defectives
Supplier	Goods inwards inspection rejects
Reasons for warranty returns	Quantity of warranty returns
Reasons for test failures	Quantity of test failures
Reasons for rework	Quantity of rectification work

The object of Pareto Analysis is to identify 'THE IMPORTANT FEW' with a view to avoiding 'THE TRIVIAL MANY'. Thus it is possible to make an 80% improvement by tackling and eliminating only 20% of the problems.

Cause and Effect Diagrams

Introduction

These diagrams provide a means of logically analysing a problem with a view to tackling the root cause. Generally the construction of a Cause and Effect Diagram is a team exercise. The diagram is to formalise and to keep a record of the team's logical approach to the problem. This provides a method by which the team's thoughts and deliberations can be documented, and provides a catalyst for discussing the problem.

Cause and Effect Guidelines

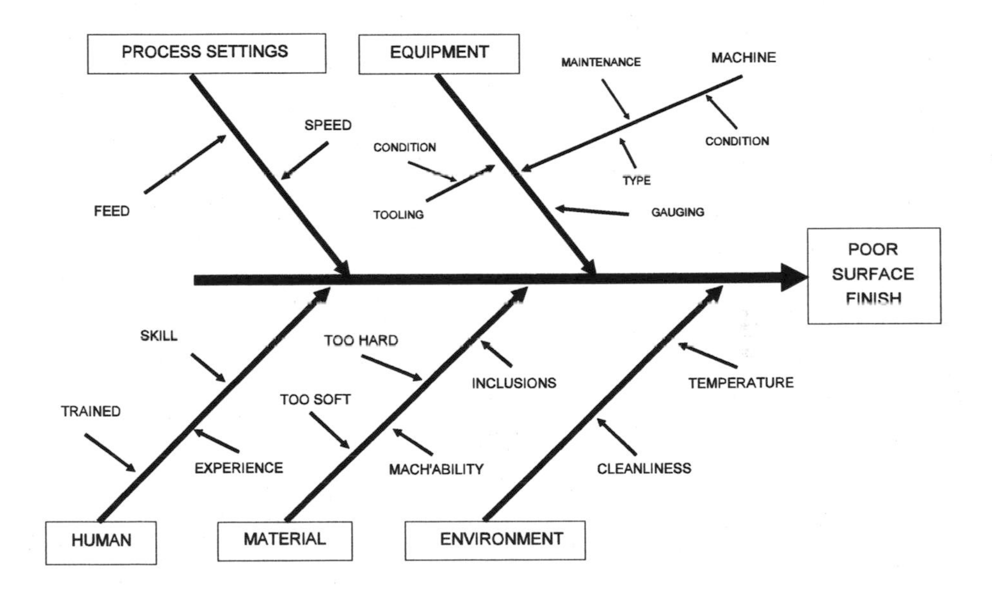

Figure 34 Cause & Effect Diagram

The first stage is to clearly define the problem. This definition may be provided from a Pareto Analysis or from statistical process control data. **Figure 34** records from a fixed point what the team considers are the main causes of the problem. Such as human, material, machines, environment, sequence, procedure, process system, equipment etc. Having determined the major group causes, the team brain storms the likely sub-causes within the major groups and possibly the further sub-causes.

Having established the team's views on possible suspects or causes of the problem, the team next needs to consider which, in their view, is the most likely culprit. The possible causes can be ranked in order of most likely, most easy to eliminate from the investigations etc.

Having prioritised the most probable culprits an action plan for investigation can be drawn up and implemented. This plan would detail the most likely causes, the method of evaluation and who is responsible for conducting the investigation. This stage would be repeated until the actual guilty party was discovered, again Pareto Analysis may be put to useful effect. (See section Pareto Analysis)

In certain cases the problem may be so complex that more sophisticated statistical methods may need to be employed, such as Taguchi Techniques; sometimes known as an analysis of variance.

Stratification

Introduction

Stratification or sampling is a technique where a small sample is taken from a large sample or batch, usually to determine the quality of the large sample.

Sampling can be used for attribute data (pass/fail) or variable data (measured). The advantages are that it provides a quick method of determining the state of the batch without having to examine every item. Often, examining every item can result in mistakes, possibly through boredom or inattention of the checker. To determine the correct sample size to use, sampling tables such as BS 6001 can be employed. The diagram **Figure 35** shows how a sample could be randomly taken from four processes.

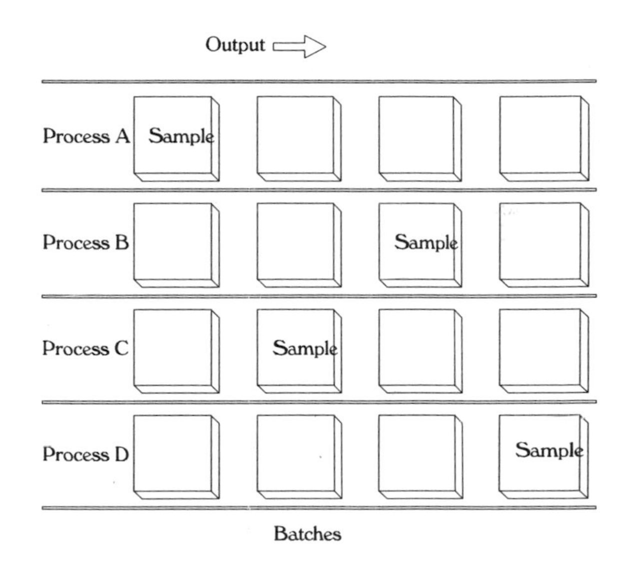

Figure 35 Sampling from batches

Guidelines for Stratification

Stratification involves:

1. Planning to identify the batch to be examined and the sample size to be taken.

2. Data collection by randomly selecting the sample and examining the selected sample. The diagram shows random selection of samples from a number of processes.

3. Analysis of the results of sampling.

Activity Sampling

Introduction

Sampling can take many forms and is used in numerous applications:

- Batch Sampling - Goods Receiving Inspection (see Stratification)
- Process Sampling - During manufacturing, charts such as attribute charts can be used to record the information gathered (see Statistical Quality Control)
- Activity Sampling - Can be used to take a snapshot of activities at any particular time.

To gather information about how much time is being spent on various activities, a study can be performed that monitors the activities or process on a 100% basis, continually examining the process and noting process changes and activities. This approach will necessarily involve a considerable full time resource and only a limited number of activities can be observed in this way. It is very difficult to monitor the process 100% of the time and while not under observation important process activities may be missed. To provide more objective results sampling can be employed, this technique gives the opportunity to quantify the current situation making the problem less subjective and more objective. The activity can be sampled at predetermined intervals to provide a more reliable and accurate account of the situation.

Activity Sampling can be used to monitor: The proportion of time spent on particular activities, waiting time, equipment utilisation time, labour utilisation time etc.

Activity Sampling Guidelines:

Pre-study Guidelines

1. Determine the process or activities to be studied - this may involve defining the problem more clearly.

2. Determine the likely scope of the study; factors to be recorded, frequency, duration, the required accuracy of the study, the recording method. It may be appropriate to conduct a pilot study first.

Table 16 A typical check list table for Activity Sampling recording

Factors\Sample Number	1	2	3	4	5	6	7	8	9	10	11	12	13	14	15
Waiting Instructions															
Waiting Work															
Break down															
Running															
Other															
Total															

In the row, Sample Number, the date and time of the activity sample can be recorded. In the column, Factors, various activities are listed that could be observed when the activity sample is taken.

3. Ensure that all the correct or agreed activity sequence, usage and method is understood.

4. Communicate the reason for conducting the study to all personnel concerned.

Analysis of Results

5. Having collated the results it may be necessary to repeat the study on the basis of the information gathered. Alternatively, the situation may now be much clearer and the appropriate course of action may now be apparent. A report can be compiled which identifies the key factors, Pareto Analysis may be useful for this.

Check or Tally Sheets

Introduction

Tally sheets or check sheets are used to gather and record data. The data may be numerical but check sheets can also be used for audit purposes, i.e. listing audit questions to be asked and recording the responses. The tally list provides the facility to record data to establish a clear picture of the situation. **Table 17** shows an example of a tally sheet used for recording the number of rejects produced each week.

Table 17 Tally Sheet

Test Rejects	Number per day					Week Total
	M	T	W	T	F	
Voltage	11	1111	1111111	1	111	17
Power	11	1111	1	111111	11	15
Speed	1	1	1	11111	11	10
Torque	1111	1	111111	0	111111111 1111	24
Total	9	10	15	12	20	66

Guidelines for Tally Sheets

Plan: Determine the reasons for collecting the data. Establish which factors are to be monitored (Brainstorming or Cause and Effect Diagrams may help). When (how frequently and sample size) and how the data is to be collected.

Implementation: Collect the data and record the quantities on the tally sheet

Analysis: Total the result over the predetermined duration. Analysis of the data can be accomplished by the use of Pareto Analysis or Scatter Diagrams.

Histograms or Bar Charts

Introduction

A histogram is a method of representing data in a bar chart format. These diagrams can be used when gathering and analysing data.

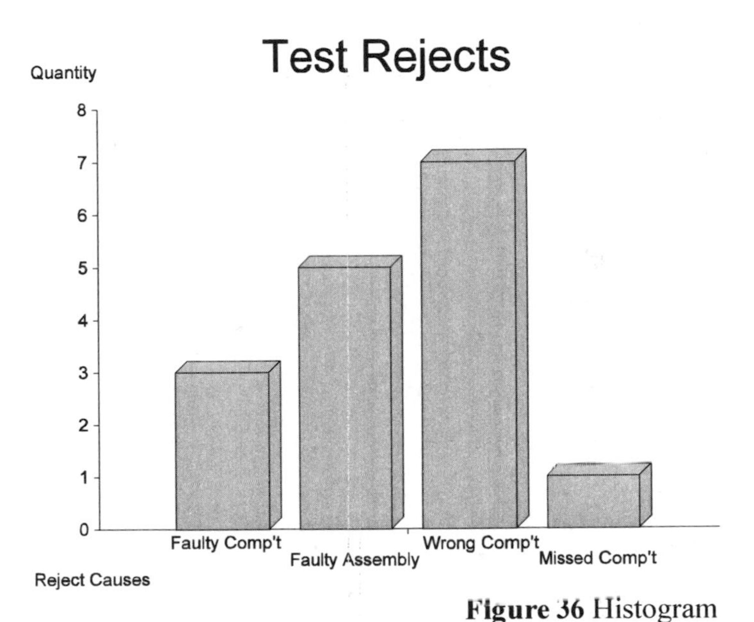

Figure 36 Histogram

The data may be discrete categories of data. This could be used to analyse numbers of customer complaints against the reason for the customer complaint or the hours spent on inspection of each operation or product. The diagram **Figure 36** opposite shows the number of rejects for each fault type. This type of histogram can be employed when performing a Pareto Analysis, in this case the causes of rejects would be listed in descending order.

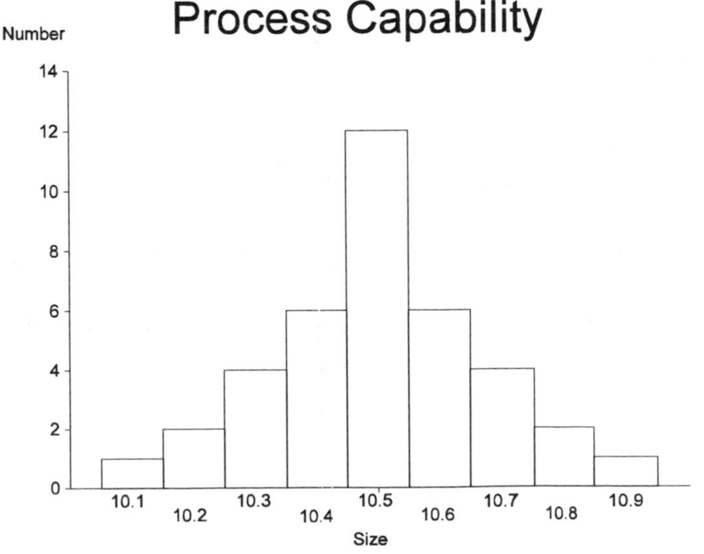

Figure 37 Histogram - Process Capability Study

Alternatively, the histogram could show data spread over a period of time or over a range of dimensions or sizes. There are numerous ways in which histograms can be usefully employed, two examples are:

To analyse the change in the cost of quality of a company by displaying the total cost of quality on a month by month basis over the past year.

Or as in **Figure 37** the number of components manufactured between a particular range of sizes (10.1 to 10.9mm). This type of histogram is particularly useful when performing a process capability study.

Guidelines for Creating Histograms

a. Determine the factors to be analysed and collect the data (possibly by the use of check sheets).

b. Rank the data in ascending or descending order.

c. Establish the appropriate horizontal scale by determining the number of columns required (normal 6 to 8 is adequate) and the width of each column.

$$\textit{Width of each column} = \frac{\textit{Largest Value} - \textit{Smallest Value}}{\textit{Number of Columns}} \qquad \textbf{(2)}$$

Establish the vertical scale. The vertical scale is often cost, quantity or frequency of an event.

Scatter Diagram

Introduction

Scatter diagrams are used to examine if there is a relationship between two factors or variables. These diagrams can be employed in gathering and analysing data, problem solving, and testing solutions.

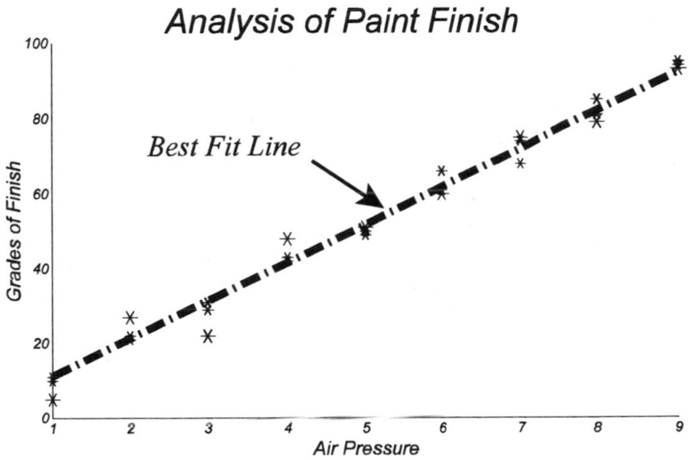

Figure 38 Scatter Diagram

When analysing a problem, it is sometimes necessary to determine if there is a relationship between two factors. For example, measurements taken by two inspectors, tool life and cutting speed or, as shown in **Figure 38**, air pressure and paint finish.

Guidelines for Scatter Diagrams

To perform this analysis:

Planning to determine the factors to be monitored, possibly using the horizontal axis for the cause and the vertical axis for the effect.

Data collection of approximately 50 or more results.

Analyse the graph and draw the 'best fit' line through the points. (There are statistical techniques which can be employed i.e. Regression Analysis to determine the best fit line).

It is important to ensure that the relationship is real, remember there are lies, damn lies and statistics. With statistics, it is probably possible to prove a direct relationship between the number of new Methodist Ministers and the number of unmarried Mothers. This relationship is obviously (hopefully) faulty, but with statistics it may be possible to demonstrate such a relationship, so care needs to be taken when attempting to determine a relationship between two variables. If there is a relationship between the factors then it should be possible to fit a line between the points plotted and consequently make predictions regarding the cause and effect. Using **Figure 38** as an example, an experiment was set up to determine if there was any relationship between paint finish and pressure of the spray gun. As can be seen from the graph, the results tend to suggest a relationship. If the variable pressure is increased then there is a corresponding improvement in grade of finish. Presumably there would be a limit to this relationship - continuing to increase pressure would eventually not improve the paint finish. But within the limit of the graph shown above the paint finish grade does improve. From this data it should be possible to determine the optimum setting for the air pressure.

Shewhart's Control Charts and Graphs - Statistical Quality Control (SQC)

Introduction

Most activities, when analysed, form some type of process or sequence, e.g. office paper work, manufacturing, construction, service or maintenance processes. All of these processes will require some form of monitoring to ensure that the process is not going out of control and to identify the causes of variation and thereby improving the overall process performance. SQC can be used as a means of process monitoring to assist in identifying causes of variation and improve process performance.

The skill of starting RIGHT! - All processes are subject to variation. This variation may be small and insignificant, alternatively the variation could be excessive causing products to be produced outside the specification. It is therefore important to understand the extent to which a process will vary before production starts, thereby avoiding costly scrap or start/stop production. To determine the extent of process variation a study can be performed measuring the amount by which processes vary. These measurements can subsequently be statistically analysed, providing a clear indication of the process's ability to meet specification, i.e. a Process Capability Study (see diagram Process Capability Study Chart).

The skill of keeping the process RIGHT and making the process world class! - Having determined the process's ability to meet specification, controls need to be applied which continually monitor the process for quality and which allow continuous improvements to be made to product quality - (Statistical Quality Control, SQC). This involves taking regular measurements of process variation and comparing these observations with predetermined control limits of variation. This comparison can best be accomplished graphically on control charts. The application of SQC gives the opportunity to implement operator quality control, assisting in reinforcing the operator's responsibility for the quality of their own work and gives a sense of pride in their work. Thus, reinforcing the need for all concerned to achieve a process of world class standard.

Guidelines

Statistical Quality Control

Process Capability Studies (PCS) - *The skill of starting RIGHT!*

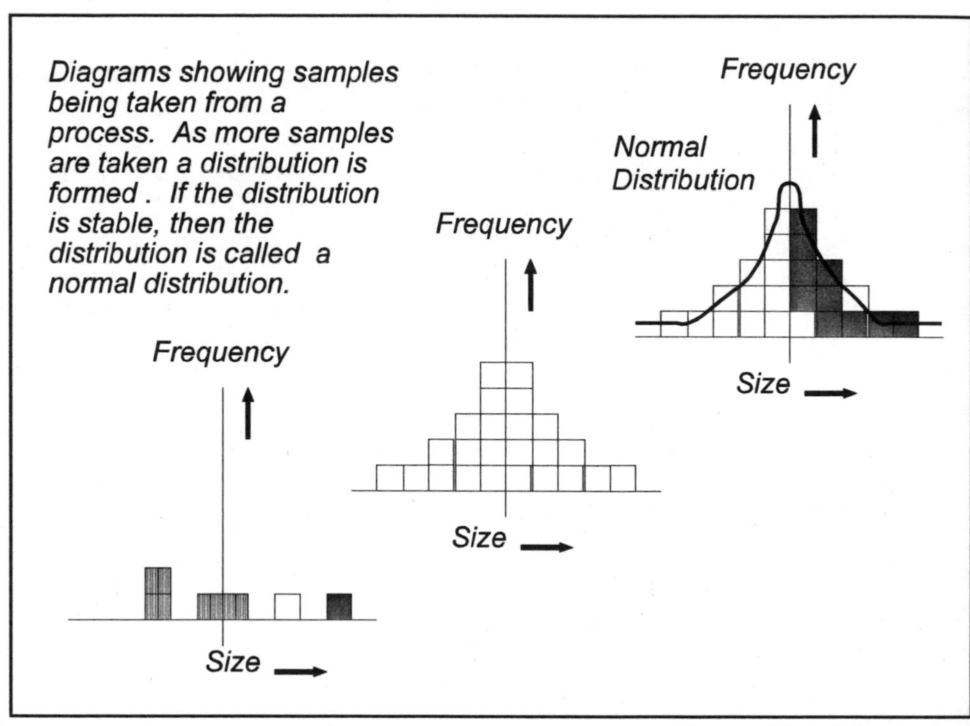

Figure 39 A Distribution

As explained, processes are subject to variation which can affect the process's ability to meet process specification. One method of determining a process's ability to meet specification is by conducting a Process Capability Study. **Figure 39** shows how data from a process can be collected and plotted on a chart. As more data is collected a picture starts to form; if the process is stable then this picture will form the shape of a normal distribution. The following procedure describes how to gather the data to produce a picture that represents the way in which the process is performing for quality.

Pre-study Guidelines

A. Determine the process to be studied - this may be on the basis of:

1. analysis of scrap or rework - internal failures
2. analysis of customer complaints - external failures
3. a modified process which has never been run before or the acceptance of a new process i.e. new capital equipment
4. the first off after setting a process

B. Determine the features to be studied - possibly on the basis of a Failure Mode and Effects Analysis[25] results or after producing a cause and effect diagram or just the inspector/setter's judgement on which are the key feature/s.

C. Ensure that all the key factors are correct against the relevant process instructions and drawings. Parameters such as pressures, temperatures, settings, equipment etc.

D. Confirm that operations carried out prior to the process under investigation have been satisfactorily completed. I.e. That the previous processes met specification and therefore will not have any detrimental effect on the process undergoing consideration. For example, excessive variation in the location dimension could have a direct effect on the result of the study.

E. It is advisable that the number of samples taken is at least 25.

F. The measuring, gauging or transducer accuracy is usually expected to be within 10% of the process specification.

G. Communicate the reason for conducting the study to all personnel concerned.

---

[25] See section Failure Mode and Effects Analysis

During the Study

The samples should be measured in the order that they are produced, otherwise trend cannot be observed. If multiple processes are being studied, then each product should be identifiable to a particular process. Should the process be reset during the study this should also be noted. Any abnormal conditions should be noted if they are likely to produce variation in the product e.g. size.

If a product is found to be 'way out of line' with the others during the study, it should be examined for an assignable cause or non-random effect which would account for its condition. Only then can the product be discarded.

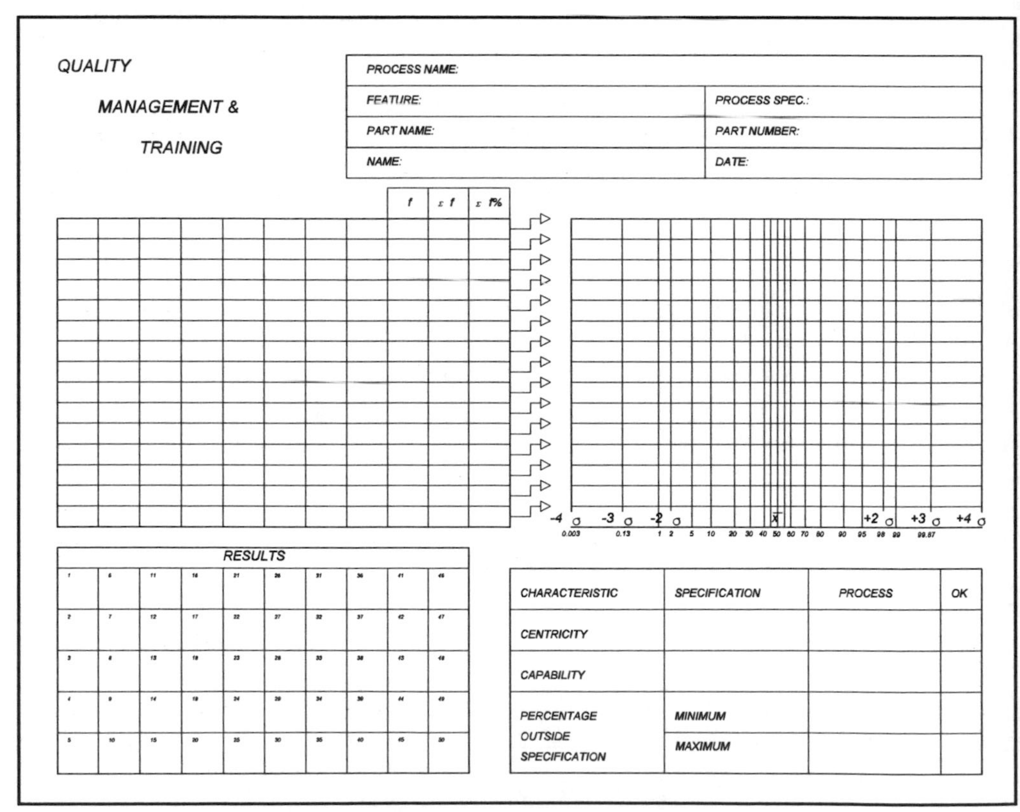

QUALITY
MANAGEMENT &
TRAINING

PROCESS NAME:	
FEATURE:	PROCESS SPEC.:
PART NAME:	PART NUMBER:
NAME:	DATE:

f | Σf | Σf%

-4σ -3σ -2σ $\bar{X}$ +2σ +3σ +4σ

0.003 0.13 1 2 5 10 20 30 40 50 60 70 80 90 95 98 99 99.87

RESULTS									
1	6	11	16	21	26	31	36	41	46
2	7	12	17	22	27	32	37	42	47
3	8	13	18	23	28	33	38	43	48
4	9	14	19	24	29	34	39	44	49
5	10	15	20	25	30	35	40	45	50

CHARACTERISTIC	SPECIFICATION	PROCESS	OK
CENTRICITY			
CAPABILITY			
PERCENTAGE OUTSIDE SPECIFICATION	MINIMUM		
	MAXIMUM		

Figure 40 Process Capability Chart

Completing the Process Capability Study Form

STEP ACTION

1. Enter the process details (see **Figure 40** Process Capability Chart).

QUALITY MANAGEMENT & TRAINING

PROCESS NAME: BONDING	
FEATURE: JOINT STRENGTH	PROCESS SPEC.: 400N 60N±
PART NAME: LEVER & SHAFT ASS.	PART NUMBER: 9167/103
NAME: Peter Vorley	DATE: 4th April 1992

				f	Σ f	Σ f%
460						
450						
440						
430						
420	II			2	50	100
410	IIIII	IIIII	IIII	14	48	96
400	IIIII	IIIII	I	11	34	68
390	IIIII	IIIII	II	12	23	46
380	IIIII	I		6	11	22
370	IIIII			5	5	10
360						
350						
340						

-4 σ -3 σ -2 σ $\bar{X}$ +2 σ +3 σ +4 σ

0.003 0.13 1 2 5 10 20 30 40 50 60 70 80 90 95 98 99 99.87

RESULTS

416	104	416	406	372	384	394	406	382	380
412	410	394	410	392	404	414	410	408	390
408	372	412	370	384	412	382	396	404	418
398	400	414	400	390	392	388	374	408	392
418	424	392	376	410	418	396	402	394	422

CHARACTERISTIC	SPECIFICATION	PROCESS	OK
CENTRICITY	400	402	✓
CAPABILITY	120	92	✓
PERCENTAGE OUTSIDE SPECIFICATION	MINIMUM	0	✓
	MAXIMUM	0.1%	

Figure 41 Completed Process Capability Chart

2. Enter the process results in the sequence that they were produced.

3. Determine the scale to be used. Experience has shown that the formula below can be used as a guide.

$$\frac{\textit{Largest Reading} - \textit{Smallest Reading}}{8} = \textit{Class Interval} \qquad (3)$$

In the example (see **Figure 41** Completed Process Capability Chart)

$$\frac{424 - 370}{8} \simeq 6.7 \textit{ rounding up gives class interval of } 10N \qquad \textbf{(4)}$$

4. Draw in the tolerance or process specification limits in a thick black line across the complete width of the chart. Enter the results on the tally chart.

5. Enter the frequency of each result in the column 'f' (zero if no value is found).

6. Working upwards in column '$\sum$f' calculate the cumulative frequency (Note $\sum$ means the sum of or cumulation).

7. Convert the cumulative frequencies 'Σf' into percentages of the total and enter the result in column '$\sum$f%'.

8. Noting the bottom figure in column '$\sum$f%' follow the arrow until the corresponding point on the probability graph is found. Mark this point with a cross. Repeat this exercise until the 100% figure is reached. To avoid losing this last number the average of the last two figures can be plotted e.g.

$$\frac{\textit{Last Reading} + \textit{Second to Last Reading}}{2}$$

$$\frac{100+96}{2} = 98 \qquad \textbf{(5)}$$

$$\textit{plot as } \textbf{98\% @ 425}N$$

9. Draw the best fit straight line through all the points (extend the line to the extremities of the graph paper). If a reasonable fit cannot be found (your own judgement is required here), then the data may contain some non-random effect or be zero limited. In these circumstances either identify the non-random effect or use special skewed distribution paper.

Interpretation of Results

10. **Figure 42** Interpretation of PCS Results indicates the desired process performance.

    The process setting should fall within 2 standard deviations. The symbol x bar is a measure of the location or setting of the process.

    The process specification should be less than or equal to the process capability (6 standard deviations). The symbol σ means standard deviation and is a measure of the spread or width of the distribution.

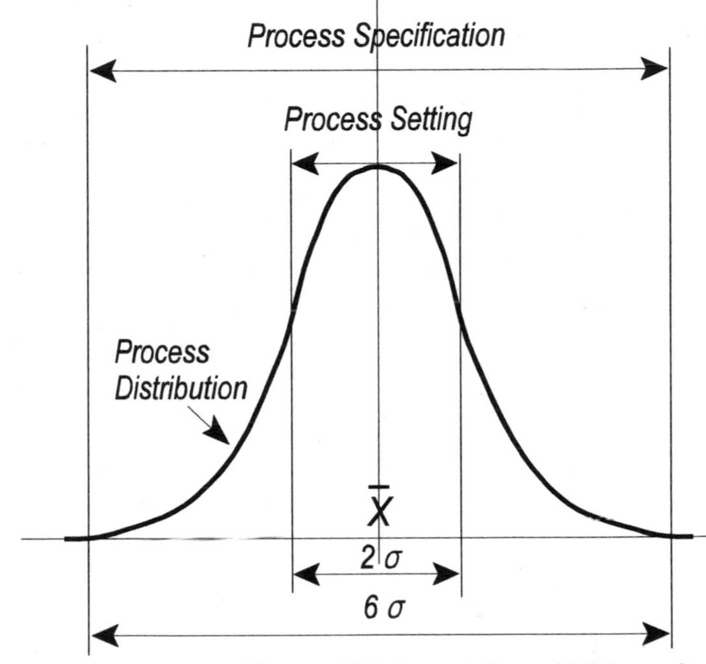

Figure 42 Interpretation of PCS results

11. Locate the 50% or x bar point on the probability paper and read off the average value from the left-hand scale. This average value will be adjacent to the intercept point on the graph *(in the example 402N)*. This gives an indication of the setting of the process and is sometimes termed the **CENTRICITY** value.

12. Enter the specified (required) centricity and process (actual) centricity in the box. *(In the example, 400N & 402N respectively)*.

13. Determine from the chart the distance that will correspond to 6σ (±3σ); this is termed **CAPABILITY**. Enter the values for specified and process capability in the box. *(In the example, 120N & 92N respectively)*.

14. Determine the number of items likely to be produced outside specification. *(In the example, the intersection of the best fit line and the process limits, i.e. minimum 0% and maximum 0.1%).*

Benefits of Process Capability Studies (and uses of a PCS)

Having gathered the data regarding the process, it is then possible to determine the extent to which the process holds the specification. In the previous example (**Figure 41**) if the process specification was changed from 340N/460N to 380N/460N then the predicted reject level will be approximately 10%. This would provide the data for a process improvement programme.

If there were a number of processes to choose from the decision on which process to choose can be on the basis of quality and price.

Table 18 Process Selection

Characteristic	Process A	Process B
Cost	£0.50 per piece	£0.25 per piece
Output Rates	10 per hour	10 per hour
Predicted reject quantities Minimum Maximum	 0 0.1%	 10% 0.1%

The PCS data and graph provides the means of assessing the process faults and the causes of any rejects.

It may be possible to establish the frequency with which the process needs to be monitored and adjusted.

A PCS could form the basis of acceptance trials for the purchase of capital equipment. If the features to be monitored were determined prior to ordering capital equipment then a PCS could be performed prior to acceptance. This PCS could be performed either by the supplier or customer to confirm the process's ability to meet specification.

As a process matures then the process's ability to meet specification can become impaired. If the original process capability was known it may be possible to predict when the process requires repair or replacement.

Statistical Quality Control

The skill of keeping the process RIGHT and making the process world class!

The previous section described how to determine whether it is possible to 'make it right'. Having established that the process can 'make it right', then the next stage is to 'keep it right' and 'make it world class'. Sometimes the PCS establishes that the process cannot produce correctly thus, in these circumstances, it is even more important to apply SQC.

The application of SQC can be used to monitor and improve the performance of the process.

Before Introducing SQC

Communication: Ensure that all personnel are aware of the need for, and the benefits of using SQC. The personnel involved in collating and analysing the data should be suitably trained.

Characteristic: Determine the features or characteristics to be controlled using SQC. From past experience it may be known which features or parameters present the most problems. Alternatively, the features may be established on the basis of:

A. Performing a Pareto analysis, identifying "the important few", internal or external quality problems, e.g. scrap, rectification, rejects, customer complaints or warranty returns.
B. Key Features - Features that could cause financial or reputational damage if they are not maintained within certain limits.
C. Features identified as a result of performing a Failure Mode and Effects Analysis.

Measuring: Establish testing, checking, measuring or gauging methods to be employed, ensuring that the equipment will be sufficiently accurate, (approximately 10% of the drawing requirements should be adequate).

Decide on the inspection criteria:

1. Check that drawings and specifications contain realistic quantifiable standards.

2. Check that the specifications are appropriate (designers have been known to set unrealistic specifications on rare occasions).

3. Check that the acceptance criteria are clearly defined.

4. Check that the reference standards, gauges, visual aids such as samples or photographs etc. are available.

5. Check that operator/inspector possesses the appropriate faculties (e.g. good eyesight) and necessary skill.

6. Check correct environment for task (e.g. good lighting).

Logistics: Install the chart holders and control charts in a prominent position, preferably adjacent to the process and within easy reach of the personnel controlling the process.

Sampling: Select an appropriate sample size and frequency for monitoring the process. It is not essential, but if a PCS has been performed the results can give a good indication of the sample size and frequency.

Select: Decide on the most appropriate charting method to use.

Chart Selection

Various types of chart are available, described below are some of the more commonly used charts, together with examples of where the charts can be usefully employed. See **Figure 43**.

VARIABLE DATA; X/R Chart (Average and Range) these charts will be used when the data is measured, i.e. readings from measuring device such as a volt meter.

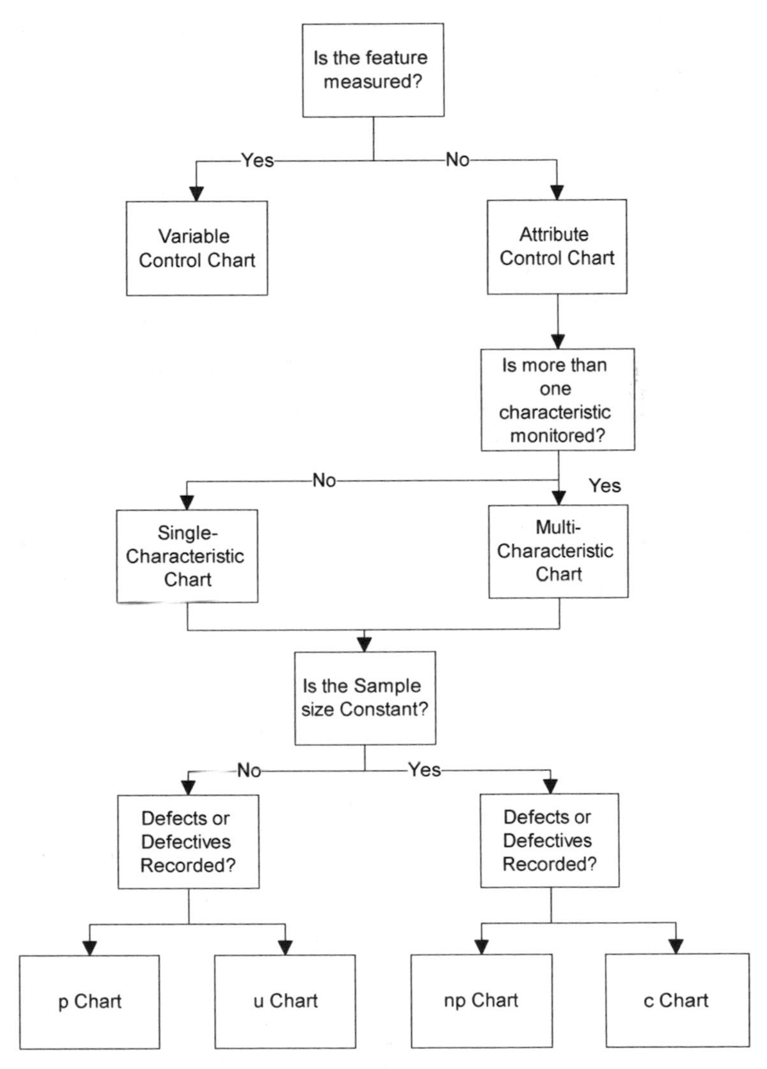

Figure 43 Chart selection

ATTRIBUTE DATA (see **Figure 43**) Single characteristic chart or Multiple characteristic chart. These charts will be used in go/nogo, pass/fail situations.

A. The p chart for proportion of Defectives where the sample is not necessarily of constant size.
B. The np chart for Number of Defectives where the sample size is constant.
C. The c chart for Number of Defects where sample size is constant.
D. The u chart for Number of Defects per Unit where the sample size is not necessarily constant.

Table 19 Attribute Chart Selection

Sample Size Varies	Sample Size Constant	Fault Type	Description
Proportion	Number		
p	np	Defectives	Accept or Reject
u	c	Defects	Number of different flaws

Note: An item may have 4 different flaws, in which case there are 4 **defects** in the item, but there is still only one **defective** item. (See **Figure 44**)

Examples in the use of single characteristic charts may be:

For p and n type charts

- pass or fail light bulb test
- go or nogo hole size
- correct or incorrect torque loading
- accept or reject weld strength

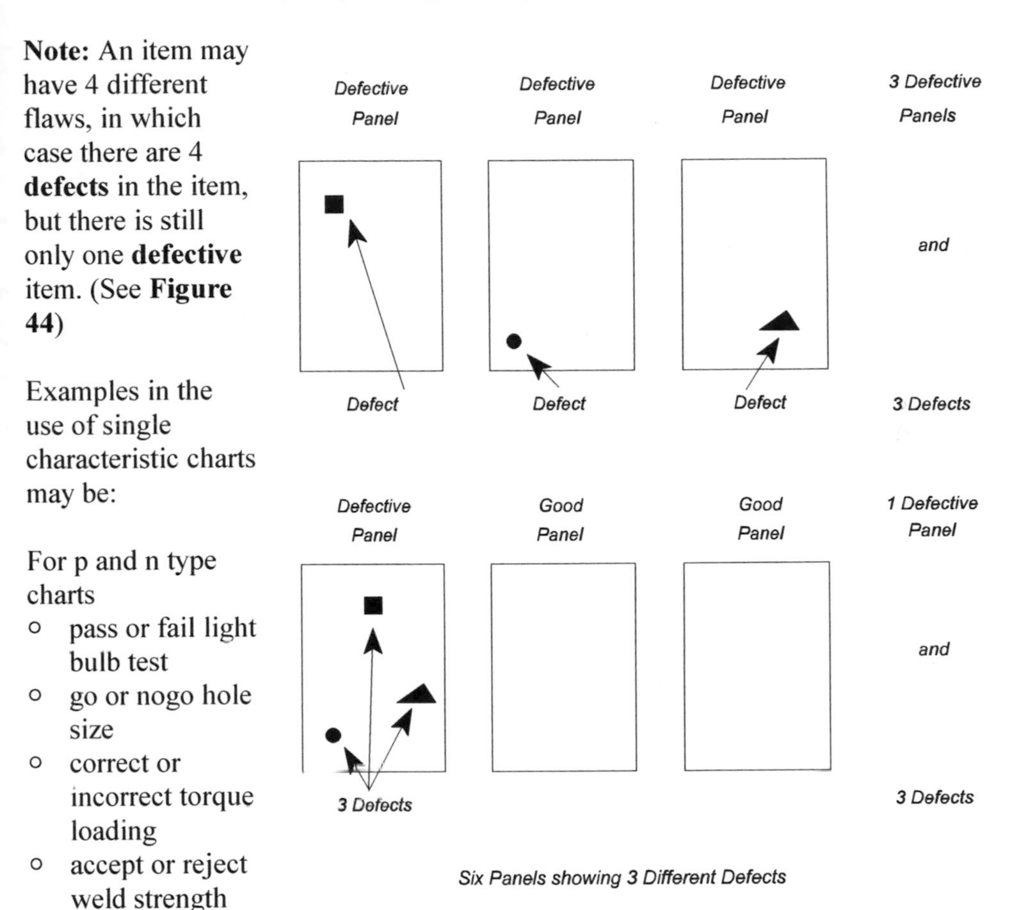

Figure 44 Defectives or Defects

For c or u type charts

- porosity or number of holes in a casting
- number of paint blemishes on a panel
- number of flaws in a sheet of glass
- number of errors on a printed circuit board
- number of faults with a washing machine

In the latter two examples (printed circuit board and washing machine) each board or machine may contain various defects.

In the case of the printed circuit board, the characteristics could be; a component missing, bad soldering, wrong component, defective components.

Or in the case of the washing machine; leaking, fails to start, motor defective, heater defective etc.

In these circumstances it may be appropriate to employ a multiple characteristic chart. With this type of chart, each of the above characteristics will be monitored individually. The result of this monitoring is then collated and the total number of defects is plotted.

Implementing SQC

This step consists of 3 key elements:

STAGE 1: Gather the data

STAGE 2: Determine the control limits

STAGE 3: Data analysis and variation reduction

These 3 stages are ceaselessly repeated for continuous improvement in process performance.

Variable Charts and data

The procedure to be observed when SQC is applied to variable data is described below.

STAGE 1 Gather the data

1. Complete the process details on the Statistical Quality Control Chart (see **Figure 45** SQC Chart) using the Statistical Quality Control Chart and from the Process Capability Study determine an appropriate scale for the average x and range R.

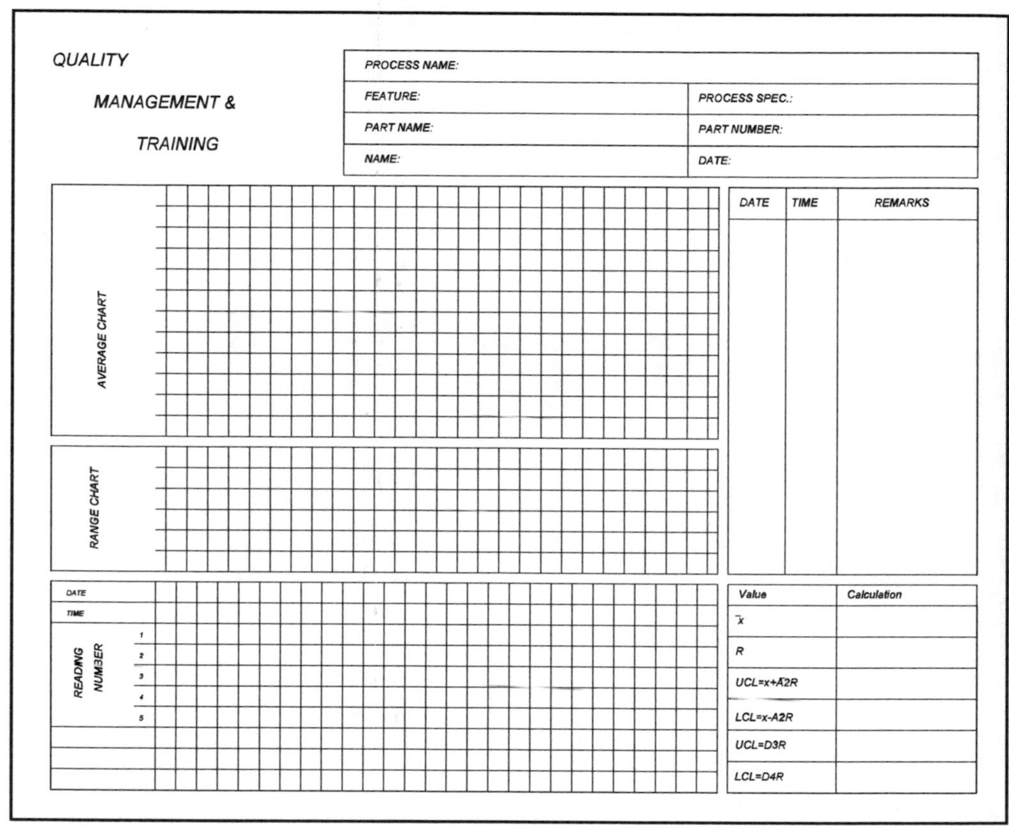
QUALITY MANAGEMENT & TRAINING

PROCESS NAME:
FEATURE: PROCESS SPEC.:
PART NAME: PART NUMBER:
NAME: DATE:

AVERAGE CHART
RANGE CHART
DATE TIME REMARKS

DATE
TIME
READING NUMBER 1 2 3 4 5

Value	Calculation
$\bar{x}$	
R	
UCL=x+A2R	
LCL=x-A2R	
UCL=D3R	
LCL=D4R	

Figure 45 SQC Chart

For the average and range chart this can be approximately 2 x Process specification.

2. Obtain first set of readings and record date, time and results. Circle or highlight any readings outside process specification.

3. Calculate average and range for each sample taken.

$$Average\ \bar{x} = \frac{\Sigma\ x_i}{n} \qquad (6)$$

Where Σx_i = the summation of each individual reading 1,2,3,...i
N = number of readings
and R = range, the difference between the highest and lowest value

Record x bar & R at the bottom of the chart.

$$\textit{For the first example } \bar{x} = \frac{51.7}{5} = 10.34 \qquad (7)$$

$$R = 10.4 - 10.3 = 0.1$$

*See **Figure 46** Completed SPC Chart*

4. Plot the value for average and range on the control chart directly above the date and time. Join the points together with a straight line.

Now repeat this exercise until approximately 25 samples or 100 readings have been obtained.

STAGE 2 Determine the control limits

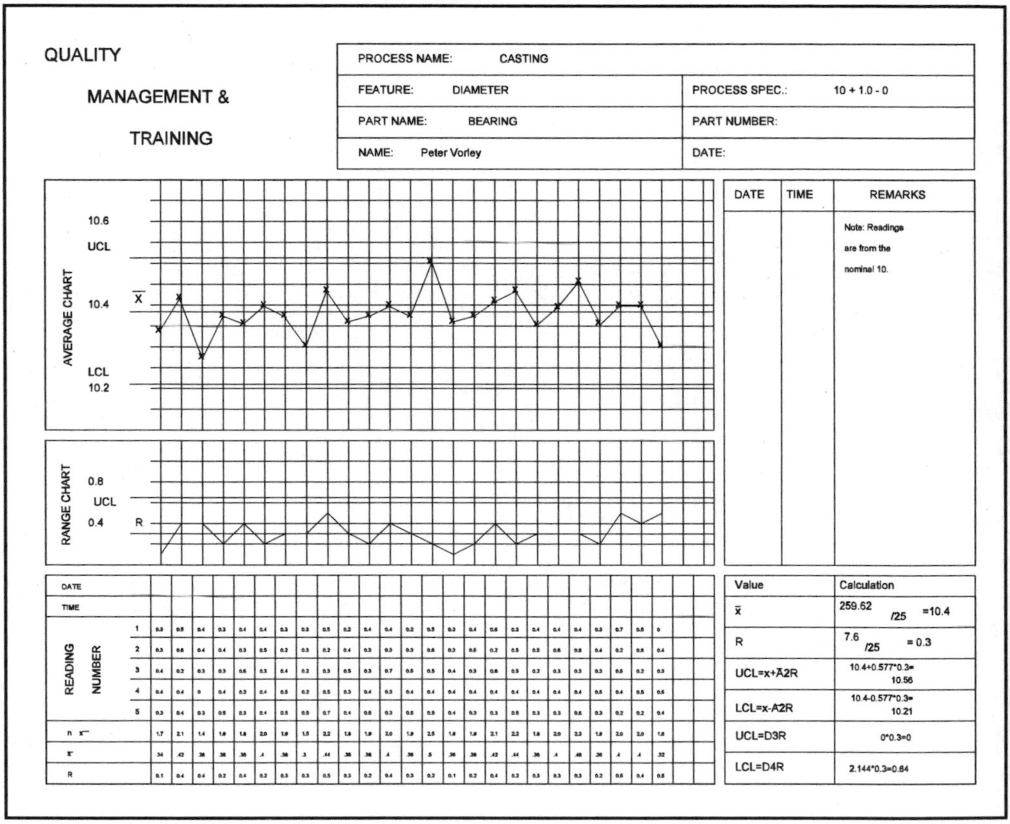

QUALITY MANAGEMENT & TRAINING

PROCESS NAME: CASTING	
FEATURE: DIAMETER	PROCESS SPEC.: 10 + 1.0 - 0
PART NAME: BEARING	PART NUMBER:
NAME: Peter Vorley	DATE:

AVERAGE CHART: 10.6, UCL, $\overline{X}$, 10.4, LCL, 10.2

RANGE CHART: 0.8, UCL, 0.4, R

DATE	TIME	REMARKS
		Note: Readings are from the nominal 10.

DATE																									
TIME																									
READING NUMBER 1	0.3	0.5	0.4	0.3	0.4	0.4	0.3	0.3	0.5	0.2	0.4	0.4	0.2	0.5	0.3	0.4	0.6	0.3	0.4	0.4	0.4	0.3	0.7	0.8	0
2	0.3	0.8	0.4	0.4	0.3	0.5	0.2	0.3	0.2	0.4	0.3	0.3	0.3	0.8	0.3	0.6	0.2	0.5	0.5	0.8	0.8	0.4	0.2	0.8	0.4
3	0.4	0.2	0.3	0.3	0.6	0.3	0.4	0.2	0.3	0.5	0.3	0.7	0.6	0.5	0.4	0.3	0.6	0.5	0.2	0.3	0.3	0.3	0.6	0.2	0.3
4	0.4	0.4	0	0.4	0.2	0.4	0.5	0.2	0.5	0.3	0.4	0.3	0.4	0.4	0.4	0.4	0.4	0.4	0.4	0.4	0.4	0.5	0.4	0.5	0.6
5	0.3	0.4	0.3	0.6	0.3	0.4	0.5	0.5	0.7	0.4	0.6	0.3	0.6	0.5	0.4	0.3	0.3	0.5	0.3	0.3	0.6	0.3	0.2	0.2	0.4
Σx	1.7	2.1	1.4	1.9	1.8	2.0	1.9	1.5	2.2	1.8	1.9	2.0	1.9	2.5	1.8	1.9	2.1	2.2	1.8	2.0	2.3	1.8	2.0	2.0	1.8
$\overline{x}$	.34	.42	.28	.38	.36	.4	.38	.3	.44	.36	.38	.4	.38	.5	.36	.38	.42	.44	.36	.4	.46	.36	.4	.4	.32
R	0.1	0.4	0.4	0.2	0.4	0.2	0.3	0.3	0.5	0.3	0.2	0.4	0.3	0.2	0.1	0.2	0.4	0.2	0.3	0.3	0.3	0.2	0.6	0.4	0.6

Value	Calculation
$\bar{x}$	259.62 /25 =10.4
R	7.6 /25 = 0.3
UCL=x+A2R	10.4+0.577*0.3= 10.56
LCL=x-A2R	10.4-0.577*0.3= 10.21
UCL=D3R	0*0.3=0
LCL=D4R	2.144*0.3=0.64

Figure 46 Completed SQC Chart

5. Calculate the average range value R.

$$\overline{R} = \frac{\Sigma R_i}{k} \tag{8}$$

Where $\sum R_i$ = the summation of each range value
and k = the number of samples taken

$$\overline{R} = \frac{7.6}{25} = 0.304 \tag{9}$$

Draw $\bar{R}$ on the range chart as a thick line

6. Calculate the control limits for the range chart.

The control limits are used as a guide to determining process performance. The use of the control limits is described in the section - STAGE 3 Data Analysis & Variation Reduction (Page 225).

In order to calculate the control limits it is necessary to use certain constants. In **Table 20** Control Limit Constants are the sample size and the other constants A_2, D_3 and D_4 which are used in the control limit calculations.

Table 20 Control Limited Constants

n	2	3	4	5	6	7	8	9	10
A_2	1.880	1.023	0.729	0.577	0.483	0.419	0.373	0.337	0.308
D_3	0	0	0	0	0	0.076	0.136	0.184	0.223
D_4	3.268	2.574	2.282	2.114	2.004	1.924	1.864	1.816	1.777

The first constant to be used is D_4 which can be found in **Table 20** by locating on row 'n' the sample size and read off the value for D_4. Record the value of D_4.

Calculate Upper Control Limit for ranges.

where $UCL_R = D_4*R$

In the example $UCL_R = 2.114*0.304 = 0.642$

Draw UCL_R on the range chart as a thick line.

Calculate the Lower Control Limit for ranges.

$$LCL_R = D_3*R$$

D_3 is given in **Table 20** and is found in a similar way to D_4.

In the example $LCL_R = 0*0.304 = 0$

Draw LCL_R on the range chart as a thick line.

7. Calculate the process average.

$$\textbf{\textit{Average}}\ \bar{\bar{x}} = \frac{\Sigma\ xi}{k} \qquad \textbf{(11)}$$

Where $\sum xi$ = the summation of each individual sample average

$$\textbf{\textit{In the example (Completed SQC Chart)}}\ \bar{\bar{x}} = \frac{259.62}{25} = 10.38 \qquad \textbf{(12)}$$

Draw x bar on the average chart as a thick line

8. Calculate the control limit for average charts.

Determine the value for A_2, where A_2 is given in the table. It is found in a similar way to D_4.

Calculate Upper Control Limit for averages

$$UCL_x = \bar{x} + (A_2 * R) \qquad \textbf{(13)}$$

In the example (Completed SQC Chart) $UCL_x = 10.38 + (0.577*0.304)$

Draw UCL_x on the average chart as a thick line.

Calculate the Lower Control Limit for averages

$$LCL_x = \bar{x} - (A_2 * R) \qquad \textbf{(14)}$$

In the example (Completed SQC Chart) $LCL_x = 10.38 - (0.577*0.304)$

Draw LCL_x on the average chart as a thick line.

STAGE 3 Data Analysis & Variation Reduction

One of the key purposes of using control charts is to improve quality by reducing variation. Consequently techniques need to be employed which can help identify any sources of variation. One such method is to identify the presence of a non-random effect, and if possible eliminate it. Non-random effects can be recognised by applying the following tests when examining the charts.

TEST 1 **Any point outside the control limit**

TEST 2 **A series of 7 points above or below the average**

TEST 3 **A trend of 7 points up or down**

TEST 4 **Any other cyclic pattern**

Once a non-random effect has been identified, its source should be investigated to determine what action is necessary to a) correct the non-conformity and b) prevent it recurring. As an aid to trouble shooting when non-random variations occur, it is important to keep a log of any changes such as resetting, change of shift, material or equipment changes.

TEST 1

Points outside the control limits. The control limits have been calculated using the constants (A_2, D_3 and D_4). These constants are calculated so that there is only a 1 in 1000 chance of points lying outside the Control Limits. It is reasonable, therefore, to presume that a non-random effect has caused the change.

A point outside the control limit (either above or below) could indicate that:
A. The point has been wrongly plotted
B. The control limit has been incorrectly calculated or plotted
C. The process has worsened or improved
D. The inspection standard has changed

TEST 2

A series of 7 points above or below the average. A change in the process average could indicate that the average has moved and stabilised at a new higher or lower level. A run of 7 points above the average could indicate that, on the average chart, the accuracy or process average has worsened. On the average chart - a run of 7 points below the average could indicate that the accuracy or process average has improved.

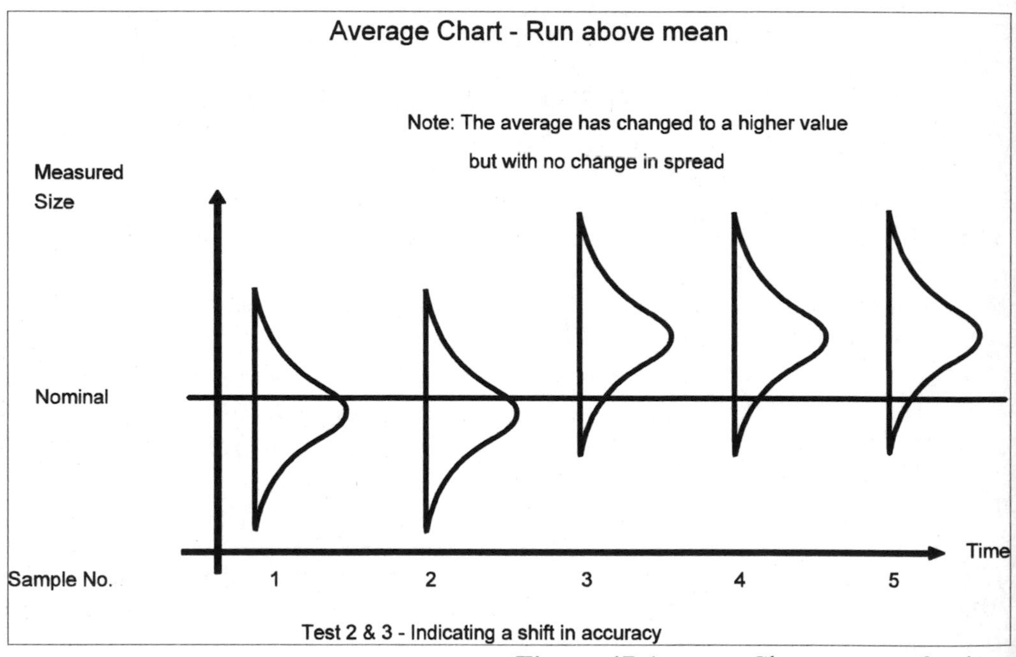

Figure 47 Average Chart - a run of points

The effect on the process distribution is shown in the diagram **Figure 47**. The spread of the process has not changed but the setting has undergone a change, resulting in a shifted average and stabilising at a new higher level.

On the range chart - a run of 7 points above the average would indicate the repeatability or spread of the process has worsened. Or the inspection standard or measuring system has changed.

On the range chart - a run of 7 points below the average would indicate that the repeatability or spread has improved. Or the inspection standard or measuring system has changed.

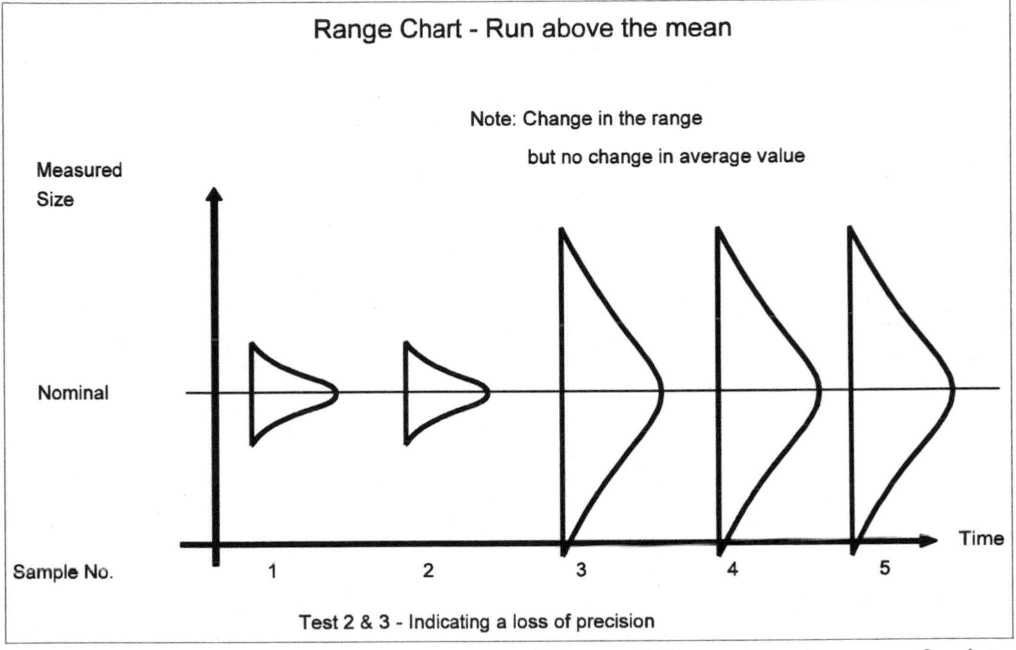

Figure 48 Range Chart - a run of points

The effect on the process spread of a run of points above the average on the range chart is represented in **Figure 48** above. The location of the spread has not changed but the width of the spread has increased. Consequently, there will be a greater variation between the individual process values.

TEST 3

Any trends within the control limits (even when all points are within the control limits) should be investigated as it may be an indication of conditions which, if ignored, could lead to the process moving outside the control limits, or an improvement opportunity that should be encouraged.

Trends - on the Average Chart.

A run of 7 points where each point is higher or lower than the previous may indicate that the accuracy or process average is changing, possibly worsening. The inspection standard or measuring system could be changing.

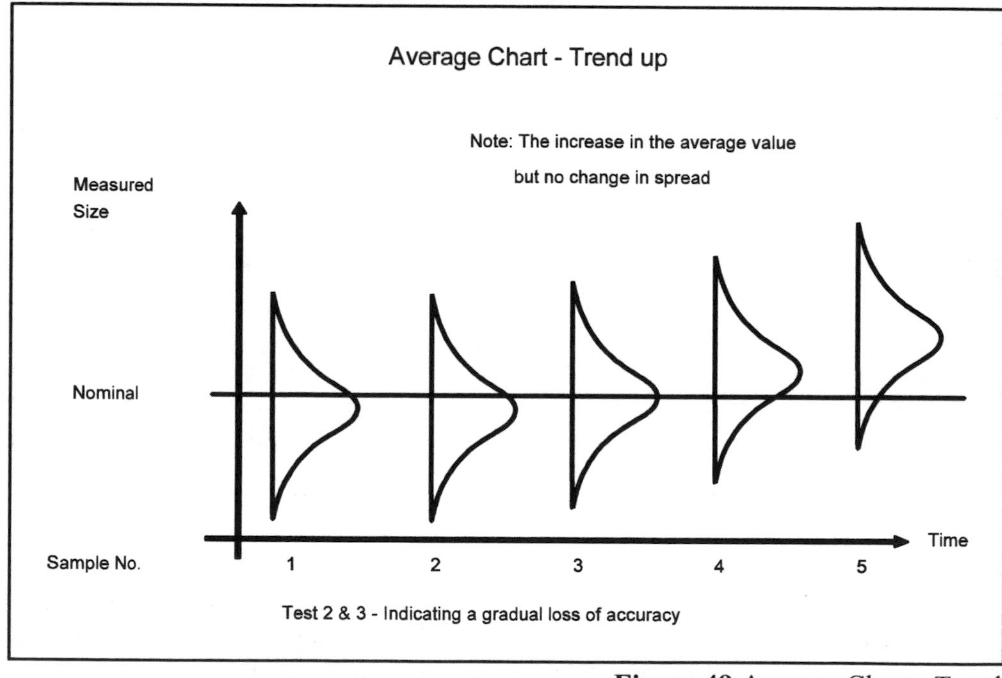

Figure 49 Average Chart - Trend

Figure 49 represents the effect on the process distribution as a result of a run of points on the average chart. There is no change in the process spread but a shift upwards of the process setting or location.

Trends - on the Range Chart.

A run of 7 points where each point is higher than the previous could indicate that the repeatability or spread has worsened and is still deteriorating. A run of 7 points where each point is lower than the previous could indicate that, the repeatability or spread has improved and is still improving - investigate and encourage this trend.

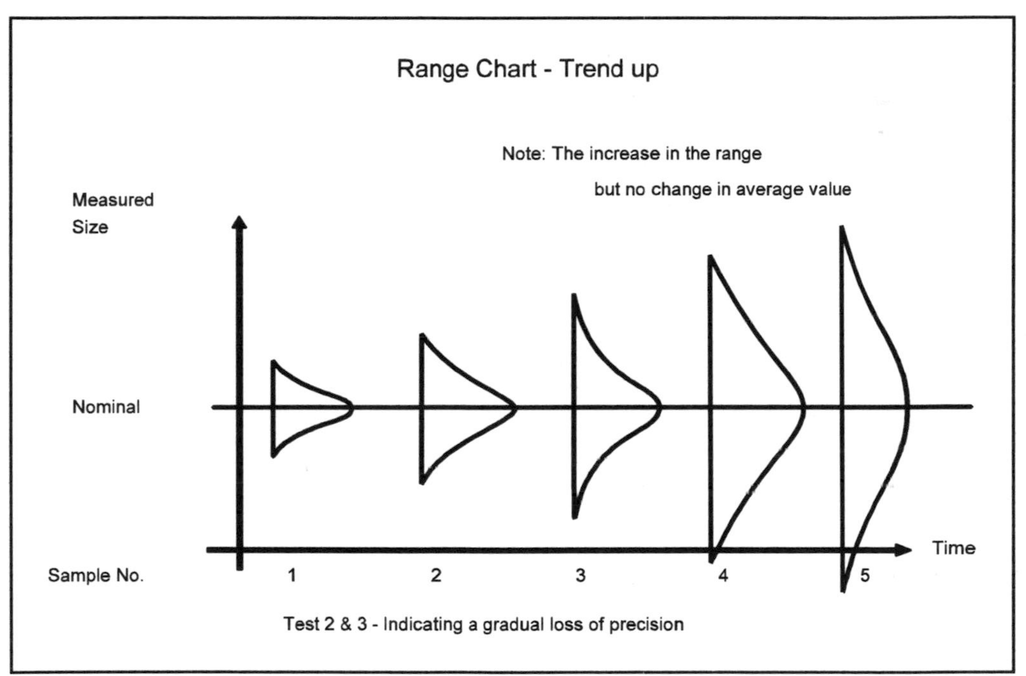

Figure 50 Range Chart - Trend

Figure 50 represents the changes to the process distribution as a consequence of a run upwards of points on the range chart. The spread of the distribution is deteriorating and there will be a steadily worsening variation between individual process values.

TEST 4

The control limits are such that approximately 2/3 of the data points should lie within the middle third region of the control limits. About 1/3 of the data points should lie in the outer two thirds of the control limits.

Cyclic patterns may be due to plotting points from samples taken from different conditions, e.g. different processes, different shifts, different batches.

Variation Reduction

Identification and Remedy: Once a non-random cause of variation has been investigated and remedied, the process should have improved. If subsequent data points are consistently below the previous average (confirming the improvement) then the control limits can be re-calculated for the new improved process performance.

Continuous Process Improvement: The data should continue to be collected, plotted on the chart and analysed to identify further process improvements. It may be appropriate to use some of the other techniques detailed in the section Ishikawa's 7 Tools of Quality to assist in achieving process improvements, particularly Pareto analysis and cause and effect diagrams.

Attribute Charts and Data

The previous section described the procedure to be observed when SQC is applied to variable data. This section shows how to apply SQC when attribute data is collected. Prior to following the procedure outlined below, check that the steps stated in the section *Before Introducing SQC* (see page 135) have been observed.

The data will need to be divided into samples or sub-groups of 'n' items. The number of items in each sample should preferably remain constant (although this is not essential). The interval between each sample should be chosen on the basis of production frequency, the importance of the operation or process. The samples need to be sufficiently large to allow defectives to appear (although hopefully none). The samples should be taken from one process, otherwise it will be difficult to identify the source or cause of any defectives. I.e. separate charts should be kept for different processes.

STAGE 1 Gather the data

1. Decide on a sample size in accordance with the above rules.

2. Record the number of defects/defectives in each sample. See **Figure 51**.

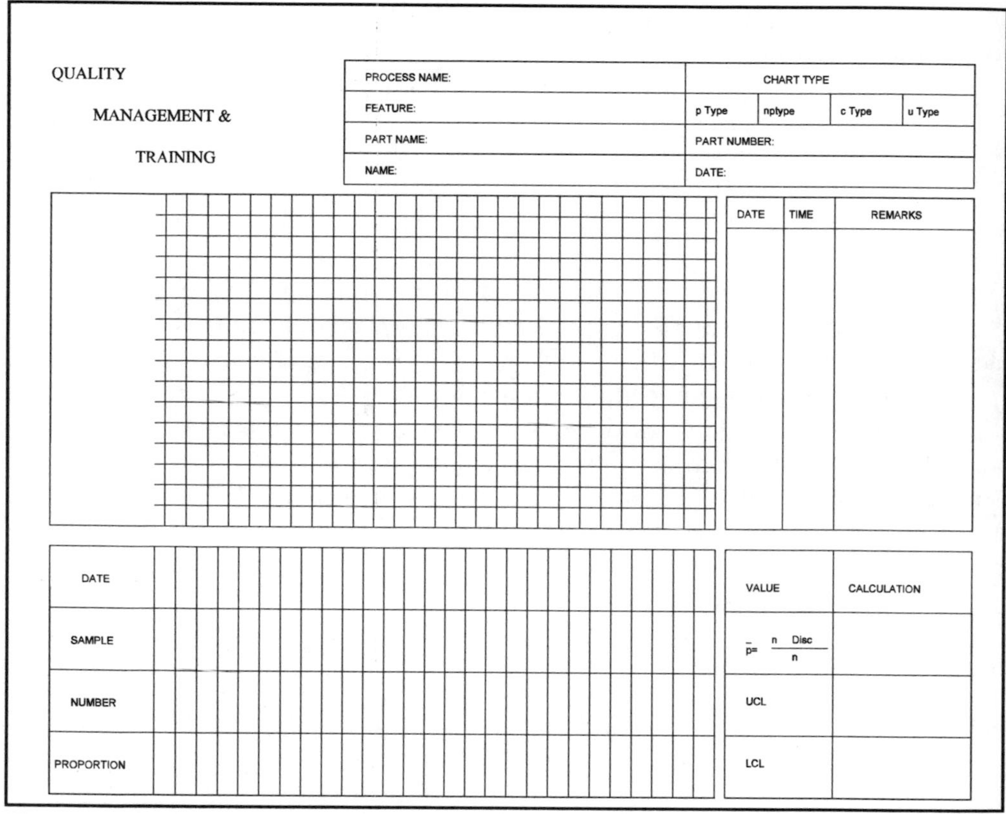

Figure 51 SQC Chart for Attributes

3. The proportion or number of defects/defectives should be shown on the vertical axis and the sample identification (hour, day etc.) on the horizontal axis. The vertical axis should extend from zero to about 1.5 times the highest point expected.

4. Depending on the chart type selected, plot the value of p, np, c or u for each sample on the chart.

STAGE 2 Determine the control limits

i) The p chart for PROPORTION OF DEFECTIVES (NON-CONFORMING UNITS)

The proportion of defectives is p, i.e. the number of defectives (np) divided by the number in the sample.

$$p = \frac{np}{n} \tag{15}$$

Calculate the average number of defectives for the process

$$p = \frac{\textit{Total number defectives}}{\textit{Total number inspected}} \tag{16}$$

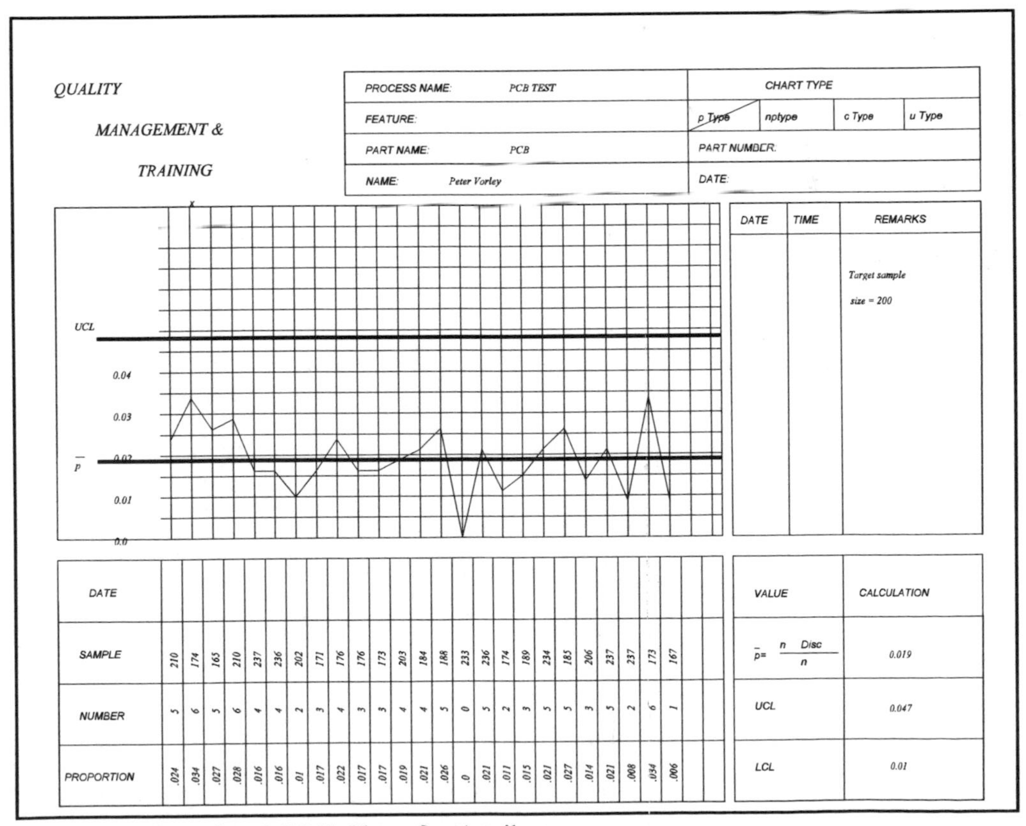

Figure 52 Completed SQC Chart for Attributes

Calculate the Control Limits (UCL, LCL):

$$UCL_p = \bar{p} + 3 * \sqrt{\frac{\bar{p}(1-\bar{p})}{\bar{n}}} \tag{17}$$

$$LCL_p = \bar{p} - 3 * \sqrt{\frac{\bar{p}(1-\bar{p})}{\bar{n}}} \tag{18}$$

Draw the process mean (p bar) and control limits on the chart and label (p, UCL_p and LCL_p).

Note 1: As the sample size can vary with p charts then this can affect the control limits. Therefore, it may be necessary to recalculate the control limits. Once calculated the new control limits should be plotted on the control charts.

Note 2: If the LCL is negative then ignore this control limit, since it is not possible to have less than zero defectives. (See **Figure 52** Completed SQC Chart for Attributes).

ii) The np chart for NUMBER OF DEFECTIVES

The number of defectives is np, i.e. the number in the sample multiplied by the proportion of defectives in the sample.

Calculate the average number of defectives for the process:

$$\overline{np} = \frac{np_1 + np_2 + np_3 + ...np_n}{m} \tag{19}$$

Where np_1, np_2 etc. are the number of defectives in each of m samples inspected.

Calculate the Control Limits (UCL, LCL):

$$UCL_{np} = \overline{np} + 3 * \sqrt{\frac{\overline{np}(1-\overline{np})}{\bar{n}}} \tag{20}$$

$$LCL_{np} = \bar{n}p - 3 * \sqrt{\frac{\bar{n}p(1-\bar{n}p)}{\bar{n}}} \quad \textbf{(21)}$$

Draw the process mean and control limits on the chart and label (np, UCL_{np} and LCL_{np}).

Note: If the LCL is negative ignore this control limit, since it is not possible to have less than zero defectives.

iii) The c chart for NUMBER OF DEFECTS (NON-CONFORMITIES)

The number of defects is c.

Calculate the average number of defects for the process

$$\bar{c} = \frac{c_1 + c_2 + c_3 + ...c_m}{m} \quad \textbf{(22)}$$

Where c_1, c_2 etc. are the number of defects in each of m samples inspected.

Calculate the Control Limits (UCL, LCL):

$$UCL_c = \bar{c} + (3 * \sqrt{\bar{c}} \quad \textbf{(23)}$$

$$LCL_c = \bar{c} - (3 * \sqrt{\bar{c}} \quad \textbf{(24)}$$

Draw the process mean and control limits on the chart and label (c, UCL_c and LCL_c).

Note: If the LCL is negative ignore this control limit since it is not possible to have less than zero defectives.

iv) The u chart for NUMBER OF DEFECTS (NON-CONFORMITIES) per unit

The number of defects per unit is u.

Calculate the average number of defects per unit for the process

$$\bar{u} = \frac{u_1 + u_2 + u_3 + ...u_m}{n_1 + n_2 + n_3 + ...n_m} \quad \textbf{(25)}$$

Where u_1, u_2 etc. are the number of defects per unit in each of m samples inspected.

Calculate the Control Limits (UCL, LCL).

$$UCL_u = \bar{u} + 3 * \sqrt{\frac{\bar{u}}{n}} \quad \textbf{(26)}$$

$$LCL_u = \bar{u} - 3 * \sqrt{\frac{\bar{u}}{n}} \quad \textbf{(27)}$$

Draw the process mean and control limits on the chart and label (u, UCL_u and LCL_u).

Note 1: As the sample size can vary with u charts then this can affect the control limits. Therefore it may be necessary to recalculate the control limits with each new sample size. Once calculated the new control limits should be plotted on the control charts.

Note 2: If the LCL is negative then ignore this control limit, since it is not possible to have less than zero defectives.

v) Multiple Characteristic Charts

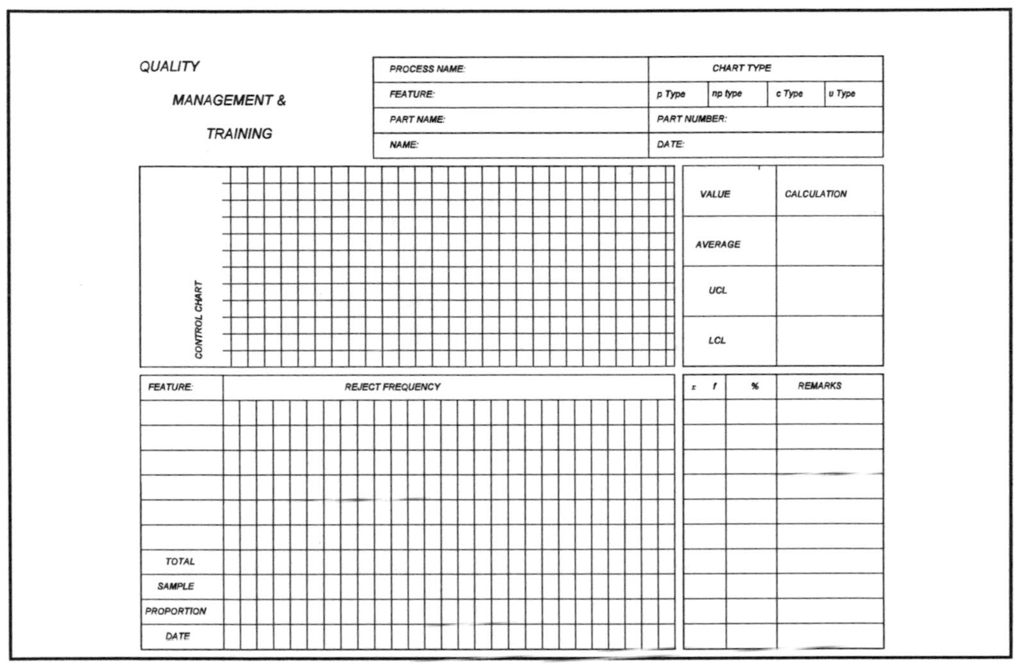

Figure 53 Attribute Control Chart - Multiple Features

With any of the above p, np, c and u charts it is only possible to monitor one characteristic. With all of these charts (p, np, c, and u) it may on occasion be necessary to monitor more than one characteristic or feature. In this situation a multiple characteristic chart can be employed which enables several characteristics to be recorded on the one chart. Thus giving a more comprehensive picture of the process performance and assisting with identifying the causes of variation (see **Figure 53** Attribute Control Chart - Multiple Features). Note that a Pareto Analysis (see section Pareto Analysis) of the various characteristics can be performed on the data calculated on the right-hand side of the chart.

STAGE 3 Data Analysis & Variation Reduction

One of the key purposes of using control charts is to improve quality by reducing variation. Consequently techniques need to be employed which can help identify any sources of variation. One method of reducing variation is to identify the presence of a non-random effect and if possible, eliminate this non-random effect. Non-random effects can be recognised by applying the following tests when examining the charts.

TEST 1 **Any point outside the control limit**

TEST 2 **A series of 7 points above or below the average**

TEST 3 **A trend of 7 points up or down**

TEST 4 **Any other cyclic pattern**

Once a non-random effect has been identified its source should be investigated to determine what action is necessary to a) correct the non-conformity and b) prevent it recurring. As an aid to trouble shooting when non-random causes of variations occur, it is important to keep a log of any changes such as resetting, change of shift, material or equipment changes. The previous section - Stage 3 Data Analysis & Variation Reduction (for Variables) described interpretation of the four "TESTS".

Benefits of SQC: Monitoring a process by the use of control charts provides the means of a process improvement programme. Giving the operators the opportunity to use their abilities to the full in controlling and improving the process performance (world class performance), facilitating the process improvement for better quality, lower costs and greater productivity. SQC assists communication and discussion regarding the process performance, giving a better understanding of the requirements and process's ability to meet requirements.

Limitations of SQC: Although there are major benefits from the introduction of SQC there can also be some limitations and problems.

The organisation may operate a piece work scheme which may prevent the operator having the time to complete the control chart. *One solution to this is for the inspector to complete the control chart - this should be avoided at all costs as it defeats one of the main objectives of SQC - getting the operator involved with the quality of the work produced. The operator needs to be provided with all the necessary facilities to perform SQC.*

The operator may not be capable of understanding or using SQC and may not wish to be involved. Not possible or able to gain appropriate commitment from all areas. *If SQC is properly explained then there will be no problems in understanding or gaining commitment - it is only when the reasoning behind SQC is not fully explained that problems will be encountered.*

There will be certain expenditure associated with the introduction of SQC: resources to implement, equipment (measuring, chart holders and charts etc.), additional time completing and analysing the charts - *but there are savings as well (quality, productivity etc.).*

The process may not be capable of meeting specification, therefore SQC cannot be applied. *Applying SQC will help identify the reasons for non-capability of the process and assist in establishing conformance to specification.*

The process may have too many features that need to be monitored. *Failure Mode and Effects Analysis may assist in identifying the key features that need monitoring and control. Alternatively, Multi-feature Attribute Charts could be employed.*

Not applicable on certain processes, i.e. no measurements are taken, only pass or fail. *Attribute control charts can be used for go/nogo situations.*

Application of Statistical Quality Control to the analysis of Processes.

Statistical Quality Control is not just a technique associated with manufacturing processes, it can be used to analyse many different processes. As an example, a very simple process - travelling to work - will be analysed using the Statistical Quality Control approach. Firstly the process needs to be understood. A basic flow charting technique will be used.

The Key Performance Indicator (KPI) for this process will be "arrival at work on time" and the objective or quality goal will be to minimise travel time.

The Stages are (based on the PDCA cycle, See Deming):

1.1 *Plan*: Define and agree the process, see **Figure 54**. Determine the measurement stages. See the clocks and durations on **Figure 54**. Agree and target the arrival at work time and travel time.

1.2 *Do*: Measure the process performance. See the Control Chart at the bottom of **Figure 54**. Analyse the data (using the TESTS - See Stage

3 Data Analysis & Variation Reduction). Implement the proposed improvements.

1.3 *Check*: Confirm the success or otherwise of the implemented changes.

1.4 *Act*: Either implement with "rules" the successful changes or if unsuccessful, repeat the cycle again.

An obvious comment is "by the time I've spent all this time recording I could have been at work 5 minutes earlier". Well, this is the first lesson in process improvement - motivation - there needs to be an imperative for change. Consequently, the first stage is missing the most important element "Management Commitment".

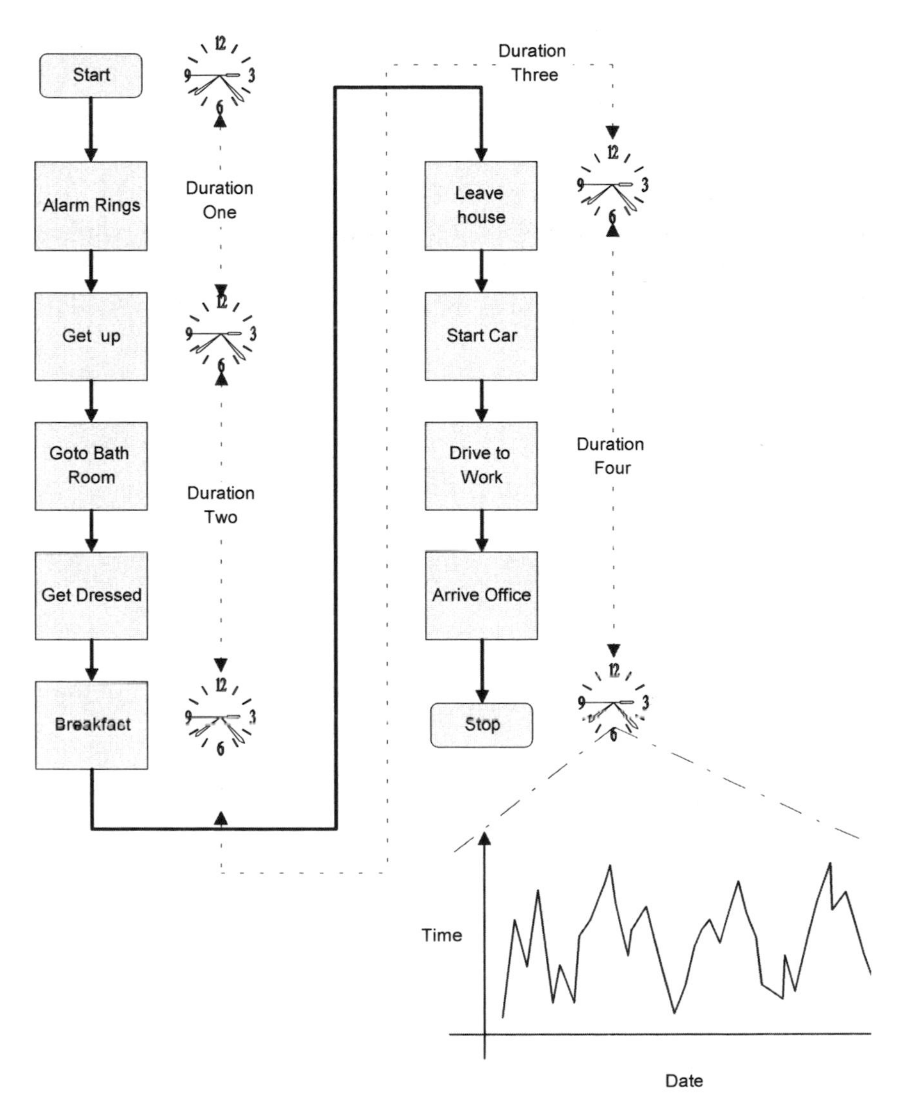

Figure 54 Travelling to Work Process

Statistical Tolerancing

Introduction

Statistical Tolerancing is a method of avoiding specifying unnecessarily tight tolerances. When assemblies consist of several mating components the designer will usually select tolerances for the individual components that will make tolerance clashes impossible. This is an understandable decision as it avoids any problems in assembling the finished product. However, in practice, the designer is worrying unnecessarily because the chance of such a tolerance clash condition actually occurring is very remote.

An example of this could be a lamination assembly.

Figure 55 shows a bracket which contains 10 laminations. The 10 laminations fit inside a bracket with a 20/20.1mm gap. If the designer uses arithmetical tolerances then the following equation would apply.

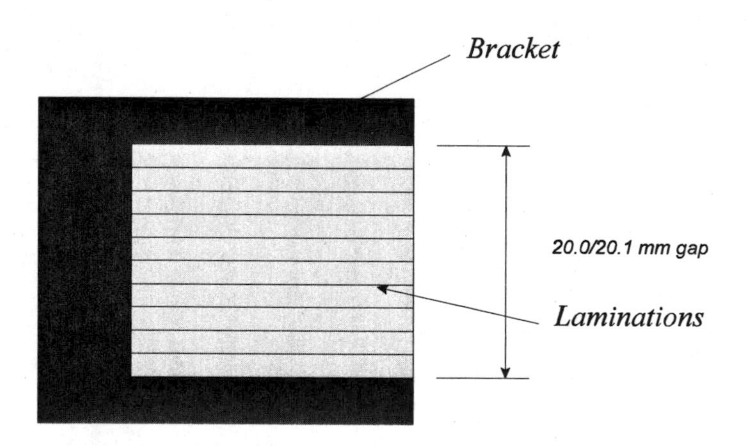

Figure 55 Lamination

$$\frac{\textit{Total tolerance}}{\textit{Number of Components}} = \textit{Component Tolerance} = \frac{0.1}{10} = 0.01mm \qquad (28$$

In effect this means that each lamination must be between 2.00 to 2.01mm in size. In practice the probability of requiring this tolerance condition is very remote. This is because this tolerance allows for the assembly being fitted with all top limit laminations, which is a very unlikely event.

Statistical tolerancing takes into consideration that this is a very unlikely event. If statistical tolerancing was applied to this example then the tolerance could be much greater.

From the section on Process Capability Studies it was suggested that for process capability the process specification should be equal to or greater than 6 standard deviations.

$$Tolerance = 6 * \sigma \qquad \textbf{(29)}$$

Statisticians have shown that the sum of the individual variance equals the total variance. As standard deviation equals the square root of the variance then:

$$\sigma_t = \sigma_1^2 + \sigma_2^2 + \sigma_3^2 + \sigma_4^2 + \text{..........} \ \sigma_n^2$$

Where $\sigma_1^2, \sigma_2^2, \sigma_3^2, \sigma_4^2, \text{..........} \ \sigma_n^2$

is the individual standard deviation of each comp.

And σ_t *is the total standard deviation* **(30)**

From equation **(29)**

$$\sigma = \frac{Tolerance\ t}{6} \qquad \textbf{(31)}$$

Then substituting equation **(31)** into equation **(30)**

$$\left(\frac{T_t}{6}\right)^2 = \left(\frac{T_1}{6}\right)^2 + \left(\frac{T_2}{6}\right)^2 + \left(\frac{T_3}{6}\right)^2 + \left(\frac{T_4}{6}\right)^2 + \text{............} \left(\frac{T_n}{6}\right)^2 \qquad \textbf{(32)}$$

Which can be simplified to

$$\left(\frac{T_t}{6}\right)^2 = \left(\frac{T_i}{6}\right)^2 * n \qquad \textbf{(33)}$$

or

$$T_i = T_t * \sqrt{\frac{1}{n}} \tag{34}$$

Where

T_i = *The individual tolerance*
T_t = *The total tolerance*
n = *The number of items*

For the lamination example, the tolerance for each individual lamination is:

$$T_i = 0.1 * \sqrt{\frac{1}{10}} = 0.032mm \tag{35}$$

This tolerance (0.032mm) is obviously an improvement on the 0.01mm which was given by arithmetical tolerancing. Statistical tolerancing can provide cost and time savings - in the example the tolerance is now over three times larger, with probably no effect on the overall assembly performance.

There are, however, certain dangers with statistical tolerancing. The process needs to be capable, the process distribution needs to be normal, and vary equally around the mean. If these criteria are not met then there will be a detrimental effect on the statistical tolerance.

Following are some other examples of the application of statistical tolerancing.

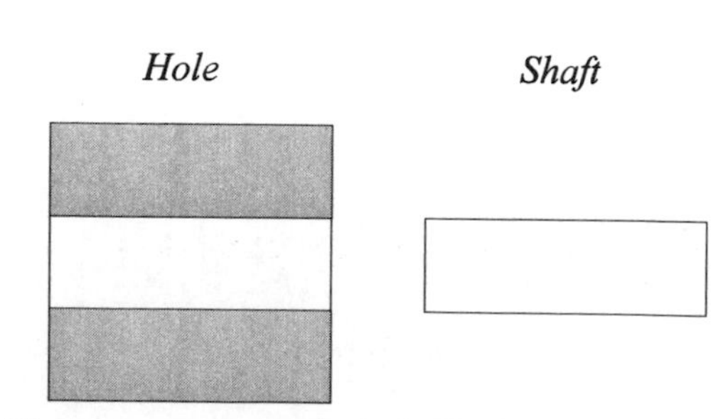

Figure 56 Hole & Shaft

The first example is of a hole and shaft. The clearance between the hole and the shaft needs to be 0.01mm to 0.05mm. Sharing the arithmetical tolerance equally between the hole and shaft would mean that the hole and shaft tolerance would be 0.02mm each.

However if the statistical tolerancing equation is used then the tolerance becomes 0.028mm.

$$\textit{Individual tolerance } T_i = 0.04 * \sqrt{\frac{1}{2}} = 0.028mm \qquad \textbf{(36)}$$

The second example is where a complete bar length is made up of three individual bars of various lengths and tolerances.

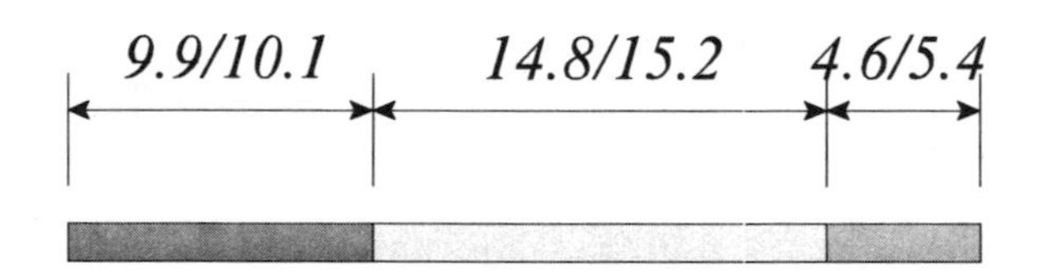

Bar length

Figure 57 Bar length

The arithmetical variation in bar length will be 0.2+0.4+0.8 = 1.4mm.

The statistical variation in bar length will be:

$$\left(\frac{T_t}{6}\right)^2 = \left(\frac{0.2}{6}\right)^2 + \left(\frac{0.4}{6}\right)^2 + \left(\frac{0.8}{6}\right)^2 \qquad \textbf{(37)}$$

$$T_t = \dot{0}.92mm$$

As previously explained there are benefits to be gained from the use of statistical tolerancing but there are also dangers. It is important that the process is confirmed to be capable, otherwise the calculation may be in error.

Quality Function Deployment

Introduction

As a project or design progresses, the greater becomes the possibility of overlooking specific customers needs and expectations. In order not to neglect or overlook "the voice of the customer", the technique of Quality Function Deployment (QFD) has been developed. The initial development work took place in the Kobe Shipyard of Mitsubishi Heavy Industry. The QFD Technique is similar to value analysis as both techniques seek to understand the basic function or customer requirements and determine how best these functions can be achieved. The analysis is performed in a very structured way considering each customer need and how the need is best realised.

The aim for QFD is to identify the key customer needs and translate these needs into controls. This is achieved by establishing what the customer requires and throughout the various stages of QFD how these various requirements will be realised. QFD is not intended to determine the function of the quality department but to provide better quality planning. QFD is not only applicable to product engineering, it can also be applied to manufacturing processes and the service industries, e.g. hotels, airlines etc.

Some of the benefits derived from QFD can include:

- i) Reduction in the number of design changes
- ii) Reduction in design time
- iii) Reduction in the development and start up costs
- iv) Reduced warranty claims

Guidelines for Quality Function Deployment

The first stage in performing QFD is to list the customer's requirements, not necessarily in terms of a product specification but in fairly general terms. E.g. the customer may require a ball point pen, giving as their requirements that the pen must write smoothly. This requirement would need to be converted into "company speak" or something the organisation manufacturing the pen can understand. Normally these requirements would be translated by means of the design or manufacturing specification, but with QFD this means translating the customer requirements into what and how. For the pen example, writing smoothly could be translated into the ball and clasp design and target values set for the ball and clasp dimensions and durability. This relationship between what (customer requirements) and how (features), will eventually become very complicated.

The basic QFD tool is a matrix chart which can be employed to simplify and represent the relationship between what the customer wants and how these needs will be achieved. See **Table 21** QFD matrix chart.

Table 21 QFD Matrix

	Customer Rating	Means to achieve (HOW)										
		Target Values										Competition Rating
Customer Requirements (WHAT)												
Importance Rating												

The matrix is relatively simple but does provide a disciplined way of representing the customer's needs and how they are to be achieved.

Completing the matrix

Completion of the matrix would normally be performed by a team of people which could be drawn from the design, marketing, production, purchasing and quality departments. The role of the team is to establish all the key customer requirements and complete the QFD matrix. These requirements would be listed down the left-hand side of the QFD matrix. How these requirements are to be achieved would be listed along the top of the QFD matrix.

Quality Function Deployment

Stages

1. Establish the *Customer Requirements* - list what the customer requires from the product. Note, different customers may require different features so the list needs to be reasonably comprehensive. For the pen example this could include: write smoothly, reliable, long life, cheap etc.

2. Having established the customer requirements, these requirements need to be given a *Customer Rating.* This rating is quantified by selecting a number between one and ten - an essential customer requirement is given a ten, a minor requirement is given a one. It may be that the weighting will vary for different customers i.e. house wife, bulk buyer etc. For the example, write smoothly may be considered to be very important and therefore given a ten, easy to grip is usually not quite so important and given a five.

3. How the customer requirements are to be achieved are detailed along the top of the matrix *(Means to achieve (How)). The means to achieve should be quantified if possible by detailing Target Values below each 'how'.* ***The Target values*** provide objective figures for the design to achieve. For the example, the means of achieving the customer requirements include: ink viscosity, number of colours, ball & clasp tolerance, ink volume etc. For ink volume the target value could be 10cc +1cc/-0cc etc.

4. Working from the customer requirements and how the requirements are to be achieved, numbers can be added to the matrix. The number selected indicates the relationship between the factors. A one to ten scale is used; selecting a ten would indicate a strong relationship, five a medium relationship and zero no relationship. In this way all the customer needs can be fully addressed ensuring that no customer need is overlooked. For the example there is a strong relationship between write smoothly and the ball & clasp tolerance, but no relationship between no leaks and the clip.

5. The right-hand side of the matrix ***Competition Rating*** is used to evaluate and appraise the competitions' ability to achieve the customer requirements. The number chosen is in direct proportion to the competition's ability to meet the customer requirements; ten fully met, five partly met, zero not met. Having completed this stage then analysis of the figures can provide an estimate of whether the competition is ahead or behind. This information can be used to identify where product improvements need to be made, to improve the design or alternatively to extend an existing lead.

6. The ***Importance Rating*** can then be calculated by multiplying the Customer Requirements by the Relationship Number and then summing each column. The number given is the Importance Rating for each feature. By applying the Pareto principle to the importance rating the key features can be established. Identification of the key features suggests where to concentrate resources (money, time and engineering effort). For the pen example the key features would appear to be Seals & Joints - 290 and Ball & Clasp tolerance - 244.

7. The ***Competition Rating*** shown on the right hand side of **Table 22** (when completed) is intended to show the ability of the competition to fulfil each of the customer requirements.

Table 22 shows the QFD analysis performed on a ball pen.

Means to achieve (How) A=Ball & Clasp tolerance, B=Ink viscosity, C=Ink volume, D=Number of colours, E=Seals & Joints, F=Shape & Size, G=Surface finish, H=Clip

Table 22 Completed QFD Matrix

Customer Requirements	Customer Rating	**A**	**B**	**C**	**D**	**E**	**F**	**G**	**H**	**Means to achieve (How)**
										Target Values
										Competit-ion Rating
Write Smoothly	10	10	2	0	2	0	3	0	0	
Reliable	10	5	1	0	4	10	0	0	4	
Long Life	7	2	8	10	3	10	2	0	0	
Colours	7	0	2	0	10	0	0	1	0	
No leaks	10	8	2	3	1	10	0	0	0	
Easy to grip	5	0	0	0	0	0	10	9	0	
Retractable	5	0	0	0	0	0	8	0	4	
Aesthetics	5	0	0	0	10	4	10	8	9	
Importance Rating		244	120	100	211	290	184	92	105	

Due to the labourious arithmetic associated with QFD, it may be appropriate to use a computer (spreadsheet) to perform these calculations. The above analysis would suggest that the important features which require special attention are Seals & Joints - 290 and Ball & Clasp tolerance - 244. The analysis would also suggest that the designer and manufacturer need to pay particular attention to these features. This may include a review to ensure that the design can achieve the requirements and manufacturing is capable of meeting the design specification.

Some organisations believe that establishing the key features has a significant effect as it provides new ways of thinking about their products. It also provides for better understanding between departments such as marketing, quality and engineering. Having realised these benefits some organisations stop at this stage, however, it is possible to continue the QFD process.

QFD can be continued throughout the various stages in the design/manufacturing process, from the customer/marketing requirements all the way through to the quality control methods. At each stage the key features (Importance Rating) are identified and selected for use in subsequent stages. If all the features identified are used, then the next stage of analysis will become bigger than the last. If this continues throughout the stages the analysis can then become very extensive and unwieldy, however, this depth of analysis may on occasion be essential. To limit the amount of work at subsequent stages only the key features may be chosen.

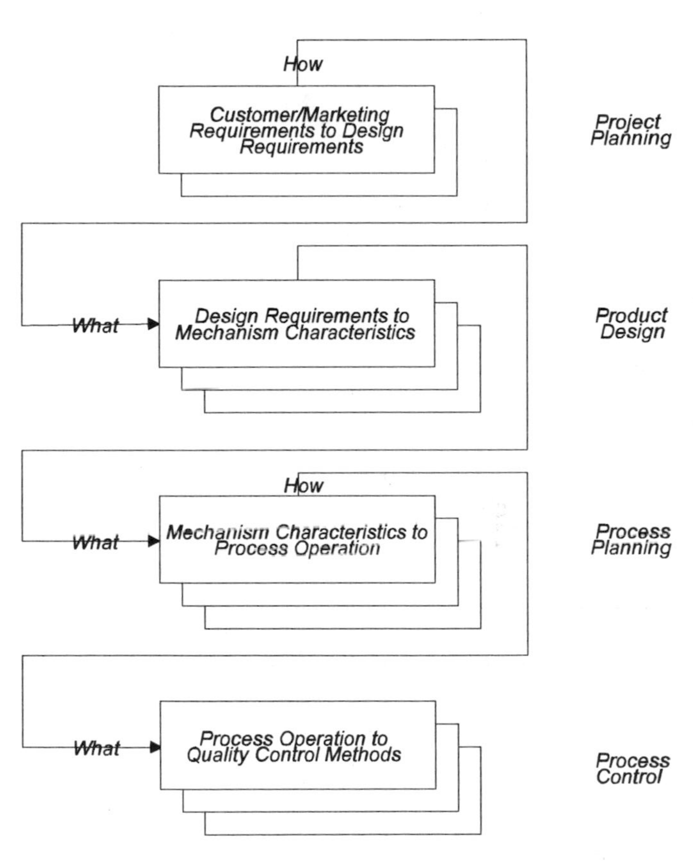

Figure 58 Voice of the Customer

Using the QFD matrix for each process stage can establish the key features and each feature's relative level of importance in satisfying the customer requirements - see **Figure 58**. The QFD can now be redrawn indicating these features throughout each stage as shown in the diagram - "Voice of the Customer". Compilation of this diagram involves the repeated application of QFD for each project stage.

For example in the Project Planning Stage it may be appropriate to use the QFD approach to interpret what the customer requires into how the design achieves these customer requirements. Next at the Product Design Stage, using QFD to interpret the Design Requirements or Functional Requirements into Detailed Design or Mechanism Characteristics. This process continues until finally (in the example shown) the Process Operation's stage interpreting the Process Operation into Quality Control Procedures and Methods. In this way the "voice of the customer" is heard all the way through the project and finally interpreted into specific quality controls. This would ensure that the voice of the customer is heard at the very point of manufacture so that personnel clearly understand which are the important features needing to be consistently and reliably maintained.

Note: Organisations may find completion of the first stage (Customer Requirements to Design Requirements) relatively simple but moving on to the subsequent stages may involve considerably more resource.

Quality Planning

Introduction

Every stage of a process or project is a possible source of poor quality. The objective of a Quality Plan is to anticipate possible sources of poor quality and to arrange for means of identifying such failure and preventing them from occurring.

A Quality Plan tends to be a project or product specific document which defines the Quality Assurance tasks to ensure meeting specific customer requirements and time scales. It enables the identification of preventive activities to provide early warning of any possible problems occurring or becoming major. It allows anticipation of any project or product risk areas and for the opportunity to take appropriate action to eliminate or mitigate any such difficulties. This differs from a Quality Manual which is project or product independent and a Quality Programme which usually describes the implementation of the Quality Manual.

A Quality Plan identifies any existing and additional procedures or activities that may be necessary. Often Quality Plans are required on large capital cost projects such as construction projects or the launch of a new product or software development etc. - where main contractors need to control the activities of sub-contractors. The Quality Plan can be used as model or method of describing the Quality Assurance activities so that everyone can comment on, criticise and develop the plan ensuring their involvement in project achievement.

Normally the project manager or project controller is responsible for the generation of the Quality Plan. The plan would then require approval by the project team and possibly the customer.

The stages involved are:

Defining the process - this can often be established by drawing a flow chart of the process showing each of the key stages and the sequence.

The next stage is to identify which parameters or key stages require control, specifying the criteria for judging conformity, deciding on the means of control, deciding on the means of assessment, preparing the appropriate documentation and monitoring the effectiveness of the plan.

Guidelines for Quality Planning

How to complete a Quality Control Plan:

a. The sequence to follow in the compilation of a Quality Control Plan is first to select a process, project or operation, e.g. a manufacturing or servicing sequence, processing a customer or purchase order, processing documentation, a project etc.

b. Identify the process or project owner or person responsible for the process. Ensure that there are adequate resources to complete the process satisfactorily in terms of:

   Labour (quantity, skills, ability etc.)
   Facilities (equipment, assets, buildings etc.)
   Time
   Budget
   Materials

c. Draw the chosen process as a flow chart. Include all stages and activities (transfer, store, inspect, test etc.).

d. Transfer the flow chart on to the Quality Control Plan Form.

   i. Numbering and describing each stage.
   ii. Selection of the appropriate quality control activities associated with each stage; trials, design reviews, project reviews, tests etc. Determination of when in the project sequence such quality control activities should take place.
   iii. *Source of Information*: Describe the source of information for the person performing the task, e.g. Quality Manual, Work Instruction Number 1234 etc. The work instruction would need to include; the activity or task description, the sequence, the resources necessary to perform the task e.g. quantity of people, skills, materials, equipment (both process and measuring), the process standard and tolerance to be achieved.
   iv. *Responsibility*: Who is responsible for performing the task?
   v. *Record*: Establish what records (if any) will be maintained showing successful completion of the task.
   vi. *Check by*: Who carries out (if anyone) the check on the task, confirming if successfully completed and what inspection and records will be maintained of this check?
   vii. *Overseen by*: Who oversaw (or audited or reviewed) the check of the task, confirming successful completion and what inspection and records were maintained of this check?

e. Re-assess the process or project commitments in the light of the information gained from the review of the necessary resources availability, the creation of the flow chart and the quality plan. Gain agreement and approval of the overall process or project quality plan from the project team members, key managers and customers.

There follows two examples of a Quality Control Plan Flow Chart, one for a Service Organisation (shown in **Figure 59**) and the other for a Software Process (shown in **Figure 60**). Both Flow Charts have been developed into Quality Plans. (The Service Organisation is shown in **Table 23** and the Software Process is shown in **Table 24**).

Service Quality Plan

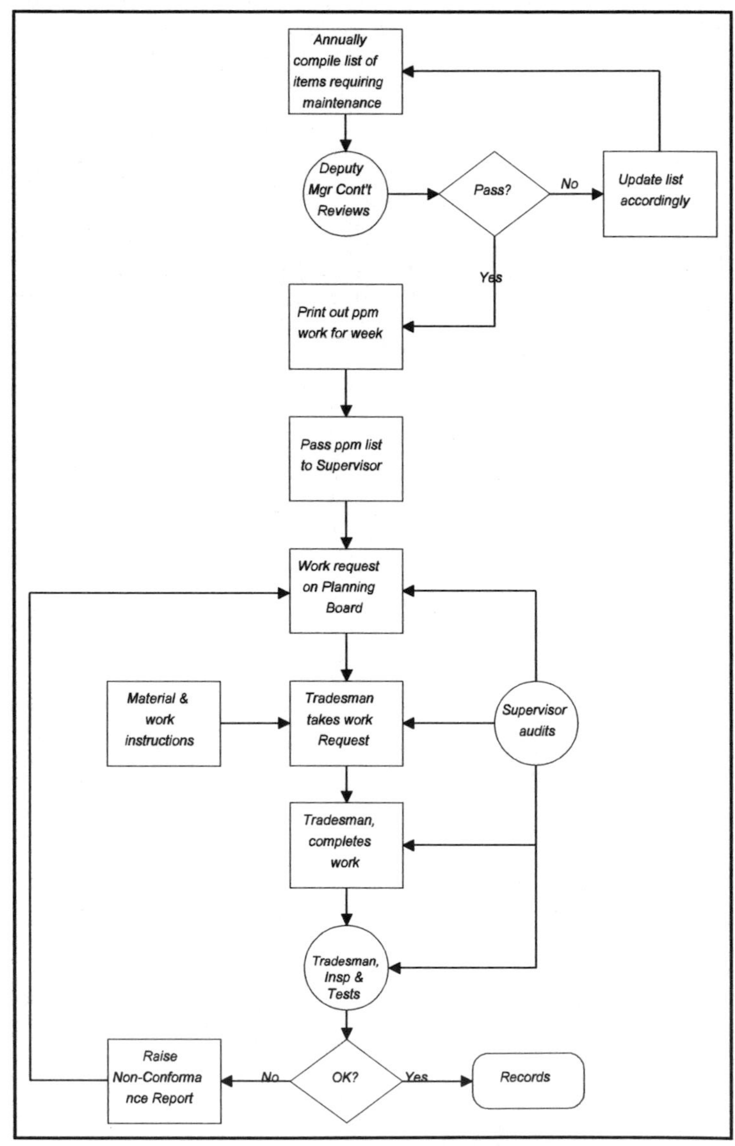

Figure 59 Flow Chart - Service

The numbers in the Quality Plan Flow Chart correspond to the stage numbers in the Quality Plan Table. This Quality Plan is for a Service organisation involved in providing Planned Preventive Maintenance (ppm) on electrical and mechanical equipment and buildings. The Flow Chart represents the initial review of the yearly overall maintenance programme for the facility or organisation. Once the programme has been agreed, the subsequent stages of the Flow Chart show the undertaking of the maintenance programme. This is with the tradesman completing the work as required by the maintenance programme and being responsible for the quality of their own work. The supervisors audit the work completed by the tradesman to ensure the work has been performed in a satisfactory manner. This Flow Chart has been developed into a Quality Plan. Having agreed the activities, stages and sequence of the Flow Chart (no easy task!) the next step is to establish:

- Where the information (work instructions) will be found to explain how to perform each stage e.g. Quality Manual, Labour Management System Operation Handbook. For stage 1 the instruction for conducting the review of the annual maintenance programme are to be found in section 3 of the Quality Manual.
- Who is responsible for completing the stage and meeting the quality standard. For stage 1 the person responsible for holding the review is the Deputy Manager of the organisation.
- What records need to be maintained, the format of the records and where the records will be kept. For stage 1 the records will be kept on the completed contract review check list. This check list is used as an aide-memoire during the contract review process (see ISO 9001). The check list will be signed by the Deputy Manager indicating satisfactory completion of the contract review stage.
- The check is performed by the Deputy Manager.
- In this case there is no need for anyone to oversee that the stage was performed satisfactorily.

Table 23 Quality Plan for a Service Process

#	Description of Stage	Source of Info.	Respon-sible	Records	Checke d by	Overs-een by
1	Contract Review for Planned Preventive Maintenance (ppm)	QM Sec-tion 3	Deputy Mgr	Check List	Deputy Mgr	
2	Weekly print of all equipment req-uiring ppm	Labour Mgt System (LMS)	Clerical Officer	Weekly List		
3	Pass list to supervisor		Superv isor			
4	Pass ppm Instruction to Tradesman	QM Sec-tion 8	Superv isor			
5	Tradesman draws material, starts work and updates job card	Ppm & stores Procedure	Trades-man	Job card	Trades man	Supe-rvisor
6	Tradesman carries out work as per job card	Service Manuals and job card	Trades-man	Signs ppm	Trade-sman	Supe-rvisor
7	Final Inspection & Test (sample)	QM Sec-tion 9	Superv isor	Com-pletes Audit Form	Deputy Mgr	
8	Raise Instructions for any defects found	QM Sec-tion 8	Super-visor	Instru-ctions	Supe-rvisor	
9	Raise Non-Conformance Report	QM Sec-tion 12	Super-visor	NCR Report	Supe-rvisor	
10	Ppm instruction to Planners for closing & updating (if necessary)	LMS	Planner	Note on ppm	Deputy Mgr	
11	Modify ppm (if necessary)	QM Section 4	Super-visor	Change Note	Deputy Mgr	
12	Ppm to Planner for computer feedback Statistics	LMS	Planner	Compu-ter Records		Deputy Mgr
13	Records updated on weekly list		Super-visor	Weekly List		

Figure 60 shows a Flow Chart outlining the process of software development. The flow chart starts with a review of the order. Having accepted the order the specification is detailed and the project reviewed. The software application is then developed and approved. On completion of the software development the software is installed and tested - on completion of successfully testing the software the project is again reviewed. The proprietary hardware and software is purchased and the developed software integrated onto the customer system. The user and maintenance manuals are created and a final project review is conducted prior to final installation and commissioning on the customer site.

With the completion of the flow chart the quality plan can be developed. The following table shows the development of the Flow Chart into a full Quality Plan. The plan includes:

- A detailed description of the various stages.
- Quality criteria and reference documents that contain the procedures to be observed.
- The responsibilities for observing the procedures and the records to be maintained.
- Identification of the responsibilities for approvals.

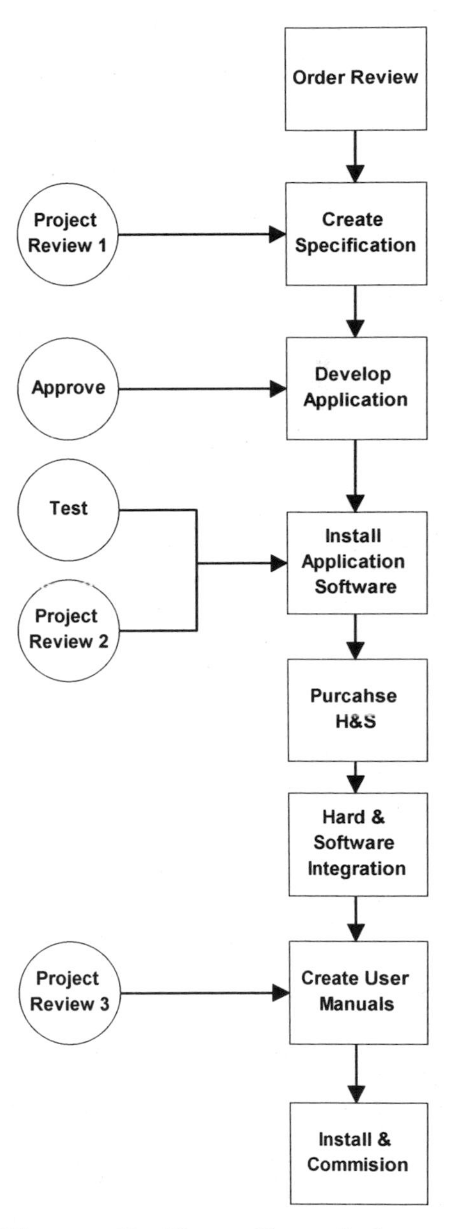

Figure 60 Flow Chart Software Project

Table 24 An example of a Quality Plan for Software Development

Quality Plan		
Client Name: **Client Order Number:**	**Plan Description:**	**Prepared by:** **Approved by:**
Client Address: **Client Telephone/Fax Number:**	**Plan Number:**	**Date of Issue:** **Rev:**

#	Stage Description	Quality Criteria	Reference Documents	Resp.	Record	Approvals	
						Org	Cust
1.	Order Acceptance	Contract Review	Order review procedure QM Section 3	Project Man-ager	Order File	DR10-0%	
	Project Mobilisation						
2.	Create Contract Specific Project & Quality Plan	Design/ Project Input	Standard Project Plan Format QM Section 4 & 5	Project Man-ager	Project Plan	DR10-0%	
3.	Project Review 1	Design/ Project Verifica-tion	Project Review Min-utes Check List	Project Man-ager	Project Review Minut-es		
	Develop Application Software						
4.	Develop Prototype Ap-plication Specification	Design/ Project Input	Standard Ap-plication Sp-ecification Format	Project Man-ager	Appli-cation Specifi-cation	DR10-0%	
5.	Create Acceptance Specification	Design/ Project Input	Standard Ac-ceptance Specification Format	Project Man-ager	Accept-ance Spe-cifica-tion	DR10-0%	

#	Stage Description	Quality Criteria	Reference Documents	Resp.	Record	Approvals	
						Org	Cust
6.	Develop Application Software	Design/ Project Process	Codes of Practice Application Development	Programmers	Code	DR(sample)	
7.	Install Application Software in house. Records of acceptance will be shown on the Acceptance Specification document, copy retained of acceptance in project file	Design/ Project Process	Codes of Practice for Installation	Programmer	Acceptance Specification	DR100%	
8.	Acceptance of Application Software. Records of acceptance will be shown on the Acceptance Specification	Design/ Project Verification		Programmer	Acceptance Specification	DA(ind)	
9.	Project Review 2	Design/ Project Verification	Project Review Minutes Check List	Project Manager	Project Review Minutes		
	Hardware & Software Procurement						
10.	Purchase Proprietary Hardware & Software	Purchasing Control	QM Section 6 Hardware & Software Schedules Approved Supplier List	Purchasing	Purchase Order	DA	
11.	Hardware & Software delivered	Verification	QM Section 10	Goods Inwards	Delivery Note	Insp	
12.	Hardware & Software Integration		Hardware & Software Integration Procedure				

#	Stage Description	Quality Criteria	Reference Documents	Resp.	Record	Approvals	
						Org	Cust
13.	Hardware & Developed Software Acceptance	Verification	QM Section 4	Programmer	Check List & Acceptance Specification	DA	Wit
14.	Create User & Maintenance Manuals	Design/ Project Control	Standard Format for User Manuals QM Section 9	Programmer	Standard format	DA	
15.	Dismantle for Shipment		QM Section 9	Tech Services	Check List	Insp	
16.	Project Review 3	Design/ Project Verification	Project Review Minutes Check List	Project Manager	Project Review Minutes		
17.	Site Survey		QM Section 9 Site Survey Procedure	Project Manager	Check List	Visit	Wit
18.	Installation & Commissioning	Verification	QM Section 9 & 10 Installation & Commissioning Procedures	Project Manager	Acceptance Specification	Insp(Full)	Wit
19.	Customer Acceptance/Handover		Handover Certification QM Section 9	Project Manager	Handover Certificate	Insp(full)	Wit
20.	Software & Documentation Archiving	Records	Archiving QM Section 9	Project Manager	Various		

#	Stage Description	Quality Criteria	Reference Documents	Resp.	Record	Approvals	
						Org	Cust
21.	Final Report	Records	Project Control QM Section 4	Project Manager	Project Summary	DA	

Description of Check		
Key	Explanation	Approved or checked by
Cust.	Customer	
DR100%	100% Examination of documentation for Review & Approval	Peer
DR(sample)	Sample Examination of the documentation for approval	Peer
DA(ind)	Independent approval of document	Project Mgr. & Peer
DA	Approval of document	Peer
Insp	Inspection activity	Peer
Insp(Full)	Full Inspection & Test of System	Project Mgr.
Org.	Organisation	
Visit	Visit Customer & Inspection	Project Mgr.
Wit	Witnessed by customer	Project Mgr. & Customer

SECTION 4 - ANALYSIS AND MAPPING TECHNIQUES

Flowcharting (including IDEF0)

Introduction

Process Flow Charting and Document Flow Charting are techniques that can be employed to provide a visual representation of a procedure. Flat text can be boring and an uninteresting way of describing a process; the reader is likely to lose interest and concentration. A picture can tell a thousand words - it can convey, in certain circumstances, a better graphical indication of the sequence and methods employed within a process. The flow chart can be used to describe a number of activities, sequence of tasks, the way documents flow around an organisation, a computer program etc. Once the chart has been completed, the Process Flow Charts can be employed to analyse all the activities involved in processes or systems. This may be used to explain why a process is done in a particular sequence or why a particular route was taken. The flow chart will also show the suppliers and customers of a particular task or activity. The flow charts can be used to determine the stages that require special quality control activities. With the flow chart being a comprehensive description of the process, identification of value added and non-value added activities and any unnecessary transportation and delays, becomes much easier. Boundaries can be added to the flow chart to denote when the responsibility for a particular set of activities changes from one person to another.

There are a number of different methods and approaches to representing a process using a flow charting method.

- ISO 5807 The specification for data processing flow chart symbols, rules and conventions.
- Cross Functional or Swimlane - A charting method that displays the process tasks, indicating the flow of information and materials across different departments. Sometimes known as swimlanes or document flow charting.
- IDEF0 - Integration Definition for Function Modelling. A method developed by the USA Air Force to graphically represent process activities, showing process activity inputs, outputs, controls and resources. IDEF0 - is the Integration Definition for Information Modelling.

When selecting the process charting method there are some considerations. What is being displayed; information, data or material? What will provide the information in a suitable format for the user? What level of detail is required? What is the business type (service, manufacturing, etc.)?

ISO 5807 - Process Flow charting

There are a number of different standards that can be used for the process flow symbols. ISO 5807 contains the most generally accepted symbols.

Process - Identifies the activity or task and contains a brief description of the work performed.
Decision - The point where a decision is made and the flow chart can slip into two paths. The paths are labelled true/false, yes/no etc. depending on the outcome.
Terminator - Identifies the beginning or end of the process.
Document - Where a document is required, used or created then this symbol can be employed.
Flow lines - Used to represent the next step in the process, connecting activities and tasks.
Connector - Used to indicate a connection between flow charts on separate pages.
Visual - When a computer is used to convey information this symbol can be used.

Guidelines for Process Flow Charting

1. Select the process or system to be examined.

2. Complete the Process Flow Chart shown in **Table 25** representing each of the activities diagrammatically with the appropriate symbol (See **Figure 61**). The table needs to be completed by discussion with the person most knowledgeable about the process under investigation (the person doing the job?).

Table 25 Process Flow Chart Form

Operation: Department: Name: Date:			
Stage	Symbol	Description	Remarks

Symbol	Activity
○	*Operation*
⃠	*Redundant Operation*
D	*Delay*
△	*Unfile*
▽	*File*
⇨	*Transport*
□	*Inspection*
◇	*Decision*

Figure 61 Process Symbols

Table 26 Activity Summary

Activity	No. of Activities	
	Current	Proposed
Operations		
Redundant Operations		
Delays		
Unfile		
Files		
Transports		
Inspections		
Decisions		
Total		

Examples of this type of Process Flow chart can be found in the section on Quality Planning - specifically a Service Quality Plan.

3. Critically analyse the chart to identify:

   a. Whether the objectives of the process are being met? Are there any omissions or duplications?
   b. Whether the activities are necessary? (Use the activity summary to show the number of current and proposed activities).
   c. Whether the process is under control? (Where could the process go wrong and have all the necessary reviews or checks been included and are they being performed?).
   d. Whether all the resources and information are available to perform the activities.
   e. Whether there are any redundant operations and unnecessary delays.
   f. Whether there are any non-value added activities (see section Non-Value Added Activities).

4. Complete **Table 26** indicating the current proposed number of activities, showing the savings made.

5. The finally completed flow chart then needs acceptance and approval by the appropriate authority.

Cross Functional Process Flow Charting

Introduction

This technique is very similar to Process Flow Charting but provides the facility to analyse the process flow of materials or information (paperwork) across different departments. Rather than use the term Cross Functional Flow Charts the shorter term swimlane, will be used.

Guidelines for Document Flow Charting

1. Select the process to be examined.

2. Complete the Swimlane chart. **Figure 62** shows a Swimlane chart for information or paperwork.

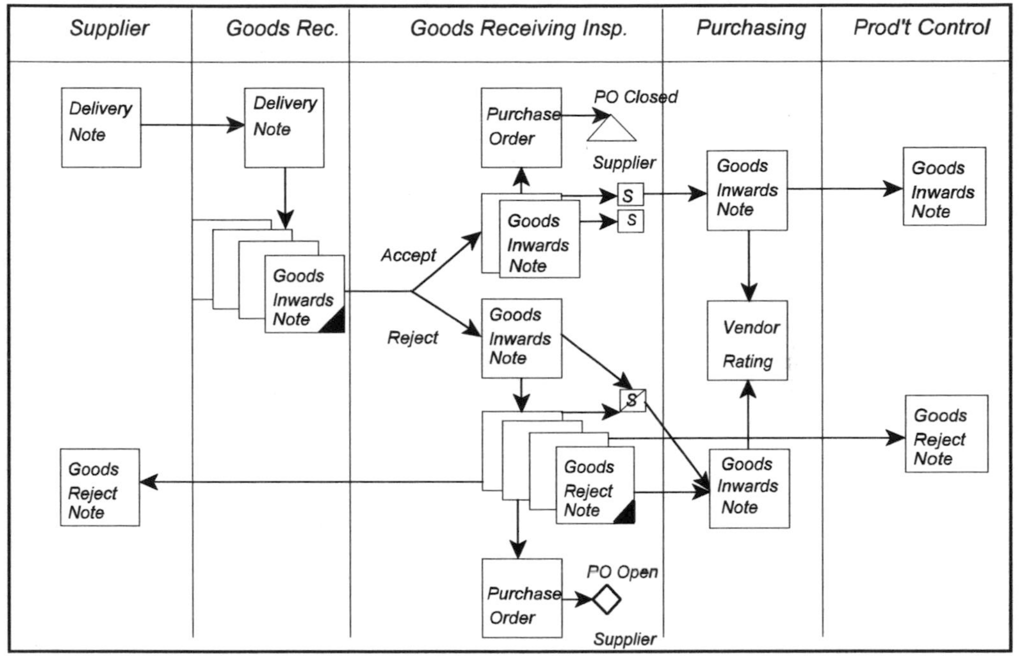

Figure 62 Document Flow Chart

Enter the name of each department, section or operator at the head of each column. Complete the chart by using a symbol to denote each stage and document employed. An arrow is drawn between the stages to indicate the flow of information around the departments. Other examples of Swimlane flow charts can be found in the section Business Process Analysis.

3. Analyse the Chart to identify:

   a. Are the objectives of the procedure being met? (Are there any omissions or duplications?)
   b. Are all the activities/documents necessary?
   c. Is the procedure under control? (Where could the process go wrong? Have all the necessary reviews or checks been included and are they being performed?)
   d. Are all the resources and information available to perform the activities?
   e. Are there any redundant operations/documents and unnecessary delays?
   f. Are there any non-value added activities (see section Non-Value Added Activities).

IDEF0 or Input/Output Diagrams

IDEF0 means Integration Definition for Function Modelling (level zero). There are other levels but level 0 is the most basic. It is a Processes Flow charting method which is based around defining the process in terms of activity or task; inputs, outputs, controls and resources. These activities are then linked together to form the process and provide a process model.

Figure 63 shows the basic IDEF0 model.

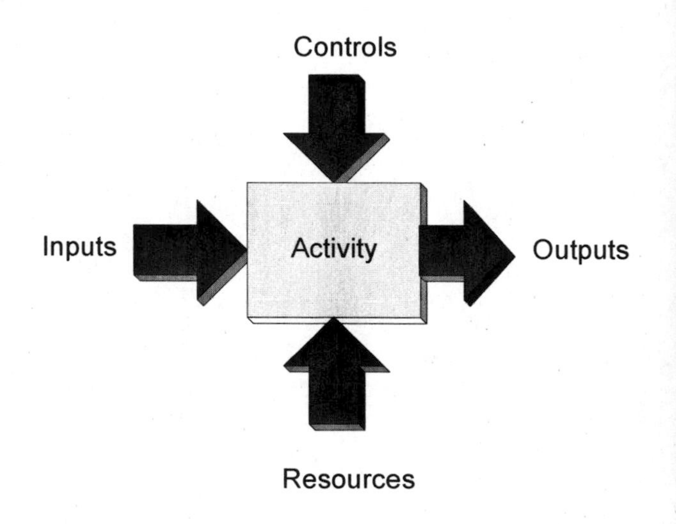

Figure 63 Basic IDEF0 diagram

As an example, **Figure 64** shows the process of making tea.

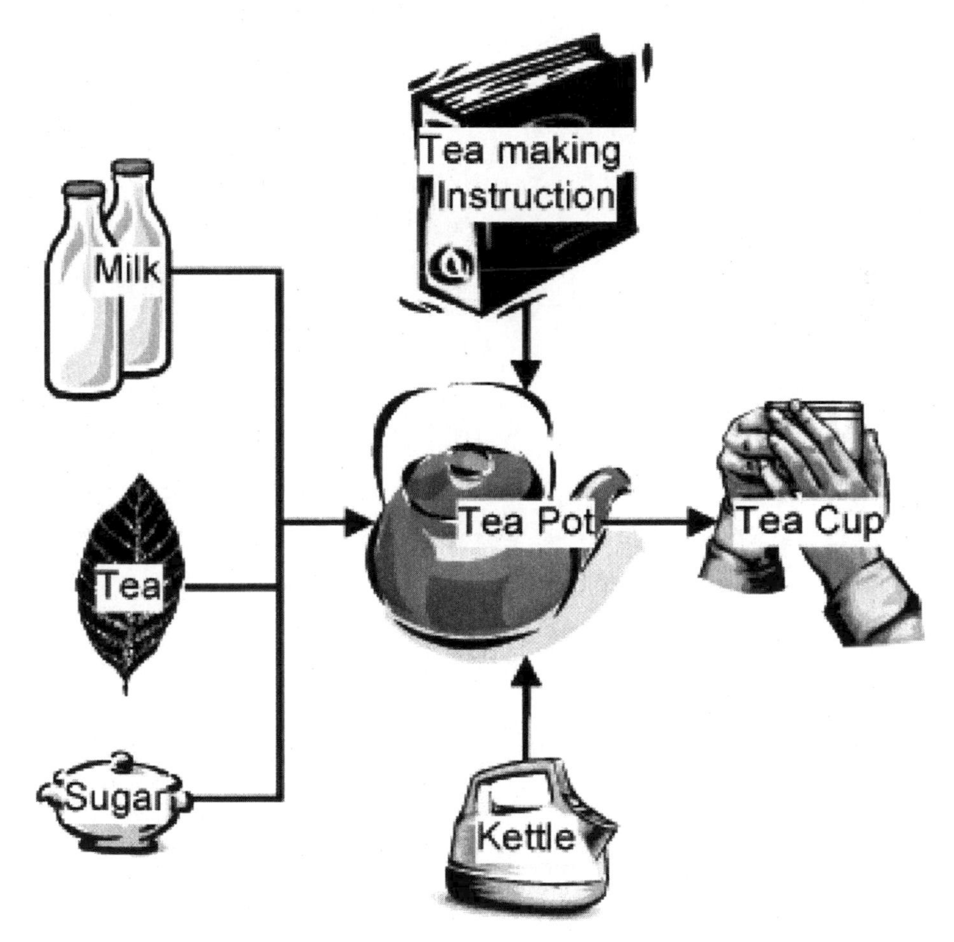

Figure 64 Making Tea

Now using IDEF0 format, **Figure 64** would become as show in **Figure 65**.

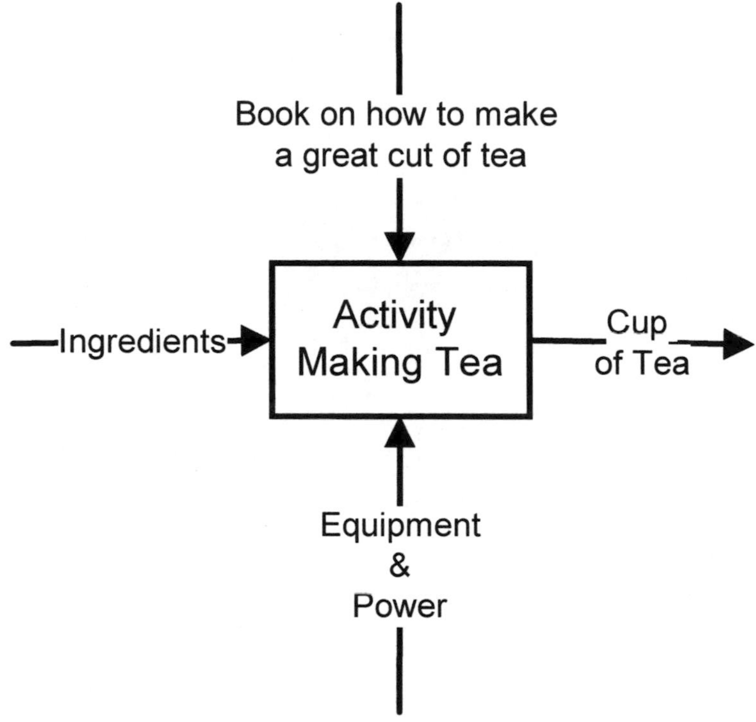

Figure 65 IDEF0 version of making tea

The arrows represent:
Inputs - Items that are used (consumed) in the activity.
Resources - Items that are used or employed in the activity but are not consumed by the activity.
Controls - Items that ensure that the activity is performed correctly for quality.
Output - The product of the activity.

The box represents
Activity - The box that is labelled with task to be performed, using the verb (making) and noun (tea) approach.

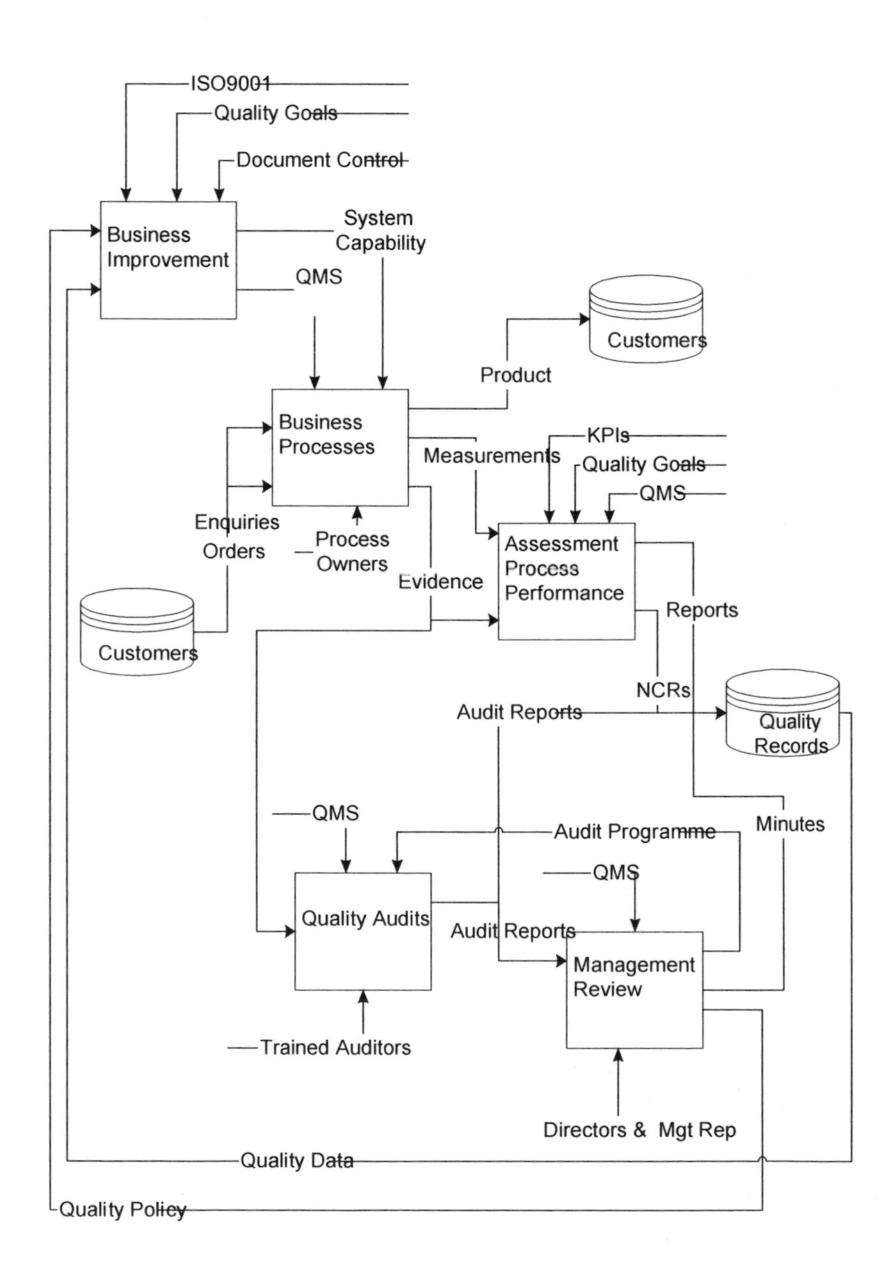

Figure 66 Quality System Model in IDEF0 Format

Figure 66 shows how a Quality System model would look if drawn in IDEF0 format. The diagram uses the same methodology of inputs, outputs, controls, resources and the verb/noun approach to describe the activities. In the bottom right hand corner of each box is the activity reference number. The process activity information can be entered into a database which, together with process performance data, can be used to measure process performance. The sort of process data that could be in each record of the process activity database includes:

- Time to complete conforming activities
- Time to complete any nonconforming activities - See Cost of Quality
- Activity waiting time
- Activity queuing time
- Activity action time - See Business Process Analysis
- Benchmarking data to compare performance against similar processes.
- Target setting and Key Performance Indicators (KPIs) - See Performance Measurement and Benchmarking.

Next is another example of IDEF0, in this case it is a software process.

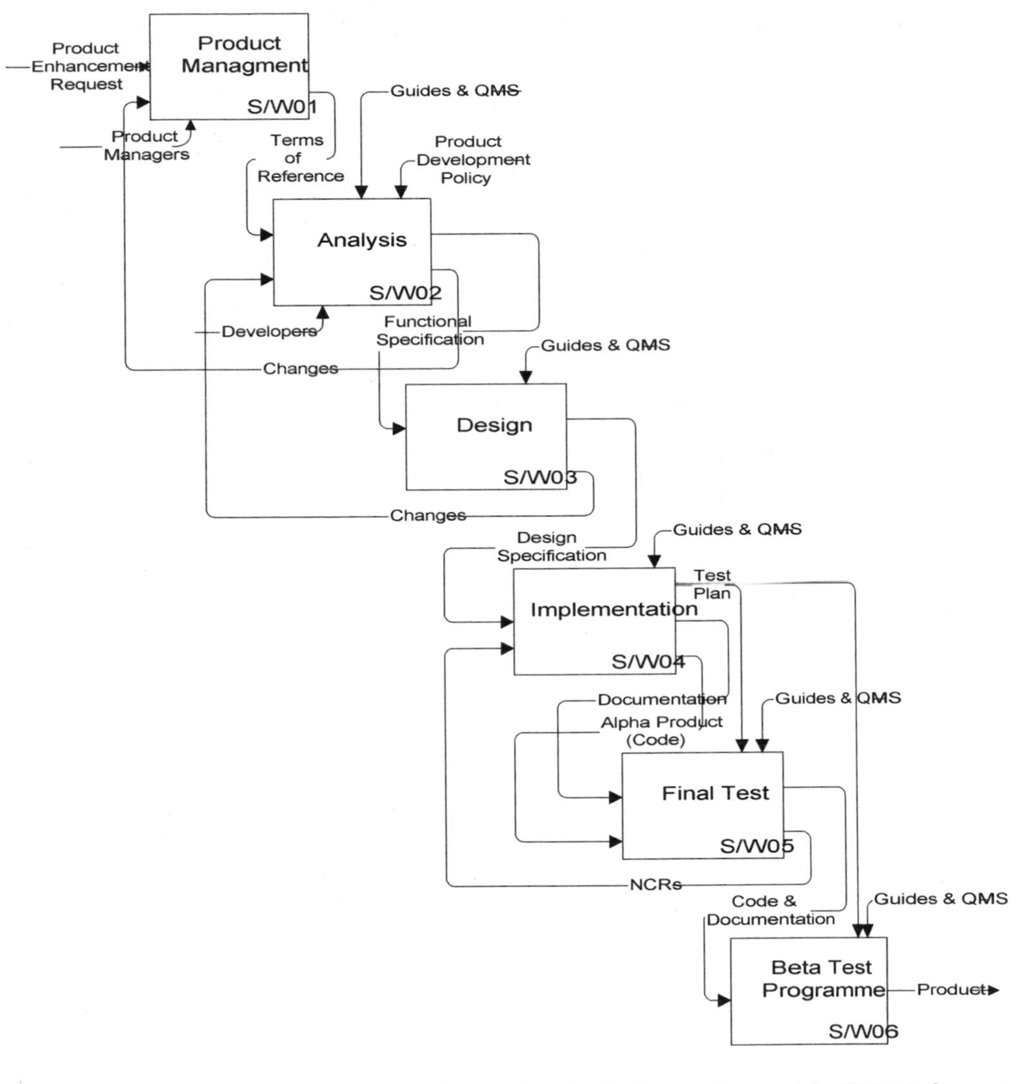

Figure 67 Example of a Software Process in IDEF0 format

In this example an input/output table has been provided below. These tables can be a useful addition to the IDFE0 process flow chart. Where the flow chart can show diagrammatically the process sequence, it is sometimes difficult to show the correct level of detail. In this situation an Input/Output table can be used to further describe the detail of the process. For example, in the Input/Output table the process user's attention is drawn to the availability of certain guides and codes of practice, terms of reference, software coding, etc.

Flowchart

#	Activity Description	Activity Input	Activity Output	Activity Control and/or Resource
SW01	Product Management	Product Enhancement Request	Product Development Policy Product Terms of Reference (ToR)	Guide for ToRs
SW02	Analysis	Product Development Policy Product Terms of Reference	Functional Specification	Guide for a Function Specification
SW03	Design	Functional Specification	Design Specification Documentation synopsis	Guide for Design Specifications
SW04	Implementation	Design Specification Documentation synopsis	Test Plans Preliminary Test results Documentation Code	Guide for Test Plans Documentation Guide Code writing code of practice
SW05	Final Test	Test Plans Code Documentation	Test Results NCRs Accepted code	Testing Code of Practice
SW06	Beta Programme	Accepted code	Product	

Risk Analysis Techniques (including Fault Tree Analysis)

There are numerous techniques available for risk analysis, some of the most popular techniques are described in the following pages.

Risk analysis is a preventive approach to determine the potential risk associated with a product, service, project or process. Typically, the aims of risk analysis are to identify the potential risks, quantify and determine an appropriate course of action to eliminate or mitigate the effects of the risk. In the case of products, not only will the organisation want to produce attractive products, the organisations need to continually strive to improve, not only the range and performance of the product, but also evaluate new techniques that prevent any possibility of customer problems (safety). The techniques listed below address these aims and objectives. Each technique has its own particular strengths and weaknesses and is often used in specific circumstances and applications.

1. Hazard Analysis Critical Control Points (HACCP) see page 199
2. Hazard and Operability study (HAZOP) see page 200
3. Failure Mode and Effects Analysis (FMEA) sometimes known as Failure Mode, Effects and Criticality Analysis (FMECA) see page 201
4. Fault Tree Analysis see page 208

---

1. Hazard Analysis Critical Control Points (HACCP)

Hazard analysis like the other analysis techniques is a preventive approach aimed at avoiding problems. The approach for Hazard Analysis Critical Control Points (HACCP) consists of:

- i Description and assessment of the hazards associated with all stages in the process, from raw material to delivery of the finished product.
- ii Identification of the critical control points.
- iii Establishment of procedures to monitor and regulate the critical control points.

One major problem of this analysis is that no account is taken of the likelihood of occurrence, the seriousness of the failure, and the likelihood of detection. The analysis also does not rank the risk or exposure to problems, not just health and safety issues but also problems of waste, inefficiency and rejects. The technique also tends to concentrate on the process and there is a need to analyse the product as well. The technique is often used to identify any possible health or safety problems with the product and its method of development, production and delivery. While this technique is successful in helping to catalogue logically the issues surrounding health and safety, it is felt that the analysis could go further, not only in terms of ensuring health and safety but also possibly improving the overall performance of the product and process.

2. HAZdard and OPerability study (HAZOP)

This technique tends to be applicable to the operation of facilities and plant, detailing the controls necessary to ensure the continued safe operation of the facilities. The HAZOP study is carried out by using guide words. These words are to identify all deviations from the objectives of the facility or plant, which will have undesirable effects on safety or operability. The overall aim of the study is to identify any potential hazards.

The HAZOP study report should contain:

- i Technical information about the facility, its design and operation of the plant or installation.
- ii Details on how safety will be managed.
- iii Information about the particular hazards of the plant or installation. These hazards will need to be systematically identified and documented by means of safety studies.
- iv Information about the safety precautions taken to prevent major accidents, together with the emergency provisions that should be taken if a safety problem or accident occurs. The object then is to reduce the effects of such accidents or safety problems.

This study will require the compilation of operating manuals. These operating manuals will need to describe:

- i Operation, control and safety procedures and instructions, including procedures for the management of changes in technology, operations and equipment.
- ii Adequate maintenance and monitoring of key operations.
- iii Adequate inspection and repair.
- iv Proper training of workers and contractors.

Part of the study will also be to determine the possible causes of accidents. This analysis of hazards should lead to the identification of potential hardware and software failures, process and design deficiencies and human error. The study should also determine what action is necessary to counteract these failures (including abnormal/normal operation, e.g. start-up and shut-down).

Such causes could include: component failure, corrosion, temperature, malfunction of control and safety devices, deviations from normal operation, failure in the monitoring of crucial process parameters, human and organisational errors, incorrect repair or maintenance work, etc.

A HAZOP study should be performed by a multi-disciplinary expert group, always including personnel familiar with the installation.

One problem with this (HAZOP) approach is that it tends to concentrate on the plant and facilities and not the process or the product. It does not provide the ability to identify areas of waste and inefficiency.

3. Failure Mode and Effects (and Critically) Analysis (FMEA or FMECA)

Introduction

Failure Mode and Effects Analysis (FMEA) is a logical technique used to identify and eliminate possible causes of failure. The technique requires a sequential, disciplined approach by engineers to assess systems, products or processes in order to establish the modes of failure and the effects of failure on the system, product or process. This is to ensure that all possible failure modes have been fully identified and ranked in order of their importance. The FMEA discipline requires the engineers to document their evaluation with regard to the failure mode, effect and criticality. The analysis work can be applied at any stage; design, manufacture, test, installation or use, but is best performed at the design stage. In a simple system the study may be performed on the total system or product but with more complex systems it may be necessary to break the product down into various sub-systems or sub-assemblies.

The addition of the "C" in FMECA refers to the criticality analysis and risk priority number generated when carrying out this analysis. The calculation of the risk priority number is included in the Guidelines for FMEA.

The reason for FMEA

With ever increasing demands to ensure that QUALITY is achieved **RIGHT FIRST TIME** then still greater pressures are placed on the Design Engineer. This is to ensure that the Engineer's design performs consistently, reliably and safely throughout the life of the product, thus providing a quality product that completely meets the demands of the customer. Designers are only human, they can make mistakes and have off days just like everyone else. FMEA ensures that any inadequacies in the design are quickly identified, preventing the possibility of releasing sub-standard products. Product testing will of course help identify any design deficiencies. There are however, possible limitations with this approach:

i) if the product fails the trial, then the modified and hopefully improved design will need to be retested - this can lead to inefficient use of resources.

i) tests and trials can usually only be performed on a limited number of products, consequently all the possible variations in specification and build standard cannot always be evaluated. Using small samples may also not be sufficiently accurate to predict field failure rates, particularly when attempting to identify causes of potentially low field failure rates (½ or 1%). These missed potential failures may result in the need for product recall or the issuing of advisory notices, (particularly in the case of safety critical failures). This can be not only expensive but also damaging for both the company and product's credibility and reputation.

So FMEA provides the potential for:

i) Reducing the likelihood of service failures
ii) Reducing the chance of campaign changes
iii) Reducing maintenance and warranty costs
iv) Reducing the possibility of safety failures
v) Reducing the potential of extended life failures
vi) Reducing the likelihood of Product Liability claims

With FMEA the emphasis is on removal of the likely cause of any potential failures. However, FMEA can also indicate to the Engineer the features in the design which require sophisticated quality control monitoring, possibly with the use of Statistical Quality Control (see section Statistical Quality Control).

Responsibility for FMEA

The analysis can be performed by either the Design, Manufacture or Quality Engineer, but the most suitable is the person who knows the system, product or process best. The Design Engineer is the person most likely to conduct this analysis as they have the most complete knowledge of the product and can therefore best anticipate the failure mode and the effect of the failure modes. The FMEA technique can be completed by an individual but is best carried out as a team exercise led by the engineer responsible for the product or sub-assembly. The team could include the Designer, Quality Engineer, Manufacturing Engineer, Customer and where appropriate any sub-contractors.

Some benefits of the application of FMEA can be:

i) Identifying potential and known failures
ii) Identifying the cause and effect of such a failure mode
iii) Ranking the identified failure modes in terms of risk factor
iv) Following up or taking action on the potential failure modes
v) Providing detailed documentation for the purpose of quality audit
vi) Checking on the FMEA decisions in the event of a major failure
vii) Making clear the accountability for the system, product or process

Limitations of FMEA

FMEA involves a considerable amount of time and labour resource in performing the study but in any case, this is only time that would need to be spent in order to satisfactorily evaluate the design. Conducting an FMEA does require the completion of paperwork but at the end of the analysis documentary evidence is available proving an assessment was performed. Even after completing an FMEA, it may be that the key design failures may have been overlooked by the team and failures still occur. However, the likelihood of such an event has been reduced. It may also be that after completing the FMEA no action is taken regarding the potential failures identified. This may be the case but clear responsibilities for taking action will have been established.

Guidelines for FMEA

The key stages in any failure mode and effects analysis on a design, product or system are detailed below and should be followed in conjunction with **Table 27** shown at the end of this section.

1. Logistics

   The system, sub-system or item and the FMEA team members need to be selected. All the relevant information needs to be collated: examples, drawings, customer brief, field failure information etc.

2. Header details

   Complete the details at the top of the form including the name of the Engineer who performed the study and is responsible for the design. Include the revision status of the drawing and the FMEA. *Note, if the study was performed by a team then the name of the team leader.*

3. Part, Process or System name and number

   Complete details regarding the part, process or system name and number.

4. Describe the function

   The engineer must identify as briefly as possible the function of the part, component or system being analysed. The question needed to be asked is: "What is the purpose of this part?"

5. Describe the anticipated failure mode

   The engineer must consider how this part could fail to complete its intended function. For example, could it break, bind, corrode, wear, deform, leak, short, etc. It is important at this stage, that the engineer should be asking the question: "How could it fail?" not whether or not it will fail.

6. Describe the effects of failure

   The engineer must describe what the effects of failure on the final component or the assembly would be. The question, "What will happen as a result of the failure mode described?" needs to be posed. Will the component or assembly be inoperative, intermittent or noisy, inefficient, not durable, inaccurate etc?

7. Cause - describe the cause of failure

   Anticipation as to the cause of failure is necessary at this stage. What is being sought is which set of conditions or factors can bring about the failure mode? For example:
   - could a foreign body jam the mechanism?
   - would poor or wrong material cause the mechanism to break?
   - would poor soldering cause the wire to short or cause an open circuit?
   - made outside specification or unable to achieve specification?

   The engineer must analyse what conditions could bring about the failure mode.

8. Estimate the frequency of occurrence of the failure

Here it is necessary to estimate the probability that a failure mode will occur. This estimation will be evaluated on a scale of 1 to 10. A one would indicate a very low probability of occurrence, ten would indicate near certainty of occurrence. The engineer needs to assess the probability of an occurrence based on his knowledge and experience of the product. The following evaluation scale is used:

1	=	1 in 1,000,000 chance of occurrence
2 & 3	=	1 in 100,000 chance of occurrence
4 & 5	=	1 in 10,000 chance of occurrence
6 & 7	=	1 in 1,000 chance of occurrence
8	=	1 in 100 chance of occurrence
9	=	1 in 10 chance of occurrence
10	=	100% chance of occurrence

9. Estimate the severity of failure

At this stage it is necessary to determine the likely severity of failure and again the scale of 1 to 10 is used, where a one would indicate a minor nuisance and ten would indicate severe consequences such as a high voltage shock. An estimate must be made of the severity of the failure. The engineer must consider the consequence of failure using the following severity scale:

1	=	unlikely to be detected
2	=	25% chance of service call
3	=	50% chance of service call
4	=	75% chance of service call
5	=	100% chance of service call
6	=	failure on installation or first use
7	=	failure results in customer complaint
8	=	failure results in a serious customer complaint
9	=	failure results in a fire, accident or injury
10	=	failure results in non-compliance with statutory safety standard or a fatality

10. Estimate the detection of failure

An estimate must be made of the probability that a potential failure will be detected before it reaches a customer. Again the evaluation scale of 1 to 10 is used. A one would indicate a very high probability that failure would be detected before reaching the customer and ten would indicate a very low probability that the failure would be detected in-house and therefore is likely to be experienced by the customer. E.g. If a 100% conclusive test is performed on the component, it is unlikely that the fault will reach the customer and is therefore assigned one. Alternatively if no checks are performed then it is highly likely that, if faulty, the defective product will reach the customer and is therefore assigned ten.

1	=	failure will be detected
2	=	80% chance of detection
3	=	70% chance of detection
4	=	60% chance of detection
5	=	50% chance of detection
6	=	40% chance of detection
7	=	30% chance of detection
8	=	20% chance of detection
9	=	10% chance of detection
10	=	no chance of detection

11. Calculate the risk priority number

By multiplying together the assessed likelihood of occurrence, severity and detection, the risk priority number (rpn) is found. The highest number being 1000, the smallest number being 1. From this number it is possible to determine which the high priority items are in terms of failure mode. The higher the risk number the more critical the component or item failure is.

12. Corrective action

The basic purpose of failure mode and effects analysis is to highlight the potential failure mode so that the engineer can take steps to eliminate or reduce the risk. At this stage it is necessary to analyse the risk number and determine what appropriate action is necessary. Obviously a high risk number would indicate immediate action, a low risk number may be ignored or could require some minor checks to be included.

13. Follow up

    Having determined what the appropriate corrective action should be it is now necessary to perform a further FMEA to ensure that the resulting risk number has been reduced to an acceptable risk. It is also advisable to confirm at some future date that the proposed action has been successfully and effectively implemented.

Table 27 FMEA Form

<table>
<tr><td colspan="5">Product:
Component Name:
Component Number:
Revision Number:
Effect on Purchasing: Yes/No</td><td colspan="5">Engineer:
Dates:
Report Number:
Sheet of Sheets:
Revision Number:
Last Updated:</td></tr>
<tr><th>Part, Process or system name & number</th><th>Function</th><th>Possible Failure Mode</th><th>Effect of Failure</th><th>Cause of failure</th><th>Occurrence</th><th>Severity</th><th>Detection</th><th>Risk</th><th>Remarks/ Action taken</th></tr>
<tr><td></td><td></td><td></td><td></td><td></td><td></td><td></td><td></td><td></td><td></td></tr>
</table>

4. Fault Tree Analysis

Introduction

Fault Tree Analysis (FTA) is a powerful, widely-recognised method for determining system reliability and possible risks. It is a logical technique for analysing and deducing the various combinations of hardware and software failures and human errors that could result in the occurrence of specified undesired events (usually referred to as the top event) at the system level. The deductive analysis begins with the top event, then attempts to determine the specific causes of this top event. The main objective of FTA is to determine the probability of this top event. The calculation involves system quantitative reliability information, such as failure probability or failure rate. FTA provides key information regarding the likelihood of failure and the means by which failure could occur. Focussing on and refining the results of the FTA can be used to minimise risk and improve system safety and reliability.

Definitions and Fundamentals

Top Event: The double box contains the description of the system level fault or undesired event. The Top Event appears only once at the end or the top of the tree and must be measurable, definable and inclusive of all lower events. The input to the Top Event double box is from a logic gate. The top undesired event is often the fault which upon occurrence results in complete failure of the system and is considered catastrophic failure.

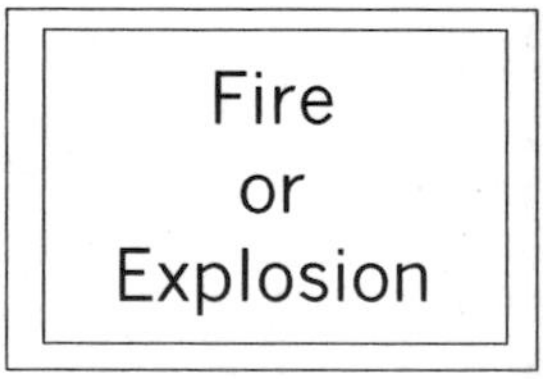

Fire
or
Explosion

Figure 68 Top event

Fault Event: The rectangle should contain a brief description of the fault event such as combustible material or source of ignition. Fault events should appear at the output or input of a logic gate.

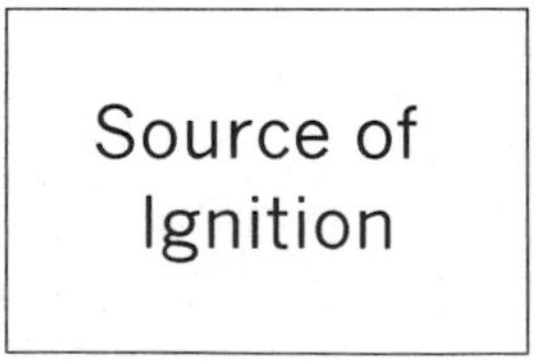

Source of
Ignition

Figure 69 Fault Event

Event Probability: The event probability figure is defined as the probability of being in a failed state or of failure to respond (possibly in the case of an operator). These figures are defined at the component level and are usually in the form of number of faults per year, e.g. EP = 0.02 faults per year. Further up the tree, the figures are calculated from combining the inputs to the AND/OR gates.

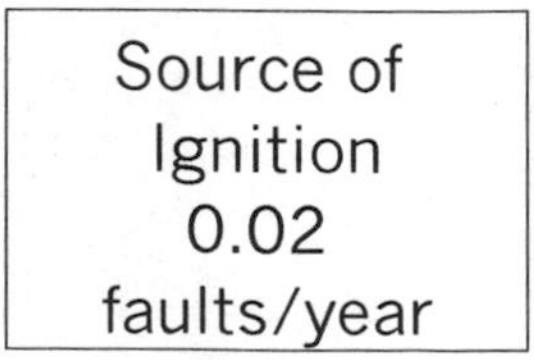

Source of
Ignition
0.02
faults/year

Figure 70 Event Probability

$$\text{AND } P_{and} = P_1 \times P_2 \times P_3 \times ...P_n$$
$$\text{OR } P_{or} = P_1 + P_2 + P_3 + ...P_n$$

Fault Tree Logic Gates: AND/OR gates are used to describe the relationship between the input and output events in a fault tree. The main gates used in FTA are described below.

Description	Symbol	Truth Table		
		Input A	Input B	Output
AND Gate. The AND gate indicates that the output occurs if all of the input events occur.		T T F F	T F T F	T F F F
OR Gate. The OR gate indicates that the output occurs if at least one of the input events occur.		T T F F	T F T F	T T T F

Fault Tree Analysis Process

a. Determine the scope and depth of the FTA.
b. Determine the system level faults.
c. Describe all events which cause this system level fault.
d. Continue to describe each lower level fault and their immediate causes, until at a component level, failure or human error can be attributed to the fault. It is usually best to complete each tree branch until component level is reached before starting a new branch.
e. Construct the fault tree using the block diagram.
f. Determine probability of each event.
g. Combine probability input to AND/ OR gates as follows:
   AND $P_{and} = P_1 \text{ X } P_2 \text{ X } P_3 \text{X}...P_n$
   OR $P_{or} = P_1 + P_2 + P_3 + ...P_n$
   until the top event probability is determined.
h. Evaluate what action can be taken to reduce the probability or eliminate the likelihood of the top event occurring.

Example of a Fault Tree Analysis for a Mixing Plant

Figure 71 shows a facility for mixing and heating two chemicals. One of the chemicals has the potential to catch fire and explode. An explosion could be caused by the inflammable material being ignited. Two materials, 1 & 2, are fed through a series of valves. The first being an isolation valve, the second controls flow rate to the heated mixing vat.

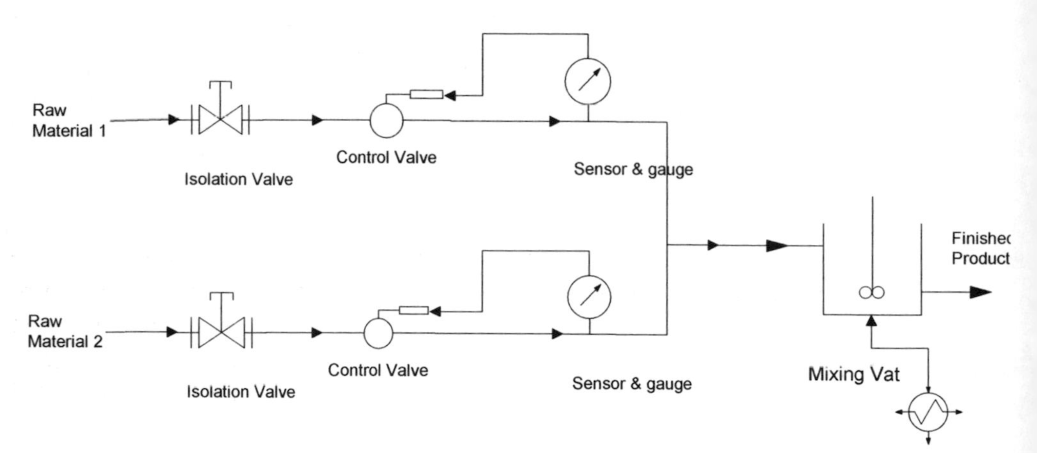

Figure 71 Chemical mixing facility

Figure 71 has been developed into a Fault Tree Analysis as shown in **Figure 72**

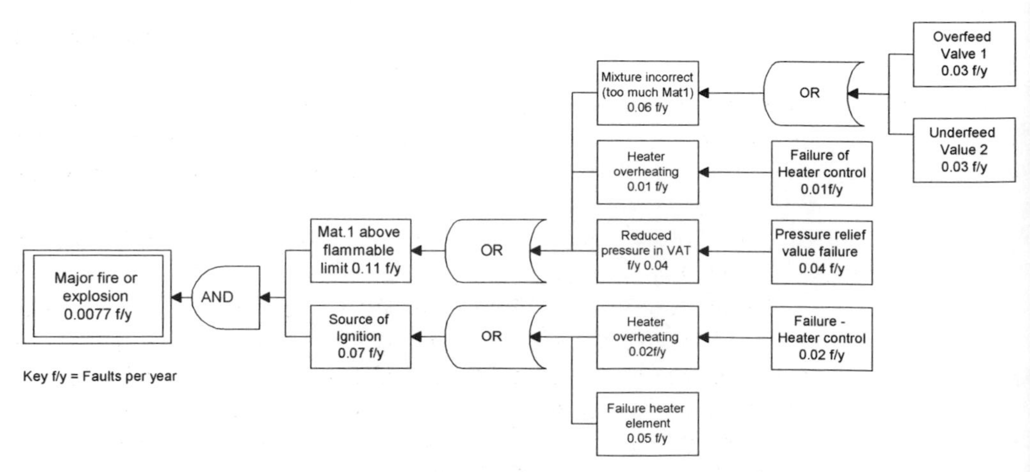

Figure 72 Fault Tree Analysis for Chemical Facility

The Top event probability is calculated to be 0.0077 faults per year, which whilst very low may be significant, it very much depends on the application and location of the facility. There are a number of actions that could be taken to reduce this risk.

Comments

This is a relatively simple fault tree and if the process was expanded to embrace the whole chemical mixing facility, a considerably more complex fault tree would result. The technique is heavily dependent on the accuracy of the data used for event probability and a good understanding of the specific process under investigation.

Implementing failure analysis

There are a number of approaches that can be adopted for the successful introduction of failure analysis. There are generally two elements to any failure analysis approach; initially a clear understanding of the responsibility and authority, then the creation of the failure analysis process, implementation and review of progress and evaluation of success. An understanding of the responsibility and authority should be established first as this will influence the approach adopted. In any event the approach adopted will require management commitment to the establishment of an environment dedicated to reliability and safety.

To achieve this:

i) Identify the authority, roles and responsibility of engineers or senior managers to complete any failure analysis.
ii) Ensure that failure analysis procedures are agreed and incorporated into any formal engineering or process manuals.
iii) The established procedures should not only clearly identify who holds overall responsibility for the failure analysis but make clear that this responsibility extends to ensuring that all recommended actions are carried out.
iv) Ensure that any resultant failure analysis actions and decisions are supported by documentary evidence justifying the action and confirming resolution or closure. Note; any design, project or process changes that have been implemented (as the result of a failure analysis), should be subjected to a further analysis on the new system.
v) The scope of the failure analysis should be made clear. Does it only apply to products or do all projects and processes needs to be included? Are all products, projects and processes subjected to this failure analysis rigour?
vi) Establish who will be involved in conducting the failure analysis.

vii) Ensure that the active participants in the failure analysis activity have been trained. Ensuring that the team members have a uniform comprehension of the FMEA methodology and rating system and a consistent interpretation of the words used in these scales.

viii) Be aware that ratings used in FMEAs are subjective and are only comparable within the subject and organisation being studied and cannot be directly compared with other.

Failure Analysis Selection

FMEA	**Fault Tree Analysis**
Assembles, subassemblies and sub-systems. Projects.	Large facilities and installation where catastrophic events are possible.
A large number of changes or variations in system functional outputs may lead to unacceptable conditions.	There is a possibility of multiple failure modes, including human errors, causing serious top event.
It is suspected that the system may produce unwanted or hazardous outputs and it is not known what these are.	A single system output giving loss of main function has been identified as being of prime importance.
The system contains new or unconventional items of equipment hardware (of known detailed design),and the effects of faults in this hardware are not fully understood.	A single unintended system output has been recognised as a possible and significant hazard.
The system contains very little or no redundant elements, standby equipment or alternative modes of operation.	The system contains an appreciable number of redundant elements, standby equipment or alternative modes of operation.
Determining the need for redundancy, design features increasing the probability of "fail safe" outcomes of failure, further derating and/or design simplification.	The fault "logic" within the system can be more conveniently represented in diagrammatic rather than tabular form.
The fault "logic" within the system can be more conveniently represented in statements on tabular form rather than diagrammatic form.	

Exercises

For a process of your choice complete an FMEA.

Nominal Group Technique and Brainstorming

Introduction

Brainstorming: The purpose of brainstorming is to generate as many ideas as possible that come from many different perspectives. The concept is that teams tend to generate more ideas than individuals. As individuals we may run out of ideas quickly. Brainstorming in teams is an effective way of obtaining more new ideas. One person's ideas may trigger ideas that others would not have thought of by themselves. It is in this way that the team build on each other's ideas which trigger off an individual's imagination. The technique is also useful in team building and cohesion. There are many ways in which brainstorming can be carried out.

Nominal Group Technique is a development of brainstorming into a problem analysis process. Nominal Group Technique (NGT), is based on a nominal group of 8 to 10 people, trained in NGT, from various functions and departments, with multi-disciplined backgrounds, who have assembled to collectively evaluate an issue, problem or opportunity for improvement. The NTG process uses all the advantages of brainstorming, i.e encouraging creativity and participation and avoiding social and psychological dynamics of group behaviour, which may inhibit group decisions. Thus, evading problems of individuals dominating the group and specific individuals doing all the talking and the rest listening. This gets a participating group to focus on very specific issues in a structured NGT process. Below is described the steps in a typical NGT process. Experience has shown following these steps and the brainstorming rules outlined in the next few pages, will greatly contribute towards a successfully managed meeting and valuable outcomes.

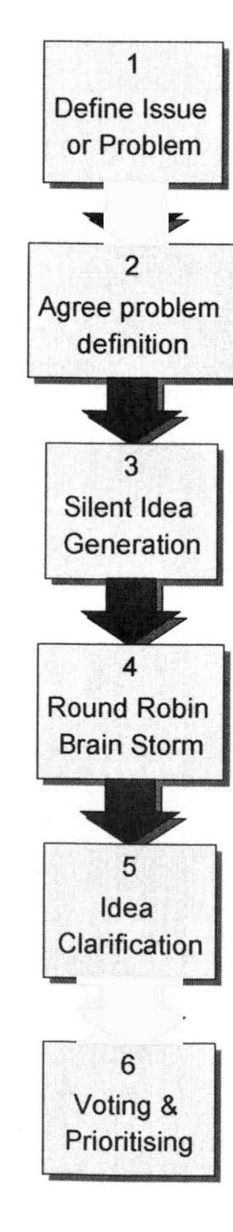

Figure 73 NGT

1. *Define the issue or problem.* The NGT leader creates a statement that predefines the issue that the group is to focus on. A copy of this problem statement is provided to each group member.
2. *Agree problem statement.* The group then evaluates the problem statement. The group is encouraged to restate and restate or clarify the statement in their own words. Care must be taken at this stage not to allow the possible vested interests to change the direction or main thrust of the stated problem. Once agreement is reached

the statement can be augmented by the NGT leader inline with the group's wishes.

3. *Silent idea generation.* The group is then given time to think about the problem. Giving the individual time for focussed and uninterrupted thought in a creative setting. Each group member is encouraged without pressurising them to write down (Notebook style) as many idea associated with the problem as they can. Creating the correct, almost academic, quiet, library like atmosphere is important for mental concentration. During this period, which usually lasts about 10 to 15 minutes, no talking should be allowed.
4. *Round Robin Brain Storm.* The NGT leader, having ended the silent generation step, will advise the group that the need for creativity has not finished yet. Each group member now in turn calls out one of their ideas, to be written down by the NGT Leader. The NGT leader may request clarification from the individual idea provider, but the other group members should remain silent during this exchange. This step is continued until each member of the group has said "pass" ie. run out of ideas.
5. *Idea Clarification.* With all the ideas recorded on a flip chart or possibly using stick-it type notes around the room. The group members are then encouraged to seek clarification of each idea in turn and suggest amendments or additions, but not criticise. At this step the ideas can also be organised into similar themes or approaches. Setting a time limit can be helpful to avoid any unnecessary discussion, but each idea should be given equal opportunity.
6. *Voting and prioritising.* Each individual group member now anonymously identifies their top five ideas. Rating them on the basis of criteria such as practicality, feasibility, simplicity, applicability, validity, ease of implementation, suitability, cost, etc. Their top idea getting five points, the next four and so on. Once voting is complete the scores are added up for each idea. This ensures that no premature decisions are made and avoids dominance by any strong group member. Now no decision has yet been made, discussion can take place of the rankings. This is where group members have the opportunity to debate the voting and the suitability of the preferred ideas, preparing themselves for the final decision. Once this brief discussion stage has been completed, anonymous voting again takes place to finalise the ideas ranking. There is now a complete written record of the idea development and selection.

This NGT provides an excellent framework for idea generation and gives the group members sense of achievement. Hopefully, motivating them for the more difficult phases of idea testing and implementation.

Brainstorming Guidelines

The following guidelines have been created to help ensure a successful brainstorming session.

The team should be sitting in a room away from distraction. Identify the theme or problem that the team wishes to discuss. Sometimes it helps to brain storm something silly before attempting to brain storm the chosen theme, e.g. *How many uses for a brick?* This can make the team more relaxed. To get the best out of brainstorming there are some simple rules which have been found to work.

Rule 1 Encourage everyone to participate by presenting only one idea per "*turn.*" One way is by taking turns to suggest one idea at a time. If an individual cannot think of anything then say "pass."

Rule 2 There are no silly or bad ideas. So, team members should not put each other down by making them feel stupid. Encourage each other to say whatever comes into their heads.

Rule 3 Criticism or judgement is not allowed. Team members should not criticise the ideas of others. The idea is to be open minded and constructive.

Rule 4 Discussion of the ideas should not take place until after the brainstorming has finished. Accept everything without comment - it could trigger off new ideas.

Rule 5 Exaggeration and enthusiasm are helpful - there is no such thing as a crazy idea. Very often so-called crazy ideas lead to new ways of thinking and imaginative solutions.

Rule 6 Look for possible combinations of ideas, in this way the team may arrive at new ideas.

Rule 7 If you run out of ideas try using the six key words - What, When, Where, Why, Who and How.

Rule 8 Build on other people's ideas where possible.

Rule 9 Record all the ideas.

There are different types of brainstorming, some are listed below. It can also help to return to the problem at some later date - *Incubation.*

Table 28

Brainstorming Approaches	
Advantages	Disadvantages
Free Style: The team calling out ideas to be written down (usually on white board or flip chart, by the team leader).	
i) Spontaneous ii) Can be more creative iii) Possible to build on each others ideas	i) Strong personalities may dominate the session ii) Can be confusing; listing ideas and too many talking at once
Round Robin: Each team member in turn calling out their idea to be written down.	
i) Difficult to dominate the session ii) Discussion tends to be more focussed iii) Everyone is encouraged to take part with equal sharing and participation iv) Possible to build on each others ideas v) Tolerates conflicting ideas	i) Difficult to wait one's turn ii) Loss of spontaneity iii) Embarrassing if cannot think of any ideas - puts participants under pressure iv) Reluctance to pass v) Not as easy to build on others ideas
Notebook Style: Each team member writes on a pad or sheet of paper their own ideas, later to be collated by the team leader.	
i) Ensures anonymity if sensitive topics are to be discussed ii) Can be used with very large groups iii) Not necessary to speak iv) Provides time to think v) Focussed and uninterrupted thought vi) Avoids competition and status differences vii) Encourages each member to search for ideas viii) Avoids conformity pressures	i) Not possible to build on ideas of others ii) Some ideas may not be legible, understandable iii) Difficult to clarify ideas iv) Not possible to hear or see ideas

Exercise: Brain storm
“Why do improvement teams sometimes fail?”

Benchmarking and Performance Measurement

Introduction:

All organisations need to establish and quantify the key factors with which to monitor their quality performance. It is not enough to believe that the organisation's quality performance has always been satisfactory. Agreement needs to be reached as to what the key factors are by which to judge the organisation's quality performance. What is the organisation's current performance against these factors and how can the current quality performance be improved? If measures of Quality Performance are not established and monitored, then adverse and possibly catastrophic trends may not be identified with possible dire consequences for the organisation concerned. Juran talks about breakthrough and control to new levels of quality performance; organisations that can achieve this objective will always be successful because they will continually be making never-ending improvements.

Quality Performance measures need to be established, not only at a corporate level but at all levels throughout the organisation, even down to an individual unit or person. Quality Performance measurement is one of the most important ways of improving the quality performance of organisations. If the current quality performance is not known then improvements can only be subjective and not quantifiable.

Having established and measured an organisation's or department's performance indicators these values need to be compared (benchmarked) against recognised leaders or pacesetters. This is to determine if the current performance is of the correct standard (*World Class*).

Guidelines for Benchmarking:

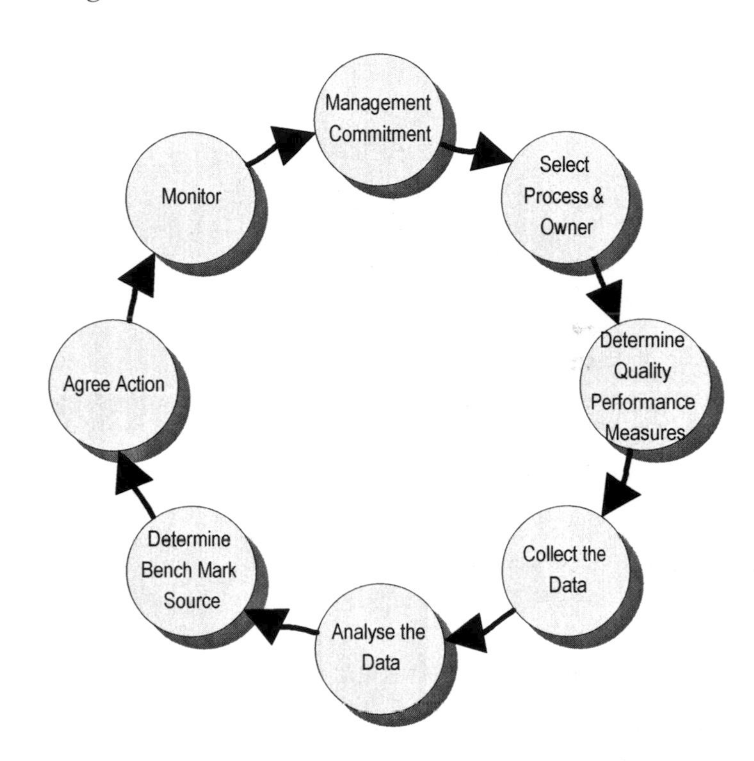

Figure 74 A Benchmarking Sequence

Firstly, there is a need to agree the necessity for establishing quality performance measures with senior management. The necessity of establishing quality performance measurement then needs to be communicated to all levels throughout the organisation to gain commitment and understanding for the need to continually make improvements in quality performance. Departmental Purpose Analysis and Customer/Supplier investigations can be used to help convince personnel of the need for quality performance measurement. The TQM team needs to agree the performance measurement.

Next, the actual processes that need to be monitored have to be established and agreed. Having established the process to be monitored then the factors critical to success need to be determined.

These critical success factors or quality performance measurements should be:

i) Suitable for the particular process, department or organisation evaluated.

ii) Consistent, so that there is no doubt about the method of calculation of the performance measure and so that the data for performance measurement can be accurately and reliably obtained.

iii) Clear and owned by a particular group or cell so that responsibility or ownership for achieving the performance criteria understood.
iv) Easily and regularly calculated, usually numbering between 3 and 7 performance measures.
v) Clearly defined start and finish.
vi) Defined direction not a solution.
vii) Achievable and within the group's capability.
viii) Possibly determined from the customer/supplier relationship and the department's purpose analysis.

The performance measurement categories can be broken down into two main categories, quantifiable "Hard Standards" and non-quantifiable (subjective) "Soft Standards". These categories can be broken down still further in terms of:

- customer satisfaction; product and service performance, reliability, complaints and claims
- process efficiency; scrap, rejects, wasted time, change, rework, labour and process utilisation
- environmental losses; pollution, unsatisfactory performance, disposal and decommissioning, waste of resources both human and energy.

"Hard Standards" are measurable such that an agreed performance target can be set. Examples of such standards could be:

Cost	a.	Costs per item, transactions per employee
Quality	b.	Number of rejects, failure rates, complaints
Service	c.	Average response and down time, lead time, delivery time

"Soft Standards", although not always directly measurable, are equally important as hard standards. These soft standards can make the difference between an existing customer returning, obtaining a new customer or placating a dissatisfied customer.

An example of soft standards could be the way in which the service engineer deals with the customer. This can often make the difference between the customer renewing their service contract and the customer advising possible new customers of the excellent service the customer has received. Or alternatively, the poor service the customer has received which may result in the customer not returning and advising potential future customers of the unsatisfactory service.

Soft Standards can include:

Personnel style	a.	Friendly, helpful, positive approach
Efficient Service	b.	Anticipate needs, be flexible, provide clear information, professionalism
Concern	c.	Manage problems - when troubles do occur understanding the customer's difficulties and help to resolve the problem.

Data collection: Having determined the quality performance standards that need to be monitored, the next stage is to agree how to quantify the current performance level and to start to collect the data on a regular basis. The data collected could include:

- customer satisfaction; which could be quantified by surveys of both existing and potential customers (see example of the customer satisfaction survey). Surveys of competing products and services. Analysis of service and product performance in terms of reliability, numbers and types of complaints and claims.
- process efficiency; by monitoring scrap, rejects and rework levels. Analysis of processes to determine wasted time, labour and process utilisation, examination of the number of changes. (See Cost of Quality).
- environmental losses; waste of resources, human and energy, could be quantified and monitored by employee surveys, interviews (e.g. exit or leaving interviews) and energy audits.

Analysis: With the current performance level determined, the TQM team or departmental personnel need to agree new targets. These new targets can either be agreed with the customer (internal or external), or alternatively, the targets may be based on other recognised leaders or pacesetters - the organisations that are seen as being World Class or best in class. This information can be obtained from; surveys (customer and competition), technical journals, review of advertisements etc.

Obtaining the Benchmark Source: There are a number of possible benchmark sources. *Internal Benchmarking;* against a similar national or international division. This is the easiest, as access to the required information should be relatively straightforward. *Industrial Benchmarking;* against the competition. This is obviously more difficult as competitors are unlikely to be keen on releasing commercially sensitive information. However, Trade Associations can be helpful but information scientists can provide useful information. Alternatively, recruiting staff from the competition could provide a more effective route. There are also best practice clubs now available, which share approaches and information.

Action Plan & Monitoring: Having obtained what is seen as being a suitable target then work can commence towards establishing an action plan for improving the performance to meet the new performance criteria.

Departmental Purpose Analysis

Introduction

Departmental purpose analysis is used to clearly understand the relationship between your department, the supply departments and user/customer departments. This analysis can extend all the way down to individuals.

The analysis will ensure:

- The department's objectives coincide with the company's objectives and plans
- The inter-relationship between internal customers and suppliers is clearly understood
- The levels of performance are understood, agreed and achieved.

A good example of this is the secretary/manager relationship. When the manager dictates a letter to the secretary, the secretary becomes the customer. The manager (the supplier), needs to supply all the information and provide all necessary resource for the secretary to successfully accomplish the task.

Subsequently, the secretary completes and returns the letter to the manager. Here the manager becomes the customer. The secretary (the supplier), needs to supply a finished product, which completely satisfies the manager's requirements and needs. The manager's requirements could include: time taken to complete the letter, letter layout, grammar and spelling. (See **Figure 75**).

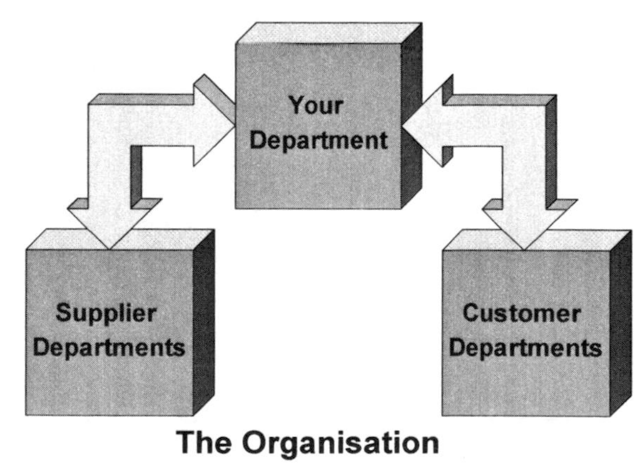

Figure 75 Internal Customers

This supplier/customer process can be extended to include everyone within the organisation from the person receiving the customer's order through to the person delivering the product or service to a satisfied customer. In this way each person in the process can be seen as an important link in a chain of events. Any breakdown or quality failure at any stage or link in the sequence will have an immediate and catastrophic effect on the process as a whole and the delivered product or service. The next person in the process is a customer of the previous person's work. As an example of this approach, possibly instead of the inspector inspecting each stage in the process, the next person in the process could be seen as the customer. The supplier or deliverer will need to completely check their own work to ensure customer satisfaction. The customer or receiver will check the incoming work as well as their own outgoing work.

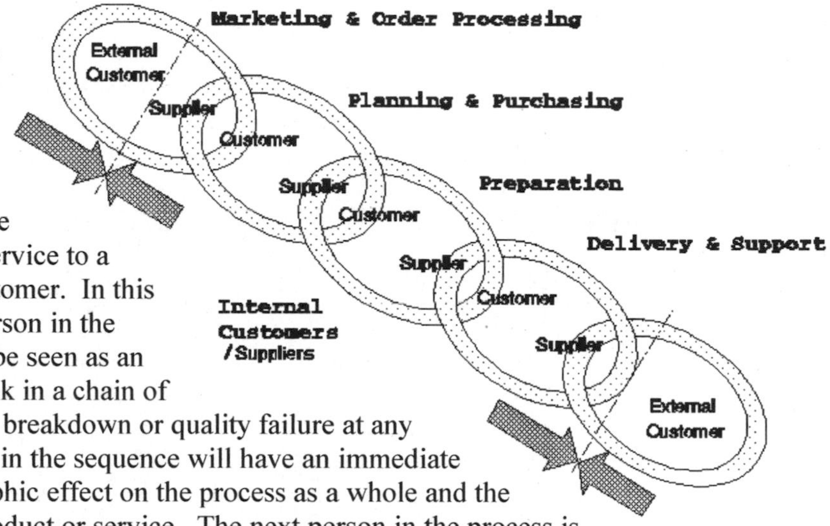

Figure 76 Customer/Supplier Chain

Figure 76 shows such a process in action. Initially from the external customer's requirements to Marketing (and hopefully a customer's order). Having reviewed and accepted the order, the next step in the chain is for Order Processing (an internal supplier) needs to supply Planning & Purchasing (an internal customer) with sufficient information. This information should be adequate (e.g. complete, accurate, reliable etc.) for Planning & Purchasing to satisfactorily complete their task in the chain. Next Purchasing (the internal supplier) to supply Preparation (the internal customer) with all the materials and facilities Preparation requires. This chain is then continued until delivery and handover to the satisfied external customer.

Departmental Purpose Analysis is an opportunity to evaluate the contribution of all departments to the overall quality performance of the organisation. For example the people in the indirect areas 'indirects' (e.g. Planning and Purchasing, Administration, Training - areas that do not directly add value) may feel that they cannot contribute to the overall quality performance of the organisation. The 'indirects' may feel that this contribution can only come from the people in the direct areas 'directs' (e.g.

manufacturing, test) - areas or functions that add value. The proportion of the salary bill is often split 60% indirect/40% direct. In monetary terms for a salary bill of £1M this means £600K is spent on indirects and £400K on directs - are the directs getting £600K worth of support from the indirects? If not why not? If not what are the indirects doing about providing value for money - Departmental Purpose Analysis? Departmental Purpose Analysis gives the opportunity to show how these indirect areas can contribute.

To assist in investigating the customer/supplier relationship the technique **Departmental Purpose Analysis** can be employed. Establishing:

- Are we doing the RIGHT tasks?
- Are we doing tasks RIGHT?
- Can we do the RIGHT tasks better?

Initially, the overall approach is to establish that the department is performing the right tasks - the tasks its customers needs (what are the department's customers needs?).

Secondly, to establish that the department is completing the tasks correctly - fulfilling the needs of the customer (what are the characteristics that the customer needs fulfilling?).

Finally, to establish if it is possible to do the tasks even better - is it possible to improve the performance of the department (what are the quality performance measures for the department, what are the important factors to achieve customer satisfaction?).

Guidelines for Departmental Purpose Analysis

Definitions

Internal Customer: People or departments inside the organisation who receive the output (product or services) from the supplier (your) department.
External Customer: People or departments outside the organisation who receive the output (product or services) from the supplier (your) department.
Customer needs: The actual products or services the customer is prepared to pay for (right tasks).
Customer Characteristics: An interpretation of products or services that the customer needs into specific individual attributes of the product or service. (Customer specification)
Quality Performance Level: The performance that the customer requires from the product or service provided.

Departmental Purpose Analysis

Note: Although reference is made throughout this section to the department, this analysis can equally be performed by an individual.

Table 29 Right Tasks

Are we doing the right tasks?	
List the Suppliers (Inputs).	List the Customers (Outputs).
Detail what is passed to the department (inputs). The information, material, products and services provided.	Detail what is passed onto the customers (the outputs). The information, material, products and services provided.
Detail all the departmental tasks - the purpose of the department.	
Confirmed by Suppliers:	Confirmed by Customer:
Name:	Name:
Date:	Date:
Title:	Title:
Department:	Company:

Are we doing the right tasks?

Using **Table 29**:

a. Detail the names of all the departments customers and suppliers. It may help to detail all the various tasks performed by the department.

b. Detail the output from the department. What are the products produced, what is the information or data supplied, what are the services provided?

c. Establish the purpose of the department. What does the department exist for, what are the aims and objectives of the department?

d. What are the tasks of the department? What work is performed to bring about the output from the department?

The tasks listed do not need to be detailed specific tasks but an overview of the major activities within the department.

e. Compare the departmental purpose with the department tasks:

- are they compatible?
- are there any inconsistencies?
- are all the departmental purposes fully addressed?
- are there any customer requirements that have been overlooked?
- are there any non-value added activities which can be eliminated? (See Non-Value Added Activities)

f. Identify which of the tasks are of highest priority.

g. Having established the above information, it is essential that the customer has the opportunity to confirm its accuracy and emphasis and to formally accept the agreed level of service.

To assist in detailing the suppliers and customers the diagram (**Figure** 77) can be drawn to show the inputs to the department (process) and the outputs from the department (process).

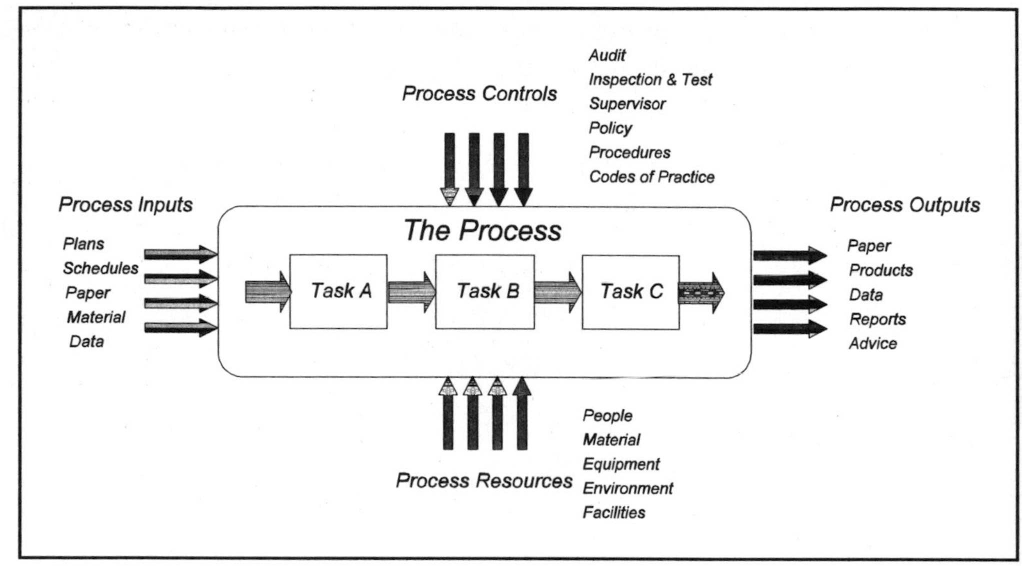

Figure 77 Process input/output diagram

Are we doing the tasks right?

Having established that only the right tasks are being performed then it is necessary to compare the actual practice with the customer specification. The activities, tasks and sequence that follows coincides with what the customer needs. **Table 30** opposite can be used in conjunction with this procedure.

Table 30 Tasks Right

Customer:	
Need	Specification or Characteristic

h. For each internal or external customer identified decide; what are the customer needs, what does the customer require in terms of a product or service?

Once these needs have been listed, how can these needs be characterised, what is the specification that the customer requires? Break down each need into specific characteristics or customer specifications.

i. Examine what is currently supplied to the customer, with what the customer needs. Are the current priorities the same as the customer priorities? For example, for the Purchasing Department the priority may be the placing of a £1M contract, whereas the Purchasing Department's customer may see the delivery of a £2.00 bolt, which is stopping production, the priority.

j. Confirm the tasks are being performed correctly and in the proper sequence, (is there an agreed method, is the method documented?). Internal quality audits may help.

k. Review any problems or complaints that the customer has identified and which are not being corrected or addressed.

Again the input/output diagram shown **Figure 77** can be used by adding to the diagram the controls and the resources necessary for the department (process) to successfully complete all the right tasks.

The output from this departmental purpose analysis stage can be to establish some Service Level Agreements (SLA) or an informal contract between the supplier and customer departments. These SLA can define a specification which the supplier commits to meet. Establishing these SLA can be a useful vehicle for debate between the internal customer and internal supplier. SLA give the opportunity for the internal customer to express clearly the level of performance expected from the internal supplier, rather than just saying things must improve, e.g minimum response time 1 hour, maximum down time 5 hours. They actually place some measurable target or performance figures against which the supplier can be judged, not only for current and future reference but against external performance, i.e. the performance of similar external bodies that do similar work (Benchmarking). How does the supplier's performance compare with the performance of an outside agency or contractor? How does the supplier's performance compare with departments doing similar activities in other organisations? Would it be cheaper and would a better service be provided by buying in the service?

Can we do the right tasks better?

Having established that the customer needs are completely understood and that the right tasks are being performed correctly, then improvements need to be made to the task efficiency. This establishes what factors need to be measured, what the current level of quality performance is and what quality performance level the customer demands and deserves.

l. Determine what factors need to be measured, e.g. average time to complete an activity, average cost of each task, average service level provided. In real terms, for the Purchasing Department, this could be average time to place an order, average time to receive goods, costs per transaction, cost per order placed. **Table 31** shows how **Table 30** has been extended to include the Quality Performance Levels required by the customer and the actual Performance Level achieved. (See section Performance Measurement)

Table 31 Tasks Better

Customer:			
Need	Specification or Characteristic	Perform-ance Level Required	Perform-ance Level Achieved

m. Having established appropriate performance criteria, the current quality performance level needs to be determined. Taking the Purchasing Department as an example again, this could be average time to place an order - six weeks, average time to receive goods - six months, costs per transaction or cost to place an order - £50 perorder. On this basis is the customer getting a satisfactory service from the Purchasing Department - would it be considered world class, is it possible to do better?

Note: Although this is for the Purchasing Department it could just as equally be applied to the Marketing, Administration or other departments.

n. These current performance levels can now be compared with what the customer requires or deserves. What performance does our customer require? Can the requirements be met, can the performance be improved still further?

o. Can tasks be combined to make the job more efficient? (See section Process Flow Charting)

Root Cause Analysis

Root cause analysis is a relatively new methodology that is currently evolving and has yet to be formalised, i.e. there are currently no established standards for it. Like other subjects covered by this book, it is not magic; "there is no silver bullet". It is the application in a different way of a series of well known, commonsense techniques. It is these techniques which when used in a different combination can produce a systematic, quantified and documented approach to the identification, understanding and resolution of underlying causes of under achieved quality in organisations. Below is a definition which encapsulates the main points of this technique:

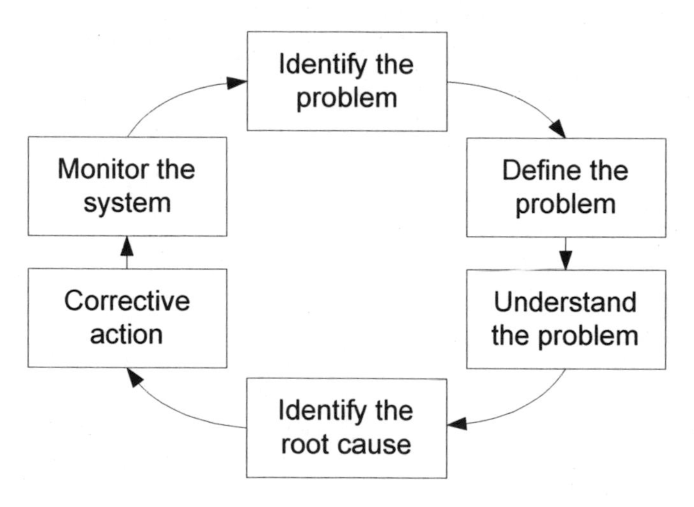

Figure 78 Root cause analysis cycle

'An objective, thorough and disciplined methodology employed to determine the most probable underlying causes of problems and undesired events within an organisation, with the aim of formulating and agreeing corrective actions to at least mitigate, if not eliminate, those causes and so produce significant long term performance improvements.'

Carrying out a root cause analysis

Root cause analysis is not just a problem solving technique. It is an overall approach to the identification, understanding and resolution of underlying causes of under achieved quality in complex organisations.

Root cause analysis is a four-phase process:

- Phase I: Problem identification
- Phase II: Problem description
- Phase III: Cause analysis
- Phase IV: Solution development

Phases I to III need to be carried out by one person or team whilst Phase IV should usually be carried out by a second team. Unlike many quality or TQM initiatives, root cause analysis is often better undertaken, particularly in Phase IV, by the people carrying out the processes following training in the techniques to be used. It is not the preserve of the Quality Manager alone. Like others however, for it to succeed, there must be an acknowledgement by the top management of the organisation that there are problems that need to be addressed and a commitment to providing the access and resources necessary to do so.

Phase I: Problem identification

In order to identify problems, the person or team carrying out the root cause analysis process must have full access to all areas of the organisation, with the freedom to communicate, where necessary, with others outside the organisation. It is also essential that there is complete visibility, i.e. they must be able to see all aspects of the situation with personal bias totally removed. In any process within an organisation, specialists associated with it are inevitably going to view it from their point of view; the manager, production engineer, store manager etc. All these subjective views need to be put aside and the overview clearly seen.

Strategies for fact gathering will include looking at customer complaints, interrogating the accounts including credit records, interviews, workshops etc. The objective is to gather as much information as possible on problems or quality deficiencies. Selection is carried out in the next phase.

Phase II: Problem description

The second phase, carried out by the same person or people conducting the first, is to fully describe the information collected. The criteria for including problems in the analysis need to be fully understood. These will include the use of flowcharts, critical incidents, spider charts, purpose and application matrices and problem understanding checklists.

Phase III: Cause analysis

Once fully described the information needs to be analysed into types. Strategies for analysis are the use of various tools, either separately or in work groups, to establish internal causes, external causes and their separate or combined effects. Root causes also need to be separated from other causes.

Cause analysis tools that may be used are histograms, pareto charts, scatter charts, relation's diagrams and affinity diagrams. Some but not all of these would be used according to their suitability in particular circumstances. Following this the cause and effect stage has been reached and the effects and therefore potential root causes, can be identified. Tools for this are cause and effect charts, matrix diagrams and the "five whys" or the "why, why" chart.

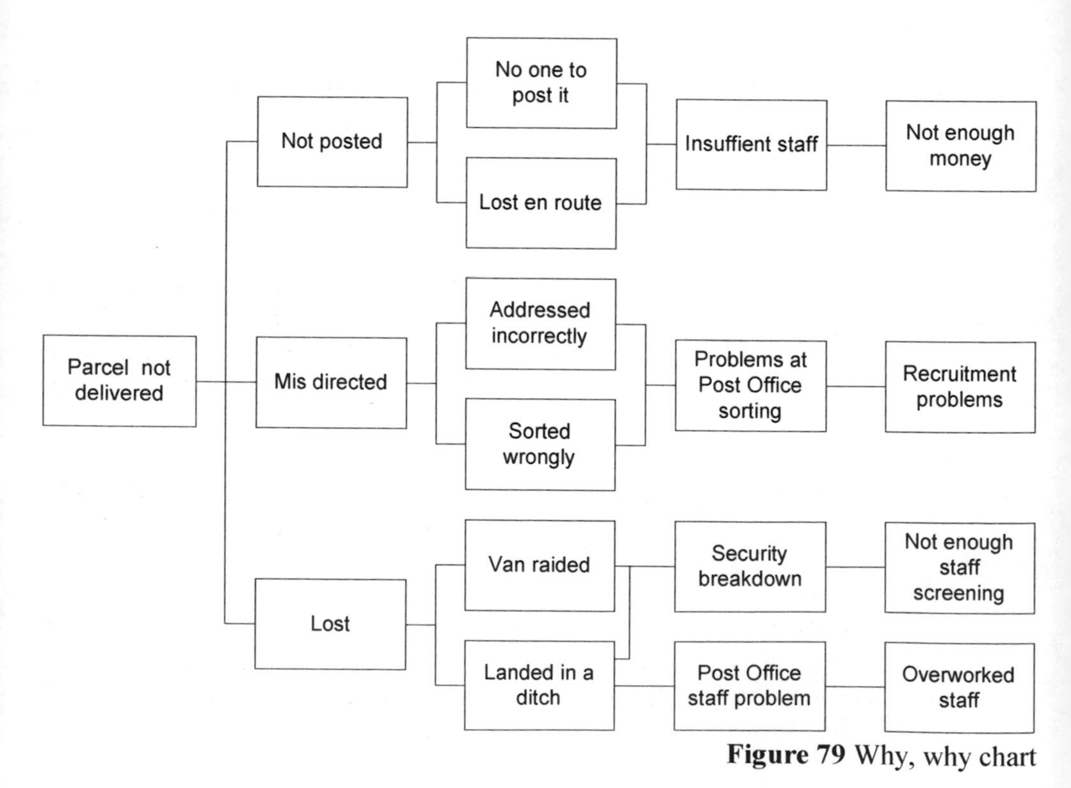

Figure 79 Why, why chart

Once identified problems need to be fully understood and ranked using techniques similar to risk analysis, i.e.

a. Identify the causes.
b. Weight the causes according to occurrence (O) 1 to 4 (where 4 occurs most often).
c. Weight the causes according to severity (S) of consequences 1 to 4 (where 4 produces the most severe consequences).
d. Calculate O x S = index for each cause.
e. List causes according to their indices to give a prioritised action list.

#	**1**	**2**	**3**	**4**
1	1	2	3	4
2	2	4	6	8
3	3	6	9	12
4	4	8	12	16

Severity →

Frequency of Occurrence→

The causes are then addressed in order.

Phase IV: Solution development

The last phase, solution development, is often done by either a different person or team. Having fully identified the problem, the solution may be developed by those who know more about the specific processes involved. Potential solutions need to be developed and presented to the decision makers and the comparative benefits and cost effectiveness of all prevention options shown.

In some circumstances the organisation may not be in control of the root cause. If this is the case then ways may need to be found to either circumvent the cause or to mitigate its effects. This will entirely depend upon the circumstances.

Another point to consider is the difference between interim action and corrective action. Solution of the root cause should result from corrective action that fully addresses the problem. Interim actions may however provide a "quick fix" which needs to be followed up by the former to ensure that the problem does not reoccur.

The last function is to ensure that controls are in place to hold the gains made. They should assure the solution prevents recurrence of the root cause.

Summary

There are a number of proprietary software and training packages available for carrying out root cause analysis, primarily from the United States where the imperative has been health and safety critical organisations, e.g. health and the petrochemical industry. The technique has yet to be applied widely in the UK.

In conclusion, root cause analysis should be the objective and systematic process of gathering and ordering all relevant data about counter quality within an organisation. It should identify the internal causes that have generated or allowed the problem and produce an analysis for decision makers that gives the comparative benefits and cost effectiveness of all prevention options. To accomplish this the analysis methodology must provide visibility of all causes and understanding of the nature of the causal systems they form, together with a way to measure and compare the causal systems and should have a visibility of all internal opportunities for the organisation to control the systems.

SECTION 5 - OPTIMISATION TECHNIQUES

Materials Requirement & Manufacturing Resources Planning

Definitions

MRP	Materials Requirements Planning	A (usually computer based) system which calculates the total material requirements (quantities, time scale) to meet a predetermined set of customer requirements.
MRP II	Manufacturing Resources Planning	A (usually computer based) system which integrates manufacturing data to calculate the total resources required to manufacture a product in specified time scales, in order to meet customer requirements.

Collectively MRP defines the total resources required to manufacture a product, in what time scale and when to order any materials to meet any such time scales. The aim of these systems is to maximise profit and performance by having all the resources planned prior to commencement of a works order and by monitoring its progress throughout the company. As each order (both customer and supplier) is logged it is possible to use this system to keep records of traceability, i.e. which orders were for which jobs, when they came in, if there were any returns etc. There can then be traceability from raw material to finished product, provided the quality of the installed system and database is initially good and is accurately and completely maintained. Then the information it contains includes all the procedures and requirements for manufacture of a given product.

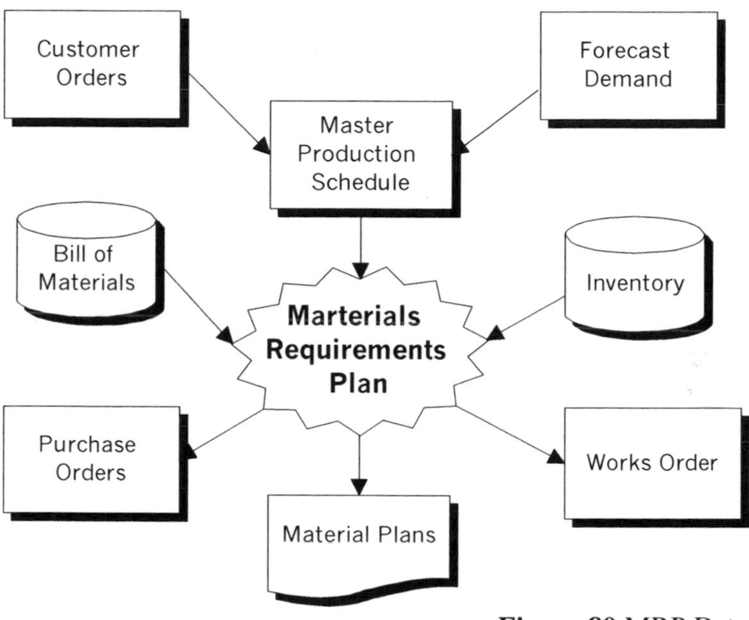

Figure 80 MRP Data

With MRP it is necessary to understand:

- What is the predicted demand for a product, consumables and spares?
- What are the items or bill of materials required to create the product?
- What is the lead time associated with each item?
- What are the current stock holdings?

Following is a typical MRP scenario which is used to explain the MRP process. A vacuum cleaner manufacturer requires 100 type A Vacuum cleaners on week 10. Below is a break down of the order processing requirements.

Firstly it is necessary to understand the Bill of material[26] requirements for the Type A Vacuum Cleaner.

---

26 A list of all the parts (part numbers and quantity) to make one product

Bill of material for vacuum cleaner type A				
Items	**Bill of Material - Quantity per cleaner**	**Lead time (weeks)**	**Source**	
Type A Vacuum cleaner	1	1	MO	Type A comprises Sub assemblies B & C
Sub-assembly B	4	2	MO	Sub assembly B comprises of items D, E & H
Item D	2	1	PO	
Item E	2	3	PO	
Item F	1	4	PO	
Sub-assembly C	1	1	MO	Sub assembly B comprises of items I, J & K
Item G	3	1	PO	
Item H	2	1	PO	
Item I	1	2	PO	
Bag (consumable)	1	1	PO	
Key				
Lead time = set up time + production time + delivery time				
PO = Purchase Order				
MO = Manufacturing Order				

Figure 81 Bill of Materials

The table in **Figure 81** shows the Bill of Materials (sub-assemblies, items and quantities) that go to make up the Vacuum Cleaner Type A. Also identified in the table is the source of those items, for example Sub-assembly B requires a Manufacturing Order (MO) as it is assembled in-house. Alternatively, items D, E & F are purchased and would therefore require a Purchase Order (PO). Information regarding the predicted lead time (the time to obtain the sub-assemblies and items) associated with each part is also detailed. Note that Sub-assembly B is made from items D, E & F. Similarly, Sub-assembly C is made from items G, H & I.

Demand Schedule			
Demand	Week number	Quantity	
Vacuum cleaner demand	10	100	Type A
Vacuum cleaner spares	8	20	Sub-assembly B and item D
Vacuum cleaner consumables	10	1000	Bag (consumable)
Vacuum cleaner consumables	6	1000	Bag (consumable)

Figure 82 Demand Schedule

The table in **Figure 82** shows the predicted demand for the Type A Vacuum Cleaner for the forthcoming month. Also included are the spares and likely consumables (cleaner bags) requirements. From this data the MRP schedule can now be developed.

MRP Schedule		Qty per Vacuum cleaner	Lead time weeks	Date (Week number)									
				1	2	3	4	5	6	7	8	9	10
Type A Vacuum cleaner	Requirement	1											100
	Order Placement		1									100	
Sub-assembly B	Requirement	4									20	400	
	Order Placement		2						20	400			
Item D	Requirement	2							40	200			
	Order Placement		1					40	200				
Item E	Requirement	2							40	200		BoM Expanded	
	Order Placement		3			40	200						
Item F	Requirement	1							20	100			
	Order Placement		4		20	100							
Sub-assembly C	Requirement	1										100	
	Order Placement		1								100		
Item G	Requirement	3									300		
	Order Placement		1							300			
Item H	Requirement	2									20+200		
	Order Placement		1							220			
Item I	Requirement	1									100		
	Order Placement		2						100				
Bag (consumable)	Requirement	1		Spares					1000			100	1000
	Order Placement		1					1000			100	1000	

Figure 83 MRP Schedule

The table in **Figure 83** shows the expansion of the Bill of materials and the Demand Schedule into the MRP schedule. In order to achieve the demanded delivery times, e.g. 100 Type A Vacuum cleaners in week 10 then the order time need to be determined. There is a lead time between order placement and receipt of the item or sub-assembly. It takes a lead time of 1 week to assemble the Type A Vacuum cleaner therefore the order placement needs to be in week 9. Type A Vacuum cleaners comprise Sub-assemblies B & C which have a lead time of 2 and 1 weeks respectively. Also there are 2 Sub-assembly (B & C) to each Type A Vacuum cleaner. Consequently, orders for Sub-assembly B need to be made in week 7 and week 8 for Sub-assembly C. Also the demand for spares and consumable needs to be planned. See 'Spares' and the row 'Bag (consumable)'in **Figure 83**. In this way a complete materials plan can be developed. The use of a computer can now be seen as important. Not only can a computer aid the calculation, but also the effects of changes in demand and forecasts on the material's plan can be readily simulated. Note, this is a relatively simple set of requirements, if a complicated type of Vacuum cleaner, with a more extensive Bill of materials were contemplated, then the calculations would quickly become very complex and a computer almost essential. Also this table has not included the additional complexity of current stores stocks, work in progress, etc.

There are other issues to be considered when placing orders - what s the most economic batch size?:

- Cost of the order process
- Discounts of quantities ordered
- Inventory costs
- Change over times

MRP makes "Time-phased requirement planing" possible for any of the organisation's products or parts. This MRP data can also form part of capacity planning, determining the capacity requirement for various processes and tasks. It should now be seen how MRP plays a central role in material planning and control, ensuring that demand is fulfilled, in the most economic manner. It converts the bill of materials and demand schedules into a coherent plan detailing the precise timing requirements. MRP can be integrated into the shop floor and procurement systems and is therefore a suitable starting point for organisations to review and overhaul their production control systems specifically with a view to computerisation.

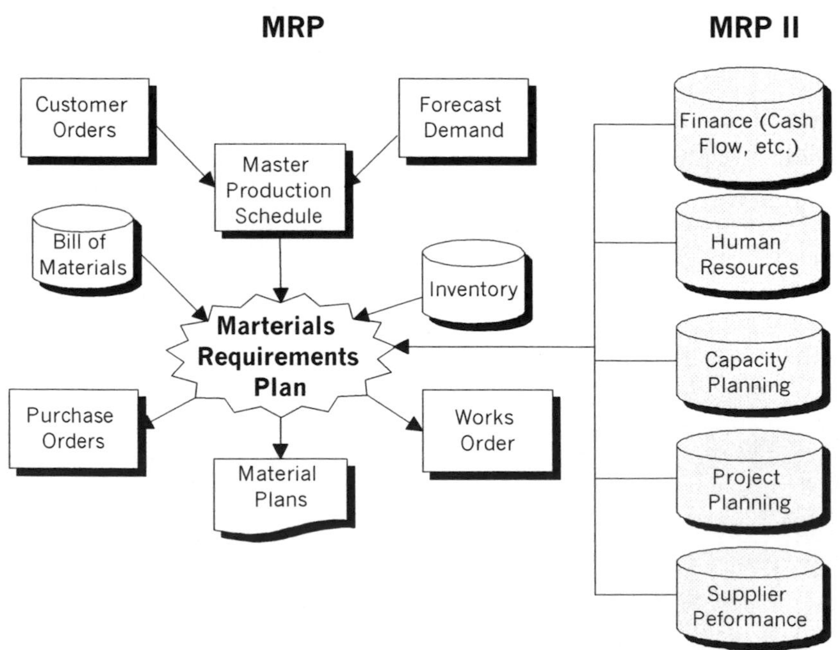

Figure 84 MRP II Data

It may have been noted that the MRP system described assumes infinite resources. It does not take into consideration other current production utilisation and is highly dependent on the accuracy of fixed data such as lead time. It does not take into account issues such as resources, material flow, financial details such as economic batch sizing and capacity planning. These issues and many more were the reason for the more powerful MRP system, MRP II, 'Manufacturing Resources Planning' of which Oliver Wight was one of the early pioneers.

So what are the Quality Assurance implications of MRP? Well they become issues of quality, quantity and time. Ensuring that exactly the right quantity and quality of items arrive at precisely the right time. The tool and technique listed below (details of which can be found in this book) need to be considered if the MRP is to work successfully. Associated with each tools and techniques is the process where the technique would most likely be applied. At the end of the tables there are some typical target performance measures (SLAs for each process).

	Order processing	**Product development**	**Purchasing**	**Production (Including Inventory)**	**Support**
Just in Time - to ensure on quantity and time delivery	X		X	X	
Change over time - to minimise and facilitate smaller economical batch quantities				X	
Process Capabilities - to ensure processes are capable of delivering to the required quality with (zero) rejects and defects			X	X	
Statistical Process Control - to monitor and maintain the required quality standard consistently batch after batch				X	
Risk analysis - to identify any potential process weaknesses and take preventive action eliminating or mitigating the effects of any failure.	X	X	X	X	
Total Productive Maintenance - to avoid or eliminate any process delays or stoppages which would affect the ability to deliver on time				X	
Requirements predictions - to give greater confidence and improve the accuracy of the demand predictions - See ISO9001 Customer Related Processes and Customer Satisfaction	X				X

	Order processing	**Product development**	**Purchasing**	**Production (Including Inventory)**	**Support**
Stock ordering system - to minimise stock holding and shorten lead time - See Kanban			X	X	
Supplier capability and integration - to ensure the procurement process deliverables are to the right quality, quantity and provided on time - See Supplier Quality Assurance			X		
Service Level Agreements (SLAs) or Key Performance Indicators (KPIs)	Accuracy of predictions and forecasts	Accuracy of data base e.g. Bill of materials, Minimise change	Time to place order, Time to receive goods, Number of defects.	Inventory accuracy, Change over time, Batch qualities, Defects, Delivery by value, Delivery by time,	Customer feedback, Spares and consumables requirements

Just in Time

Introduction

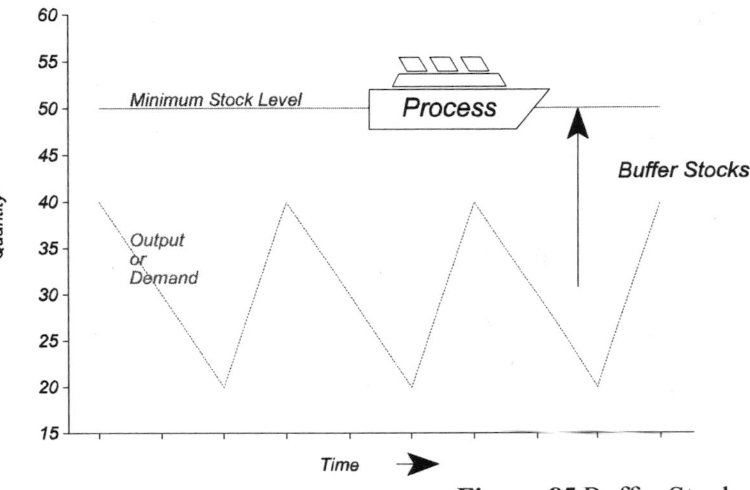

Figure 85 Buffer Stocks

Just in Time (JIT) is an approach to ensuring that the customer's requirements in terms of quality and service (deliveries and quantities) are exactly matched. The customer receives the precise quantities required (no more no less) at the time required. It involves the implementation of a programme that affects all aspects of the product or service, from the purchase of raw material through to on time delivery. Many of the techniques described in TQM can be usefully employed in the introduction of JIT. JIT by its very nature has a significant effect on buffer stocks, work in-progress etc, reducing these stock levels to a minimum. The consequence of this stock reduction is where allowances could be made for late or faulty deliveries by the use of the "slack in the system," using the buffer stocks to solve inefficiencies in the system; post JIT these buffer stocks are no longer available, allowances can no longer be made for late or faulty deliveries.

Figure 85 shows how the process can negotiate the vagaries of the market requirements in terms of output and demand by holding excessively high, inefficient and expensive stock levels. The process and output can be maintained by holding excessive buffer stocks which can be used to overcome system problems.

Figure 86 shows that the implementation of JIT should hopefully achieve a reduction of stock levels. If the system problems are not resolved, then with the reduction of these stock levels the inefficiencies in the system will be exposed and the process, as a consequence, will suffer stoppages and material shortages.

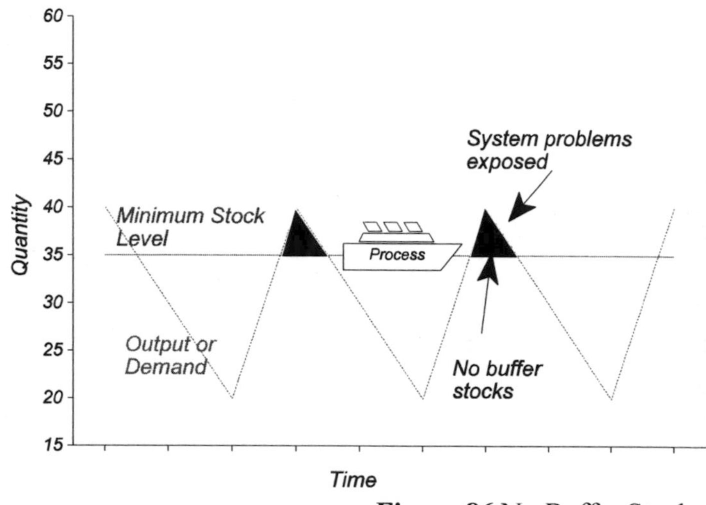

Figure 86 No Buffer Stocks

JIT needs to focus not only on how to reduce stock levels but also on how to resolve problems of inefficiency within the system.

The concepts and philosophy behind JIT includes:

Kanban - This is the method employed to pull work through the system rather than the usual approach of pushing the work through the system. Often the phrase is heard from a Manager, "I am the highest paid progress chaser in this company," meaning that much of management time is spent chasing (pushing) work through the system, as opposed to being pulled through the organisation by a system of Kanban Cards. Kanban Cards are used by the customer to let the supplier know more material is required (internal as well as external customers). The objective is that only the absolute minimum required quantities are made and that the operator is involved in progressing the work through the organisation. The Kanban card is the trigger to release work and work cannot be released unless a Kanban Card is received. Work travels in one direction, Kanban Cards in the other.

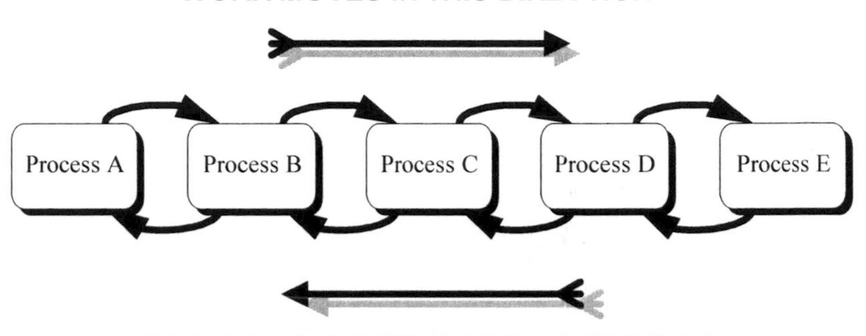

Figure 87 Kanban Cards

The Kanban Card can be attached to the container that carries the work. The card will contain the following information: Quantity, Identification, Inspection Status (on leaving), Source and Destination. Often the quantities requested will be much smaller than usually expected, in order to maintain productivity at the correct level the process switch-over times will need to be radically improved.

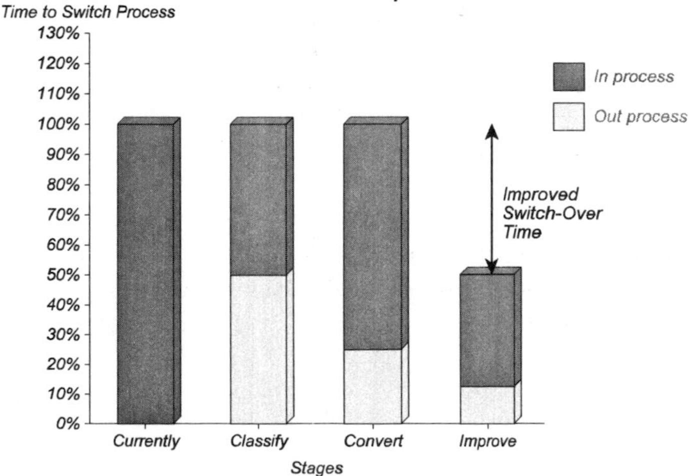

Figure 88 Process Switch-Over Improvement

Process Switch-Over Improvement - One of the major factors which limit the product variety is the time it takes to change from producing one product to another. Another consequence of larger batch quantities can be, if there are any quality problems these may not become apparent until the batch has labouriously and finally reached the assembly stage. If smaller batch quantities could be employed as a consequence of quicker process switch-over, then the time to discover a quality problem would be greatly reduced. JIT, because it works on much smaller batch sizes, means that any inefficiencies or bottle necks in the system are quickly exposed.

The procedure (see **Figure 88**) that can be followed in improving process switch over times can be:

To investigate the CURRENT situation, Pareto Analysis could be usefully employed to determine which processes take the longest to changeover and what factors have the greatest influence on the changeover time. **Figure 88** shows the current situation to be that 100% of the time is spent completing tasks while the process has stopped. Some of these tasks could be performed while the process is running. The tasks could be; obtaining material, equipment, labour, work instructions, stopping the process, changing the equipment over (i.e. removing the existing equipment and installing the following equipment) and restarting the process. Together with detailing the correct or approved changeover method.

Having established the current situation regarding the factors involved, in-process switch-over need to be CLASSIFIED into out-process (activities that could be performed while the process has stopped) and in-process (activities that could be performed while the process is running). Analysis of what actually happens as opposed to what should happen may be appropriate. **Figure 88** shows the classified (actual) situation to be, 50% activities with the process stopped (out-process), 50% of the activities with the process running (in-process). The actual situation could be determined by the use of activity sampling.

The out process activities now need CONVERTING into in process activities so that the process waiting time is minimised. **Figure 88** indicates 30% more of the activities could be or should be performed while the process is running.

Finally, the overall activities can be analysed to determine if it is possible to complete the process switch-over more effectively and efficiently; IMPROVING the overall process switch-over time. This may involve closely examining the logistics associated with the process switch-over, involving the coordination and management of activities, design of equipment for ease of switch-over, fool-proofing the equipment etc. **Figure 88** indicates a further 50% saving, reducing the out-process time still further.

If the group in charge of process switch-over were told to achieve a 300% improvement in switch-over time, it may be interpreted as needing to work 300% harder. What the above example suggests is that they work 300% smarter. ***Work smarter, not harder!***

Supplier Development - Mass production industries used to vertically integrate the supplier into their own manufacturing facilities by buying the supplier. Today it is considered better to develop a continuous process/supplier improvement relationship with supplier, where the supplier is seen as a key element in the overall process, thereby ensuring that the supplier completely understands the customer's particular requirements and needs. The section Supplier Quality Assurance, describes some of the techniques which can be usefully employed.

Some other techniques involved in JIT are: Flow Charting, Continuous Improvement, Material Planning Resources (all of these techniques are described in other sections of this book).

Total Productive Maintenance and Overall Equipment Effectiveness

i) Introduction to Total Productive Maintenance
ii) Definitions associate with Total Productive Maintenance
iii) Implementation of Total Productive Maintenance
iv) Evaluation of Overall Equipment Effectiveness

Total Productive Maintenance

Introduction to Total Productive Maintenance

Total Productive Maintenance (TPM) is an approach very similar to Total Quality Management in its philosophy including principles such as:

i) Management commitment and constancy of purpose (it takes a long time to fully implement)
ii) Measurement, benchmarking and improvement in performance (in this case maintenance rather than quality)
iii) Team building
iv) Involve all
v) Use established problem solving tools

Total Productive Maintenance Aims & Objectives:

i) Zero unplanned downtime
ii) Zero performance loss
iii) Zero defects
iv) Zero energy loss
v) Zero accidents

Maintenance is a non-value adding, non revenue earning activity but the lack of it will fairly soon affect income and the ability to satisfactorily complete tasks on time. It is because it is seen as non revenue earning that often there is a lack of attention to this area and the issues associated with breakdown and downtime. Traditionally, maintenance is the province of the maintenance department, operators have no role to play other than to report a problem or breakdown. TPM is about changing these attitudes. On a maintenance evolutionary scale, maintenance and the need for it has always been necessary. The next step in maintenance evolution is planned preventive maintenance (ppm) which has been around for about 40 years. TPM is the next natural evolution and extension of ppm.

Planned preventive maintenance involved setting maintenance schedules for machines and equipment, writing procedures to be rigorously adhered to and records maintained. This approach has been successful and reduced breakdown problems but did not prevent them all together and did not totally involve all people associated with the process. I.e. ppm and maintenance still belonged to the Maintenance Department.

TPM means bringing maintenance into the production[27] process such that it becomes integrated and part of the natural activities associated with producing the process deliverables and not some independent "bolt on" activity. Maintenance therefore is just another aspect of the production process activities and not something that happens when there is an emergency or there happens to be a break in production.

TPM grew out of Deming's and other Quality Philosopher's (Ishikawa's) work on Total Quality Management (TQM), with techniques such as statistical quality control and approaches like Quality Circles and Root Cause Analysis, establishing that many quality problems had their causes rooted in equipment reliability and repeatability. Consequently, improving equipment reliability became a focus of attention, with the application of techniques such as 5Ss and Poka-yoke.

The actual origins of the term "Total Productive Maintenance" is unclear with claims being made in both Japan (Nipondenso) and the USA.

Definitions associate with Total Productive Maintenance:

i) Maintenance: Work undertaken to support, keep or restore equipment and facilities to a defined standard.

ii) Planned Maintenance: Pre-planned, scheduled work including controls, methods and records designed to avoid equipment and facility failure.

iii) Preventive Maintenance: Pre-planned, scheduled work including controls, methods and records designed to prevent equipment and facility failure. It includes both running and shut-down maintenance.

iv) Corrective Maintenance: When equipment and facilities have deteriorated below or failed to meet a satisfactory standard, corrective, shut down or breakdown maintenance work is undertaken to return equipment and facility to a satisfactory standard.

v) Running Maintenance: Work performed while the equipment or facility is in operation or use.

vi) Shut-down Maintenance: Work performed while the equipment or facility is out of operation or use.

---

[27] "Production" does not mean that this approach is only manufacturing based. The word production should be read in its widest context including any processes that rely on equipment.

vii) Breakdown Maintenance: Work performed after a failure, but which had been predicted as a potential problem and contingency arrangements had been made possibly in the form of materials, labour and equipment.

Implementation of Total Productive Maintenance (See **figure 89**)

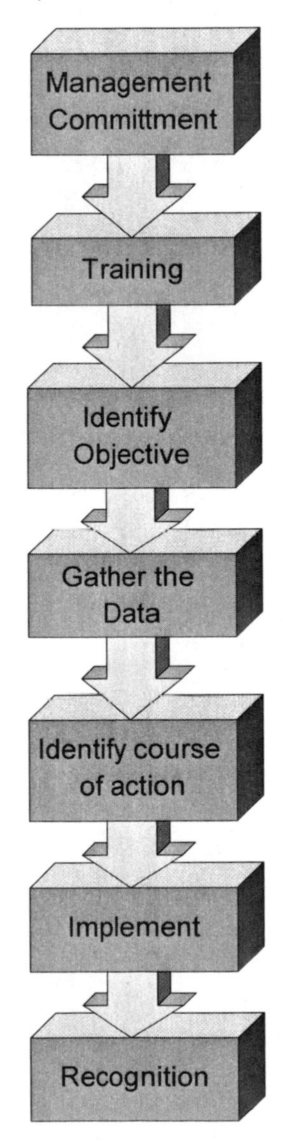

Figure 89 TPM Implementation

1. Management Commitment: As with any (quality) improvement initiative the first stage is always commitment, not only by management but also by all staff (maintenance, operators, supervisors, etc.) associated with the smooth operation of the process. These staff are often known as stakeholders, each with their own particular agenda, role and responsibility and are part of the team who are concerned with the smooth operation and quality of the process. Initially all of these people need to be convinced of the benefits to be gained in embarking on a TPM initiative. Having established some clear terms of reference, authority, scope and objective for the TPM initiative, the TPM coordinator (who is the person who facilitates the programme) needs to identify the TPM team from the process stakeholders[28].

2. *Training*: The TPM team will require training in team building, principles of TPM, data recording, and presentation, problem solving techniques, Benchmarking, Poka-Yoke, etc.

3. *Identify a team objective*: The TPM Team needs to agree the problems or issues that they would like to resolve first 'pick where the berries are sweetest'.

   In one food processing plant the filling machine, filling cartons with soup was selected. This was because this machine was key to the continuity, of the overall factory operation.

4. *Gather the Data*: Initially gather and analyse data regarding the current performance of the plant or facility situation.

---

28 Parallels are immediately obvious with Quality Circles

In the case of the filling machine this was studied in great detail by the team, recording productive and non-productive time and breaking the non-productive time down into its various categories. Visits were made to other non competing plants using similar equipment, to determine their performance and if more productive methods were available. The objective being to benchmark the existing plant performance against other organisations. The next stage was to evaluate this information and to determine what was the most appropriate course of action for the organisation's own filling machine.

5. *Identify a course of action*: This work involved establishing what immediate preventive maintenance work was necessary; cleaning, adjustment, repair, replace, etc. What preventive maintenance scheme could be implemented (instructions, check lists, frequency, records) and what training (operators, supervisors, etc.) would be required? Extending, in certain cases, the operator's responsibilities into maintaining equipment.

6. *Implement the predetermined course of action*: A plan of action needs to be established that implements the above preventive maintenance scheme including responsibilities, time scales and reviews.

7. Recognition; A presentation of the TPM Team's achievement and programme is given to management and selected staff, to show the successful results of the exercise - what was the previous plant performance and what is the new performance. Determine what next? What is the next process or machine that would be subjected to this TPM approach by this now highly skilled and experienced TPM team and how to pass this new found knowledge and skill to other TPM teams.

There are many examples of the successful implementation of the TPM approach, including organisations such as Ford, Kodak and Allen Bradley with the following reported results:

- i) Programmes costing some £3M have provided savings of some £10M,
- ii) Significantly reduced change over time
- iii) Improved productivity of up to 80%
- iv) Down time reduced by some 50%
- v) Improved utilisation and plant availability, reducing the need for outsourcing or buying or leasing addition plant capacity
- vi) Reduced spares and stock inventory (as part of the Just in Time programme)

The biggest danger is that the programme becomes just another flavour of the month or as Deming would say, 'management lack constancy of purpose' and consequently the programme fails through lack of attention and active participation.

Overall Equipment Effectiveness (OEM)

'If you do not measure it, you cannot improve it'

In order to establish the effectiveness of the TPM programme it is necessary to measure performance. Usually organisations have some kind of performance measurement system on their equipment that measures criteria such as; quantities, operating time, cycle time, etc. These criteria are fine but they are measures of equipment output and not necessarily capability which is what TPM requires. I.e how much more could we achieve from this equipment? How effective is this equipment - overall equipment effectiveness?

Overall Equipment Effectiveness (OEE) provides a metric or measure to continually monitor how effectively the equipment is performing and where the losses are with the potential for improvement.

Performance Criteria: At this stage it is necessary to detail what is expected of the equipment. Not the design specification but what is expected in terms of; output, throughput or volume, physical properties (both attribute and variable) the equipment output must achieve (see Statistical Process control), operating characteristics that are important to the equipment user, the safety considerations, the availability, etc.

To assist analysis, the factors associated with establishing the performance criteria can be broken down into; Inspection, Measurement or Demonstration. Ie.:

a) Criteria that require *inspection* - often a visual check to confirm availability and condition. Sometimes the operational aspects of the equipment.
b) Criteria that require *measurement* - key performance factors that can be appraised e.g. output rate, reliability, accuracy etc. Often the functional or safety aspects of the equipment.
c) Criteria that require *demonstration* - often the measured criteria but demonstrated during a trial, test or commissioning.

Performance Targets: Having established the performance criteria the target associated with these criteria needs to be determined. In the case of variable criteria this could be a measured value possibly plotted on a control chart.

Below is an example of a Schedule of Performance Criteria - note that these figures are only an example and in some industries these values may be unacceptable (either too tight or loose). The criteria availability, performance and quality may not be adequate and could be developed to include other measures of process performance e.g. service support.

For our facility a target for OEE needs to be established. The requirements being that the facility will achieve an OEE of 95%.

This being the sum of the ① Availability x ② Performance Rate x ③ Quality of Products Rate giving the Overall Equipment Effectiveness targeted at 95%.

Each of these elements (availability, performance and quality are calculated in the manner detailed in the following in example. Note, no one element (Availability, Performance Rate or Quality of Products) should contribute more than 50% to the overall figure of 95%.

Example of the calculation for the overall efficiency of the Plant

①Availability

$$Availability = \frac{Total\ Operating\ Time - Down\ Time}{Total\ Available\ time} \times 100$$

Example

$$97\% = \frac{400mins - 8mins}{400mins} \times 100$$

Operating Time is defined as loading, operating and unloading time including any maintenance or repair work. Down time is defined as time spent on maintenance or repairing work.

② Performance Rate

$$Performance\ Rate = \frac{Required\ or\ Specificied\ Cycle\ Time}{Actual\ Cycle\ Time} \times 100$$

Example

$$96\% = \frac{2.0\ Units\ per\ min}{2.083\ Units\ per\ min} \times 100$$

Required Cycle time is defined in the specification.
Actual Cycle time is calculated as the total number of units processed over a predetermined time divided by the total operating time. Note, if the figure is greater than 100% i.e. the cycle time is greater than specifie,d then the figure used in the overall calculation will be 100%.

③ Quality of Products

$$Quality\ Rate = \frac{Total\ number\ of\ units\ processed\ -\ Number\ of\ defect\ units}{Total\ number\ of\ units\ processed} \times 100$$

Example

$$99\% = \frac{10000\ units\ -\ 100\ defects}{10000\ Units} \times 100$$

A defect unit is defined as a unit that does not meet the agreed acceptance criteria.

Overall Equipment Effectiveness

$$OEE = Availability \times Performance\ Rate \times Quality\ rate$$

Example

$$OEE = 92\% = 97\%\ x\ 96\%\ x\ 99\%$$

The principal goal of measuring OEE is to improve the effectiveness of equipment. Since one of the major influences on equipment effectiveness is the equipment operator (possibly more than any other person). It is appropriate for them to have a significant role and responsibility in monitoring OEE, including the planning and implementing of any equipment improvements aimed at reducing lost effectiveness and waste.

Some means of gaining operator involvement include:

- Training and education programme about the equipment
- Focussing attention on the losses
- Developing the feeling of ownership of the equipment

Supervisors and Managers can help by:

- Obtaining operating and analysing data to calculate the OEE
- Feeding back to the operators and others involved in equipment performance
- Encouraging improvement

Exercises:

1. What are the key aims of a TPM programme?

   Answer: No unplanned downtime, no speed loss, no defects, no energy loss, no accidents.

2. What are the benefits to be derived from a TPM initiative?

   Answer: Cost savings, reduced change over time, improved productivity, down time reduced, improved utilisation and plant availability, reduced spares and stock inventory.

3. Define the following:
   a. Maintenance:
   b. Planned Maintenance:
   c. Preventive Maintenance:
   d. Corrective Maintenance:
   e. Running Maintenance:
   f. Shut-down Maintenance:
   g. Breakdown Maintenance:

   Answer: See TPM definitions in text.

4. List the sequence of events in a TPM programme.

   Answer: Management commitment, training the tpm team, identify a team objective, gather the data, identify a course of action, implement the predetermined course of action, recognition.

5. Explain why TPM programmes may fail?

   Answer: The group was not from the correct disciplines. The group was not allowed to choose their own problem. The group had to meet in their own time. Not all the information had been collected or was inaccurate etc. Lack of active management participation. No buy in from management or staff. Lack of group motivation. Lack of implementation of solution, impractical or too expensive solutions.

SECTION 6 - SUPPLIERS AND DISTRIBUTION

Supplier Quality Assurance

"For the want of a nail a horseshoe was lost,
For the want of a horseshoe a horse was lost,
For the want of a horse a rider was lost,
For the want of a rider a battle was lost,
For the want of a battle a kingdom was lost."

There is a wide range of approaches and techniques that can be adopted in controlling suppliers (Supplier Quality Assurance) from the fairly basic approach as described in 'ISO 9001 Purchasing' to a comprehensive approach, such as QS 9000 - the Automotive Quality System Standard. Both approaches have features that make them attractive to buyers; the simple approach will be less demanding in terms of resource but may be considered too vague and not sufficiently product or service specific.

A Basic Purchasing Control System

a) *Assessment of suppliers*

This could include:

i) An audit against the requirements of a recognised Quality Assurance System Standard like ISO 9001 and assessing the supplier's ability to meet the customer's requirements.

ii) Selection of the supplier from an approved list of suppliers. This may be an internally created list produced as a result of Vendor Rating or from commercially available lists of companies of assessed capability provided by organisations such as BSI or the Department of Trade & Industry.

iii) Sending questionnaires to existing or prospective suppliers requesting information about the supplier's Quality Assurance Management System.

iv) Examination of the supplier's historical performance by the use of techniques such as Vendor Rating.

Vendor Rating: Views on supplier's performance can be very subjective when making a decision on the selection of a supplier. The supplier may be selected on the basis of one person's judgement of a particular supplier's performance. This judgement may be on the basis of price alone. Price alone is not a good criteria on which to place an order. Many organisations would willingly (and do) pay a price premium for supplies that are to the correct quality and delivered on time. In fact studies have shown that the customer is willing to pay up to a 30% price premium if the perceived quality standard is higher than the competitors.

There are a number of factors which may be considered other than price alone, although price does need to be included when making a judgement on supplier's performance. These factors can include:

Price — The rating needs to include price as a factor but because there are various types of suppliers (e.g. suppliers of apples and suppliers of pears) comparing the price of apples with the price of pears is not appropriate. Also, often the items are obtained from a single source so comparing different suppliers on the basis of price is impossible. One way of overcoming the problem of comparing suppliers with suppliers can be to monitor changes in price from the original order price to current order price.

On time Delivery — Number of deliveries on time against the number of late deliveries.

Quality

i) The number of batches rejected against the number of orders accepted (this can include any subsequent problems found with deliveries at a later date).
ii) The results of any external assessment by giving the supplier a rating on a scale from zero - poor, to ten - excellent.

Service — A subjective judgement on the supplier's ability to react to problems (quality, schedule changes, technical support etc.). This may require discussion with buyers and engineers to determine the quality of service provided using a rating scale of zero - poor, to ten - excellent.

Each of these factors needs to be given a weighting for example:

Price 30%
Delivery 20%
Quality 30% (if no audit rating figure)
15% for rejects + 15% for external audit rating (the audit rating is a numerical interpretation of the results of an external audit)
Service 20%

Note: This weighting may need to vary for different industries.

Table 34 An example of Vendor Rating Analysis

Factor	W'ghting	Formula	Supplier A	Supplier B
Price	30%	Original Price * 30% Current Price	10*30%=25 12	12*30%=24 15
Delivery	20%	On time delivery * 20% Total no. of Deliveries	54*20%=18 60	50*20%=20 50
Quality	30%	No of batches accepted * 15% Total no of batches + Audit Rating * 15%	32*15=8 60 + 6*15=9 10	45*30=27 50 (No audit)
Service	20%	Service Rating * 20%	5*20=10 10	9*20=18 10
Rating	100%		70	89

It is important to remember to keep the analysis relatively simple as the Vendor Rating is only a guide to the supplier's performance and does not replace communication, discussion and generally working with the supplier towards the common objective of improving the overall quality performance.

b) *Purchase Order*

Ensuring that the Purchase Order contains all necessary information for the supplier to satisfactorily fulfil the customer's requirements.

The order could contain:

Identification, description and technical (drawing specification etc.) information.
Any Inspection and Test criteria (including certification) or Quality Standards to be applied.
Delivery instructions.
Review of the order (checking and approval).

c) *Goods Receiving Inspection (GRI):*

Almost all organisations perform some form of GRI. It may take the form of a complete inspection and test of the items received against a specification, possibly employing a sampling scheme such as BS 6001. Alternatively, GRI may consist of a check only on quantity, documentation, identification and damage.

Although it may be considered important to perform a dimensional or functional inspection or test at the Goods Receiving stage, the decision to carry out a formal GRI requires careful consideration. For example, take a typical company, say they receive one thousand different batches per month, containing on average one thousand components, each component may have approximately twenty different features that could be checked. If all components are checked, then the number of checks will be:

> 1000 different batches per month * 1000 components per batch * 20 features per component
> = 20,000,000 features to be checked per month - (This will obviously require a considerable inspection resource)

Due to the number of checks involved the organisation may decide:

- Not to check every batch or type, but who decides which batch to check, the inspector?
- Not to check 100%, this can be reduced by sampling (BS6001) but there are a number of risks with sampling.
- Not to check all the different features on an item - only the key features, but again who decides what a key feature is, the inspector?

Say the above gives a 1000% reduction giving 20,000 features per month to be checked, even at one minute per feature this is still approximately two inspectors' work per month. Is it any wonder that organisations are often complaining that GRI does not stop poor quality entering the factory?

The above basic approach to Purchasing Control may be considered inadequate when considering large orders for one off contracts or for high volume supplies. In these circumstances other more comprehensive approaches may be appropriate. Many large organisations produce their own “supplier quality assurance standard”. Often these are based on ISO 9001 interpreted for the specific, individual industry needs and requirements. Organisations defining a suitable and appropriate supplier quality standard and providing a not inconsiderable resource to control the suppliers is neither usual or surprising, particularly when considering, often 60 to 70% of the total manufacturing cost stem from the purchased goods and services. Discussed are two approaches one for the Aerospace industry standard AS 9100 and one for the automotive industry standard QS 9000.

Aerospace - AS 9100 is the model for quality assurance in design, development, production, installation and servicing. The standard is supported by Boeing and most of the key European aerospace companies. The standard is based on ISO9001:1994 which clarifies and adds a number of key requirements such as:

- Configuration management (A more comprehensive version of change control that embraces issues such as the effect on the performance of associated component, field and store stocks etc.)
- First article inspection (Details regarding the quality performance of the first item produced)
- Authorised signatures (Control of Inspector stamps)

Automotive - QS 9000 and ISO TS 16949. These are the standards developed and adopted by Chrysler, Ford, General Motors and a number of automotive manufacturers. This standard replaces Chrysler's - "Suppliers Quality Assurance Manual", Ford's - "Q101" and General Motor's - "Target for Excellence". The QS 9000 and ISO TS 16949 standards are based on an interpretation of ISO 9001 for the Automotive Industry, with additional elements for sector (automotive) and customer's specific needs. The sector specific requirements include:

- Product Approval Process
- Continuous Improvement
- Process Capabilities

This standard may be considered only applicable for the Automotive industries - that would be rather short sighted. While this standard is aimed at volume suppliers, it is equally applicable to one off high cost projects. The standard also provides an invaluable insight into how influential customers view supplier quality assurance.

A Supplier Quality Assurance System

Introduction

Although there are numerous approaches that can be adopted regarding supplier quality assurance (SQA), the approach outlined below is initially fairly general but the latter section concentrates on one influential supplier quality assurance standard, namely QS 9000. Whilst QS 9000 is automotive based it has many applications in other industries as well.

Possibly the typical stages in managing the supply chain are:

a. analysing the requirements
b. supplier selection & management
c. market testing and tendering
d. negotiating
e. supplier partnerships
f. cost reduction. See page 273 and Quality Operating System

Analysing the Requirements: The objective of this stage is to collate, analyse and prioritise all the key information relevant to the product or service being purchased. This can include the methods by which the purchase order or tender specification is established and agreed. It may also be appropriate to establish procurement policy with regard to a quality standard to be employed. "We only buy from companies with a recognised Quality Management System e.g ISO 9001". Alternatively, the organisation may devise their own procurement QMS, e.g Boeing D1-9000. The organisation, as part of a trade association, could agree their own procurement QMS, e.g Automotive - QS 9000, Health - Guide to Good Manufacturing or Laboratory Practice or develop an industry standard or Technical Specification, e.g. Automotive - ISO TS 16949 or Software - ISO 9000-3. Invoking these standards in the contract or tendering document is one element of quality assuring the procurement process. It gives the buyer powerful rights even, in certain circumstances, the right of entry to investigate the supplier testing activities. An additional way is to include TCATs - Test Commissioning and Acceptance Trials in the Tendering document - particularly useful in the case of large capital cost purchases.

Supplier selection & management: Selection of the supplier can be assisted through the use of supplier questionnaires to determine initial suitability. Use of a vendor rating system can also help to ensure that the supplier's historical performance is satisfactory. Visits and quality surveys can be employed to establish supplier suitability. However, there can be serious short comings with vendor quality surveys. A study carried out by Mr. E H Brainard in *"Quality Assurance"* gave the results shown in the graph, Vendor Surveys. Of 151 vendors, the vendor survey correctly predicted 77 vendors, i.e. 26 vendors predicted good were good and 51 vendors predicted bad were bad. But, more seriously, 74 vendors were wrongly predicted. (Either predicted good and actual performance was bad or predicted bad and actual performance was good.) This may confirm what many people have always thought, that vendor surveys are not good at predicting vendor performance and should not be solely relied on.

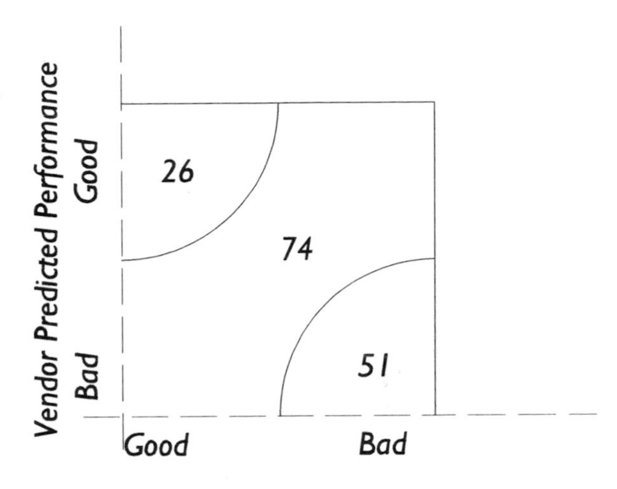

Figure 94 Vendor Surveys

Supply positioning is a technique which can assist in ensuring that the buyers concentrate effort on the *important* suppliers and that the buyer's organisation is not exposed to any risks associated with any particular supplier. To determine the importance of any particular supplier, Pareto analysis (probably completed on the basis of cost) can be employed to identify the important few suppliers. Resource and time can then be spent concentrating on the important few suppliers rather than the trivial many. One of the problems with this approach is that cost is not the only criteria. Some purchased products and services, while cheap, can have a disproportionate effect (if they break down) on the buyer's organisation. "For the want of a nail....." Also the Pareto analysis approach does not take into consideration the implications of single or multi suppliers.

If, rather than a Pareto analysis, a supplier position analysis is performed, then a much clearer picture of the key suppliers emerges (see **Figure 95**). The supplier position analysis is completed by plotting risk of exposure against relative cost. Relative cost is the cost expenditure per annum, not the individual item cost, which can be misleading. The buying objectives for the suppliers in **Figure 95** would seem to be:

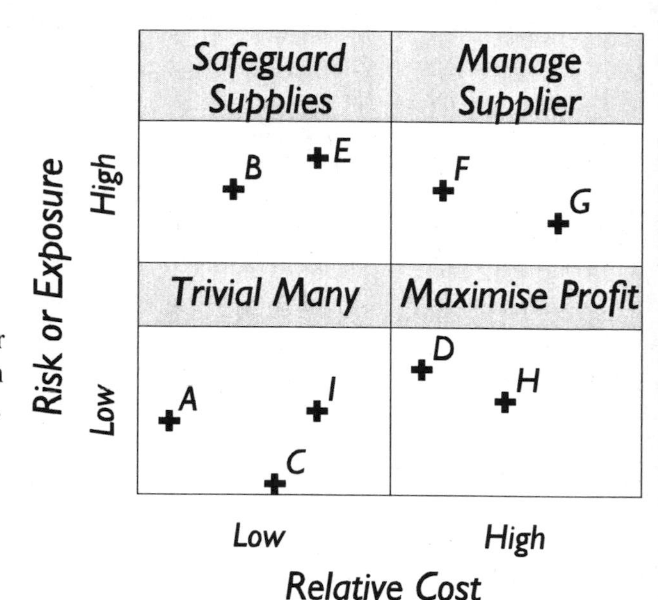

Figure 95 Supplier Position Analysis

For Suppliers B & E, although the relative cost is low, the risks are high and alternative sources of supply may be needed to safeguard supplies.

For Suppliers F & G, both the relative cost and the risks are high, these suppliers will need careful management.

For Suppliers D & H, the risks are low and the costs high, so driving for lower prices would seem appropriate.

For suppliers A, C & I, the risks and costs are low and these suppliers can be generally ignored.

Supplier Partnerships and Integrated Suppliers

Why develop a relationship with our supplier? What is the point, we only want to drive the price down. We may as well see it as a competition with each supplier competing with each other to achieve the cheapest price and winning the tender process. Many organisations have successfully reduced the price of purchased goods and services in this way but at what cost? Suppliers see this as a competition as well and hope to regain some of their revenue by way of extras or items or services which were not clearly specified in the tender documents and yet will still be required to complete the contract. This gives the supplier the opportunity to gain extra margin on the contract. The obvious problem with this approach is that the price is only one element of cost, and to reduce cost, all of its components must be controlled (delivery time, value for money, quality, through life cost, service support, etc.). Consequently it may be the cheapest but it is not the best solution.

i) A low price may conceal a high cost
ii) Cost reduction is best achieved through improved supplier expertise
iii) Meeting delivery and quality requirements
iv) Long term relationship based on trust and mutual benefit

Supplier Partnerships have a role to play in developing the organisation's supplier quality assurance strategy. This is developing relationships with suppliers to ensure that they understand the customer's specific requirements and needs. Further reducing the number of suppliers provides better control and fosters a mutually beneficial climate of continuous improvement. This climate can be used to prevent defects, reduce variation and waste in the supply chain. Often customers will link this continuous improvement and waste reduction to cost and price reduction, i.e. the customer has actively guided and assisted suppliers in reducing waste and improving efficiency. Now, is it unreasonable for the customer to expect some price benefit? It is this (price reduction) side of partnership sourcing and SQA which is difficult for the suppliers to accept. Customers acting as consultants and telling suppliers what is good for them, under the name of improving quality performance and then asking for a price reduction is sometimes hard for suppliers to accept. Never the less this should not detract from what is a widely accepted and respected approach to supplier quality assurance.

Quality System-9000

The key elements of a Supplier Quality Assurance System are often based on the interpretation of ISO 9000 for a particular industrial sector, together with some additional customer specific requirements. QS 9000 is no exception to this. There are three elements. The first is based on ISO 9000, the second Sector or Industry Specific requirements and the third on Specific Individual Customer requirements.

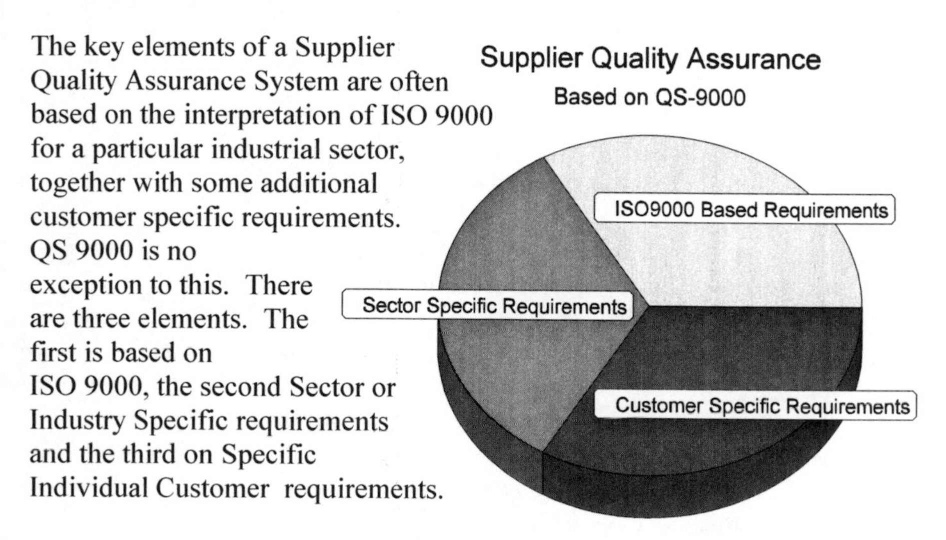

Figure 96 QS9000

These key elements can form part of an approach to ensuring supplier quality, even to the extent that the standard is made part of the contractual conditions contained in the Purchase Order.

One of the main criticisms of ISO 9000 is that the standard is not sufficiently product or process specific. I.e. ISO 9000 is too general and does not describe specific quality controls to the product or service that are needed to guarantee satisfactory supplies. The application of the following approach should ensure the identification and implementation of very specific quality control actions. This approach may be seen as augmenting ISO 9000 as the chosen Quality Assurance Management System of the organisation.

An overview of QS 9000

ISO 9000 Based Requirements

The interpretation of ISO 9000 for the automotive industry, is very similar to the original document, with the following main additions:

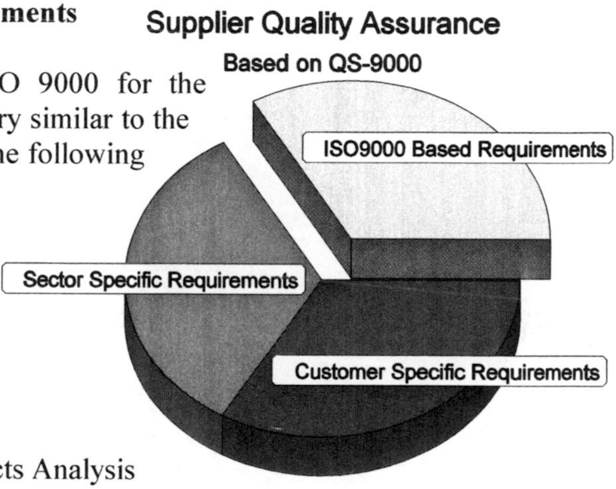

Management Responsibility
Business Planning
Customer Satisfaction
Quality System
Quality Planning
Failure Mode and Effects Analysis
Design Control
Quality Function Deployment
Value Engineering
Design of Experiments (Taguchi)
Design for Production
Reliability Engineering
Purchasing Control
100% on time delivery
Process Control
Safety & Environment Regulations
Planned Preventive Maintenance
Process Capability Studies
Statistical Techniques
Application of fundamental statistical process control

Figure 97 ISO9001 Based Requirements

Most of the above requirements can be found by reference to the relevant section of this book. The main theme behind these additions is prevention and quality improvement. In fact, these themes are enlarged still further with the next element - Sector Specific Requirements.

Sector Specific Requirements

The Sector Specific Element of QS9000 covers such issues as:

Product Approval: This usually involves the submission of product approval data and results. These results can be obtained either by self-assessment or from some recognised third party (possibly a test house, see NAMAS). These results could include process capability data from preproduction trials. This data should confirm the process's ability to reliability and consistently produce the product to specification, usually within ±four standard deviations of the product specification.

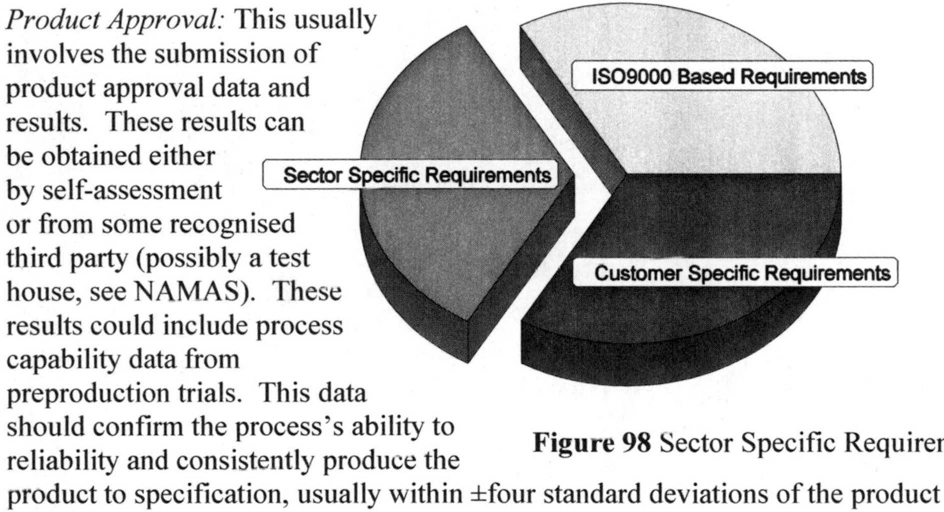
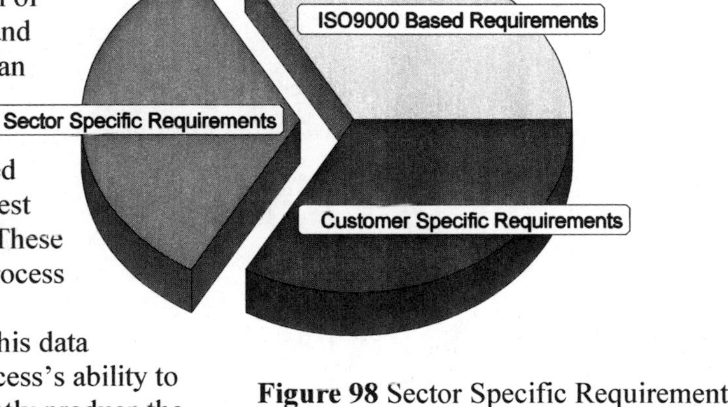

Figure 98 Sector Specific Requirements

Continuous Improvement: Having demonstrated the processes ability to consistently produce to specification, the next stage is to improve the processes quality performance and reduce variation. Techniques such as Just in Time and Process Cost Modelling are suitable methods to be employed to improve quality and productivity. Reduction in process variation and continuous improvement may be achieved by the use of Statistical Quality Control and other typical Quality Circle techniques.

Manufacturing Capability: This aspect of QS 9000 is concerned with optimising and quality assuring the processes, resources and facilities. One example of this could be such as fool-proofing equipment to ensure that mistakes cannot be made when operating the equipment. (In Japan this is known as Poka-Yoke).

Customer Specific Requirements

The Customer Specific Element of QS 9000 is concerned with issues key to that individual customer's needs. For example in Ford's case, one of the main requirements is the introduction of a *Quality Operating System* (QOS). This is a very simple technique and one which employs techniques which are well known but in an immensely powerful way.

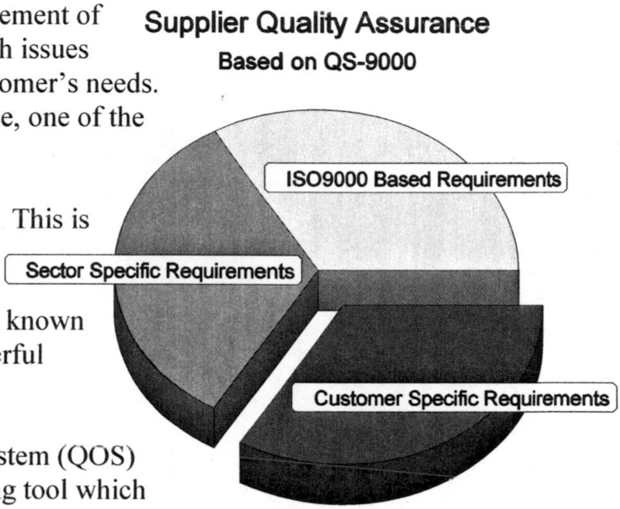

Figure 99 Customer Specific Requirements

The Quality Operating System (QOS) is a simple problem solving tool which can be used to drive the continuous improvement programme. It is based on collecting and analysing data in a consistent way and can, in certain circumstances, be used as an alternative to Statistical Quality Control (SQC). Some organisations have great difficulty in applying SQC to their processes. (The sheer volume of processes or variables to monitor, is usually cited as the most difficult problem).

QOS can be broken down into four phases: Measurement & Targets, Pareto Analysis, Action Planning and Performance Monitoring. There is nothing new in these phases but applied consistently it provides a common method of assessing quality improvement projects progress. Also this assessment can be contained on one sheet of paper and be quickly understood and analysed by almost anyone.

Figure 100 Phase One - Measurement & Targets

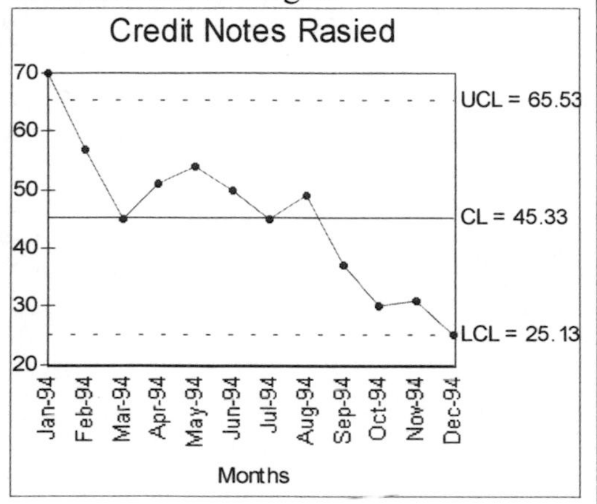

Table 36 Phase Three - Action Plan

Problem	Action	% Completed				Date
		¼	½	¾	1	
Misinterpretation	Training for Sales men					Jul 94
Price Error	Create Pricing Procedure					Mar 94
Wrong Customer Details	Up date data base					Jul 94

Figure 101 Phase Two - Pareto Analysis

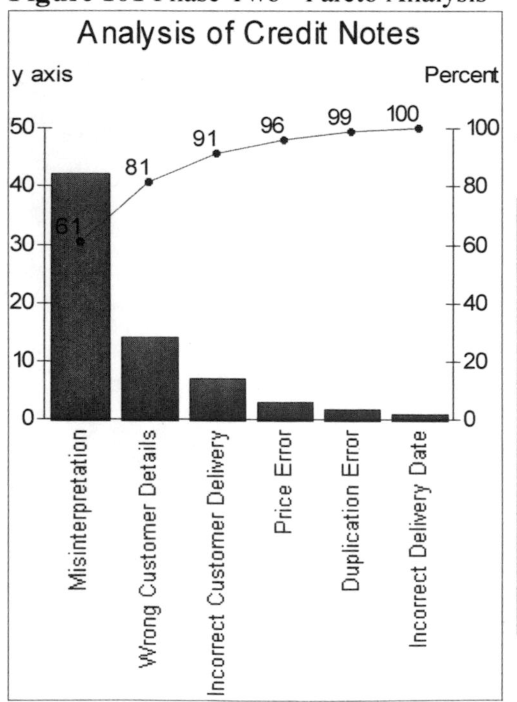

Table 35 Phase Four - Performance Monitoring

Jan	Feb	Mar	Apr	May	Jun	Jul	Aug	Sep	Oct	Nov	Dec
42	34	27	31	33	30	27	30	22	18	19	15
14	12	9	11	11	10	9	10	8	6	6	5
7	6	5	5	6	5	5	5	4	3	3	3
3	3	2	2	2	2	2	2	2	1	1	1
2	2	1	2	2	1	1	1	1	1	1	1
1	1	1	1	1	1	1	1	1	0	0	0
69	56	45	52	55	44	45	49	38	29	30	25

Figures **Figure 100** & **Figure 101** and tables **Table 36** & **Table 35** show an example of a completed QOS sheet. Phase one, the measurement and targets, shows the monitoring of performance with time. In this case the number of credit notes issued monthly. Phase two, is a Pareto analysis of credit note data to identify the important few reasons for raising credit notes. From this Pareto analysis, an Action Plan (Phase three) has been established in an attempt to reduce and eliminate the specific causes for issuing a credit note. Phase four is the raw data collected on a monthly basis detailing the breakdown of the reasons for issuing credit notes. Phase four row data labels (not shown) are the same as the horizontal axis in Phase Two - Pareto Analysis. Also included in phase four can be flags, which indicate that one of the items on the action plan has been implemented. The effect of this action should be seen (hopefully positively) on the measurement and targets chart.

Coordinating QS9000

To see QS 9000 as an overall process **Figure 102** has been drawn. The figure represents typically the sequence that could be followed in coordinating QS9000 (assuming ISO9000 certification has already been achieved).

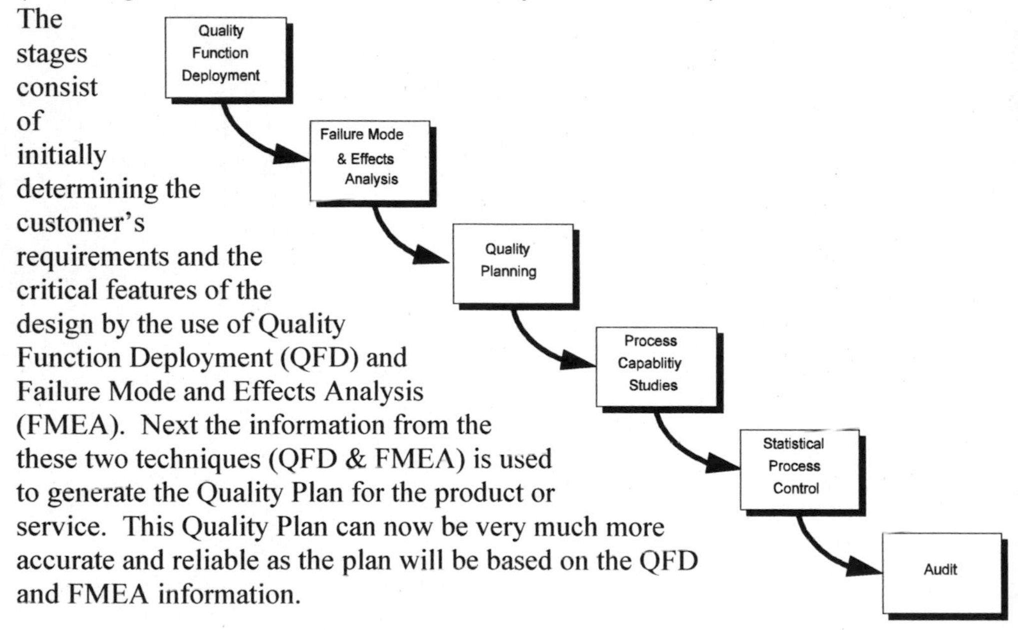

The stages consist of initially determining the customer's requirements and the critical features of the design by the use of Quality Function Deployment (QFD) and Failure Mode and Effects Analysis (FMEA). Next the information from the these two techniques (QFD & FMEA) is used to generate the Quality Plan for the product or service. This Quality Plan can now be very much more accurate and reliable as the plan will be based on the QFD and FMEA information.

Figure 102 Supplier Quality Control Steps

The Quality Plan can detail the quality control elements and records that will be needed at each stage in the production of the service process. Examples of the sort of controls specified in the Quality Plan may be Process Capability Studies or Statistical Quality Control (variable or attribute control charts) etc.

Finally, instead of what may be considered a rather nebulous audit as required by ISO 9000, a product or process based specific audit can be performed against the precise requirements of the Quality Plan.

Quality Function Deployment: As a project or design progresses, the greater the chance that specific customers needs and expectations are overlooked or not satisfied. In order not to neglect or overlook *'the voice of the customer'*, the technique Quality Function Deployment (QFD) has been developed. The aim of QFD is to identify the key customer needs and translate these needs into controls. This control is achieved by establishing what the customer requires and through the various stages of QFD how these requirements will be achieved. (See section Quality Function Deployment).

Failure Mode and Effects Analysis (FMEA): This technique is used to identify and eliminate possible causes of failure. FMEA requires a sequential, disciplined approach by engineers to assess systems, products or processes. The technique involves establishing the modes of failure and the effects of failure on the system, product or process. This ensures that all possible failure modes have been fully identified and ranked in order of their importance. (See section FMEA).

Quality Control Planning: Having completed the QFD and FMEA an excellent understanding of the customer needs and expectations will have been gained. Any potential system or product failures will also have been identified. Consequently, the process or project can be properly planned.

Process capability studies: Processes can be subject to variation. This variation may be small and insignificant. Alternatively, the variation could be excessive allowing products to be manufactured outside the specification. It is therefore important to understand the extent to which a process will vary before starting manufacture, thereby avoiding costly scrap or start/stop manufacture.

One method of determining a process's ability to meet specification is by conducting a Process Capability Study, where the process is statistically evaluated for the process's ability to conform to specification. (See section Statistical Quality Control).

Statistical Quality Control (SQC): Having determined the process's ability to meet specification, controls need to be applied which continually monitor the process for quality and to make continuous improvements to product quality. This involves taking regular measurements of process variation and comparing these observations with predetermined control limits of variation. This comparison can best be accomplished graphically on control charts. The application of SQC gives the opportunity to implement operator quality control, assisting in reinforcing the operator's responsibility for the quality of their own work and gives a sense of pride in their work. (See section Statistical Quality Control).

Problem Solving: The use of the seven stage approach is a powerful tool in problem solving.

i. Use the team approach.
ii. Understand the problem.
iii. Implement and confirm provisional corrective action.
iv. Establish and verify the root cause.
v. Confirm the viability of permanent corrective action.
vi. Implement permanent corrective action to prevent recurrence of the problem.
vii. Recognise thc team's achievements.

Assessment, review and evaluation: Having established a product specific Quality Control Plan, then perform an audit to confirm compliance with the agreed Quality Plan including the application of SQC. Review and evaluate the results of the assessment to identify any areas for possible improvement.

As can be surmised, time resource for such a programme is considerable, but the final analysis must be - how seriously is supplier quality assurance to be taken?

Supplier Associations

Supplier associations or "Supplier Clubs" are similar or like-minded suppliers who form a group to mutually help and learn from each other. Members of the supplier association could be providers to one organisation, a group of local companies or providers of similar products or services.

These supplier associations can serve various functions, from just being a list of suppliers to sophisticated supplier clubs, with rigorous joining criteria and a policy of continually developing and demanding ever higher standards for their members. This is not just to stop additional competition but to raise the standard and profile of the association and its members performance. In fact it may be seen as a honour to be a member of such a prestigious association.

Some of the aims and benefits of such associations can be to:

i) Increase the reputation, trust, social responsibility and perceived professionalism of the members, products and services.

ii) Agree common standards and rules and regulations to ensure its members act in a professional and ethical manner. Possibly include an appeals and disputes tribunal procedures.

iii) Agree common product and service standards which could be continually developed, raised and improved.

iv) Monitor customer and market development.

v) Provide a product and service development, training and support facilities. Particularly important where the club members are small to medium size organisations and may not be able to individually justify the expense but collectively as an association this becomes feasible.

vi) Improve performance in terms of cost, quality and delivery. Including the provision of a Benchmarking service, consultancy and database. Pooling knowledge and expertise and providing a benchmark for various aspects of their business and processes.

vii) Improving skills and gaining knowledge by the application and interpretation of recognised tools and techniques (described in this book) developed to meet their members particular needs and processes. Tools and techniques such as JIT, Value Analysis, Statistical process Control, Kanban, Kaizen, etc.

viii) Agree a common supply system to gain from the economies of scale when the club members purchase their goods and services. Possibly encouraging their suppliers to form such clubs as well. (Purchasing associations). Agree common purchasing standards for frequently purchased products, catalogue items, parts and services.

ix) Attract government support and funding.

x) Hold conference and discussion groups providing the opportunity to exchange ideas and approaches.

Index